"I am thankful for *IRL*. Chris Stedman is equal parts caring and indicting, and I hope this is a book that remains at the forefront of the discussion about our lives—digital and otherwise—for years to come."

—Hanif Abdurraqib, author of *They Can't Kill Us Until They Kill Us* and *Go Ahead in the Rain*

"Chris Stedman's newest book is a strangely prescient and timely guide to being more real digitally as we enter an era where we will need to be. His idea of digital life as drag has entirely reoriented my sense of self-presentation there, even as this brilliant book does more than that. By turns playful and wise, he makes us legible to ourselves and each other in new ways."

—Alexander Chee, author of *How to Write an Autobiographical Novel* and *The Queen of the Night*

"At first, the premise of this book—*Finding Realness, Meaning, and Belonging in Our Digital Lives*—was of exactly zero interest to me because I'm too shallow and morally bankrupt to read any book with *belonging* and *meaning* in the title. However, I was unexpectedly riveted by Chris Stedman's fascinating and surprising insights into authenticity both online and off, and I was especially moved by his vulnerability. I think so many people are going to relate to this work of memoir and cultural commentary, especially dismissive and judgmental people like me."

—Augusten Burroughs, author of *Running with Scissors* and *Dry*

"*IRL* is a brilliant and captivating meditation on the complexities of identity in the digital age. Chris Stedman offers a refreshingly nuanced account of how digital spaces both satisfy and complicate the innate human need for community and recognition—particularly for a generation that can no longer find such fulfillment in religion or other traditional spaces. *IRL* interrogates conventional binaries—the real versus the fake, the fleeting versus the lasting—and asks us to imagine our online lives as a frontier rich with possibility."

—Meghan O'Gieblyn, author of *Interior States*

"Chris Stedman's *IRL* is full of insight and honesty, but its greatest achievement lies in furthering our vocabulary of what it means to be real. *IRL* provides the side of the story many think pieces ignore: that for many of us, our digital lives were where we first learned to live most fully."

—Garrard Conley, author of *Boy Erased*

"Chris Stedman's *IRL* is a deft interrogation of how our increasingly digital lives have reshaped our sense of what's real, within ourselves and around us. Drawing from equally deep wells of research and reflection, Stedman probes and provokes our expectations of our changing world, and how we fit in it."

—Sam Lansky, author of *The Gilded Razor* and *Broken People*

"*IRL* takes the shame out of our dependence on the internet and helps us imagine new kinds of consolation and community for a fragmented and sometimes lonely world."

—Briallen Hopper, author of *Hard to Love*

"Chris Stedman embraces (rather than resists) the unity of opposite impulses that define our social lives online: critical engagement alongside mob mentality, surprising intimacies and algorithmic bubbles, selfies as vanity projects and selfies as spiritual opportunities. Reading this book made me think more deeply and ethically about the life I lead online and—relatedly, I now see—what it is to be human."

—Thomas Page McBee, author of *Amateur*

"By reckoning with his own complicated relationship to social media, Chris Stedman ponders notions of community, friendship, heartache, and, above all, how to live a meaningful life. Filled with humane candor and clear-eyed prose, these pages show a brilliant mind at work on some of the thorniest issues today."

—Nick White, author of *How to Survive a Summer* and *Sweet and Low*

"Chris Stedman brings a compelling combination of intimacy, vulnerability, irony, and brutal honesty to his search for what it means to be 'real' both in and out of virtual spaces. His testimony opens a space for all of us to stop fetishizing discipline and false coherence and instead dig deeper into uncertainty and connection."

—Ana Marie Cox, culture critic and host of *With Friends Like These*

"Chris Stedman draws on his work as a fierce activist and trailblazing thinker to illuminate a path forward for us all. He shows how the internet offers us an opportunity to approach the most central questions of life in new ways. This book is essential reading for understanding what it means to be human in our digital world."

—Valarie Kaur, author of *See No Stranger*

"It's easy to passively let social media run our lives (as many of us do when we start our day by scrolling through it). It takes a wise person to find the good and edifying within it, to identify a constructive way to use and to think about it. Chris Stedman is that person, and we're lucky to have his rational voice in these rancorous times."

—Dave Holmes, author of *Party of One*

"In *IRL*, Chris Stedman is getting after the real questions—and best of all, he's not answering them for us, but encouraging us to ask them too. He's a mapmaker charting intangible paths between the digital and physical realms."

—Dylan Marron, host of *Conversations with People Who Hate Me* and creator of *Every Single Word*

"I, like many of my millennial compatriots, spend a good chunk of my life online. Few are able to write as lucidly on the subject as Chris Stedman, bringing clarity to the often-chaotic lifestyle of the 'terminally online.' I highly recommend this book, and I think it will play an important part in shaping how we discuss online interactions moving forward."

—John Paul Brammer, columnist and author of *¡Hola Papi!*

"Chris Stedman's perspective on humanness is so wise, vulnerable, and insightful. While the internet can bring us together and make us feel like we know strangers, true intimacy is a rare and magical thing. This surprising book possesses that magic, and generously offers it to the reader."

—R. Eric Thomas, author of *Here for It*

"We contain multitudes. Seeing all of those multitudes spun together with a combination of personal memoir and academic interest kept me turning page after page. Ultimately, Chris Stedman does for our digital worlds what he does for atheism—asks us to expand our thinking beyond just one thing or the other, good or bad, and see that we're all of us . . . just real."

—Nora McInerny, author of *It's Okay to Laugh*
and host of *Terrible, Thanks for Asking*

"This is a book of warmth and wisdom, a book about what it means to be human. It will expand your mind and comfort your spirit. I loved it."

—Eboo Patel, author of *Acts of Faith*

"Chris Stedman writes from a very personal, empathetic place of genuine curiosity, which inspired me to reflect on my own life online."

—Cole Escola, actor and comedian

"What does it mean to be real? This is the question that launches author and activist Chris Stedman on a personal and philosophical journey through the ways social media has changed our very sense of self."

—Reza Aslan, author of *Zealot* and *God: A Human History*

IRL

FINDING
REALNESS,
MEANING,
AND BELONGING
IN OUR
DIGITAL LIVES

CHRIS STEDMAN

 Broadleaf Books

Minneapolis

IRL
Finding Realness, Meaning, and Belonging in Our Digital Lives

Cover design: Faceout Studios

Print ISBN: 978-1-5064-6351-3
eBook ISBN: 978-1-5064-6352-0

For my mom, who, whenever I ask if she's cool with me posting a picture of us online, responds, "What do I care, I don't have a Twitter." And for Charlie, and Halden, Henrik, and Hazel, who have never had Twitter accounts, either.

For my sweet Alex Small, who was on Twitter but got repeatedly banned, because in life he broke almost every rule. You taught me so much about realness. I miss you (and your memes) fiercely.

Finally, for my dog, Tuna, who has no clue what Twitter is.

CONTENTS

"In real life, unlike in Shakespeare, the sweetness of the rose depends upon the name it bears. Things are not only what they are. They are, in very important respects, what they seem to be."
—Hubert H. Humphrey

"Our virtual and physical lives are intertwined, inseparable, equally 'real.'"
—Astra Taylor

1

AMATEURS

What does it mean to be "real"?

"Realness" has always been a slippery concept, one so big and complicated it's dealt with as a central problem in religious traditions like Buddhism and Christian Science. But it feels especially loaded these days, in our ever-more-digital lives, when the platforms we increasingly use to connect, express ourselves, and find information are so often cast as "fake." The already inherently difficult question of realness—*How can I know who I* really *am?*—feels almost unanswerable now.

Given the impossible immensity of the question, there are many places I could begin. I start with a drag show. It was amateur night at a gay bar, when performers just dipping their toes into the drag waters get their start. I was newly single and begrudgingly following friends' advice to put myself back out there. Like many of the queens on stage that night, I felt very much like a novice. A woefully out-of-practice flirt, I mostly kept to myself. Whenever I glanced up from my phone, I focused almost entirely on the gritty, glittering performers.

New to the stage and not yet sure what the crowd would reward and what it would reject, many of these amateur queens were boldly, unapologetically messy. Others were more like me, broadcasting the same tentativeness as my furtive glances away from the glow of my phone screen, unable to hide the nervousness behind their masks of generously applied makeup. (Tip for the uninitiated: the makeup on your face needs to match your neck.) From cocksure to crushingly insecure, the queens were all over the map.

But there was a magic in the messiness of amateur night, its combination of audacity and naked vulnerability, that overtook me. Maybe it's how chaotic my own life felt at that moment—my boyfriend of nearly five years had just moved out of the apartment we shared, I was navigating thorny challenges at work, and everything around me seemed uncertain. Whatever the reason, something about the atmosphere of the show clicked. It felt more *real* than many of the more practiced drag performances I'd attended.

I could see the queens taking risks, experimenting; I could see their nerves, their excitement, and their courage. It was clear that, in both their confidence and their hesitance, they were thinking less about what might earn them a paycheck and more about what they wanted to *say*. None of them exhibited the perfection that was exhausting me in my social media feeds, the digital boasts and brags—the job announcements, engagement photo shoots, new houses, vacations—that made me feel worse about my own life, one that seemed determined not to go according to plan. Instead, they embodied the growing part of me that felt like maybe it was time to tear up the playbook, all the rules about what I should and shouldn't do, what I should and shouldn't value—what made my life matter, what made it real—and try something new.

In drag, the concept of "realness" doesn't necessarily mean what you might think. For many drag artists, realness isn't about trying to "pass"—to blend in with the crowd without notice—but rather about standing out and apart. By disrupting and shining a light on our assumptions, drag realness can expose that what is most real is in the in-between, in the blurring itself, in tearing up the playbook of gender. The realness of drag is that it heightens, dramatizes, and deviates in order to reveal—it holds up a mirror to us, showing us the gender baggage we inherit and inviting us to discard our conventions.

This is what the digital pieces of our lives can do, too. If we look at them honestly, they can be a mirror that reveals what we're attached to, what scripts we follow, and what these things say about how we understand ourselves. Our digital drag shows us what our culture considers perfection—perfect beauty, perfect relationships, perfect lives—and then asks if we want to discard these things, too. It is a laboratory, a space where we can experiment. A space to try things that might not work, things we're not good at yet, and see what we learn from them.

Perhaps the most famous quote about drag is RuPaul's: "You're born naked, and the rest is drag." We're born a blank slate and then spend our lives layering ourselves with costumes, masks, outfits. We all eventually face a choice: live by the scripts we've inherited or forge our own way. At its best, drag shows us the flimsiness of those scripts and how much our sense of self is shaped by the world around us. Only when we see that influence for what it is—as with drag's hyperrealness, its exaggeration, its camp and humor—can we try another way.

The internet shows us the flimsiness of our scripts, too—not regarding gender specifically (though sometimes!), but rather in terms of what we think makes us real, what makes us human. The catfishes (people who assume an online identity different from who they are offline), the filters (software that alters the shades or colors of a photo to enhance it—or, increasingly, goes much further in enabling people to dramatically manipulate their physical appearance), the deepfakes (videos created using artificial intelligence that look deceptively real), the curated digital selves we create. All these things fundamentally uproot what we've thought constitutes realness and show how incomplete that understanding was. This uprooting presents us with an opportunity to imagine another way forward. If we let it, the internet can reveal us to ourselves, all the posing and hiding we do, and give us a chance to ask ourselves who we really are, how we see ourselves, and how much of that is shaped by the scripts we've internalized. As a result, we have a chance to write some new code.

"In the beginner's mind there are many possibilities," writes Zen teacher Shunryū Suzuki, "but in the expert's there are few." To be human is to forever be a beginner—tripping around in the dark, trying to understand who we are and what animates our lives. It is only in recognizing we don't have the answers that we can ask ourselves the questions that matter.

We're all building ourselves, online and off. But when it comes to the digital realm, none of us really know how we're coming off, how we appear. It's like we think we're ready for the headliner slot when, in actuality, we're performers on amateur night: trying things out, making fools of ourselves, exposing our humanity in the process. Which is exactly why the internet may be the best venue we've ever had for exploring questions of realness. In our messy attempts to stage a show, social media gives us a chance to see that, when it comes to being human, we're all amateurs.

—■—

I'm far from a technology expert—I still don't really get how a Virtual Private Network (VPN) works and couldn't order the different bytes from smallest to largest if I tried—but there's at least one good reason for me to write a book on the digital search for realness: I owe my career to the internet. Like many writers today, I built my platform, found my voice, and first connected with an audience, critics, and peers online.

I never imagined I'd forge a career through social media. When it happened, I was a graduate student studying religion at a small theological school. But after launching a blog focused on elevating the stories and perspectives of atheists who aren't antireligious, my career quickly took off in ways I never anticipated. Within three years I went from totally unknown to a cable-news talking head with a book contract and a job at Harvard.

I was offering an underrepresented perspective, but it's also clear that my voice would never have been elevated like this if it weren't for digital tools. Without the internet, I wouldn't have sparred with best-selling atheist author Sam Harris online, debated popular atheist blogger PZ Myers, or woken up with a pit in my stomach for years, wondering if another atheist writer had ripped me apart in one of their near-daily critiques—all before I reached the age of twenty-four.

Almost everything that followed my blog's unexpected success—*Faitheist*, my book about going from fundamentalist

Christianity to inclusive atheism; invitations to appear on networks like PBS, CNN, and MSNBC, and even on the (thankfully) now defunct *The O'Reilly Factor* on Fox News—largely came about because the people extending these opportunities came across my work online.

My story reads like an example of what the internet's champions say it does: give voice to those whose perspectives have historically been absent in broader discussions and debates. I of course benefited from being a white cisgender man in a world where those voices are consistently elevated and rewarded, but as a young, queer atheist with a day job working alongside Muslims, Christians, and Hindus to promote interfaith cooperation, I didn't have the academic pedigree of my interlocutors. I looked and sounded nothing like the atheists that dominated the bestseller list. Hell, I wasn't even making a living wage at the time. While writing *Faitheist*, I worked long days and spent my nights typing away on a mattress in a partitioned section of an apartment living room. But online, none of that mattered. I bypassed the gatekeepers and injected a new perspective into a debate that had typically kept people like me out.

I owe a lot of other, arguably more important, things to the internet, beyond my career. I've made some of my closest friends on Twitter and have dated several guys I met on Instagram. But the most important thing I owe the internet may be my life. As a gay teen, I found spaces online where I could share my queer identity and find support. I not only practiced what it would be like to come out to people in the nondigital areas of my life—I also forged real, meaningful friendships with other queer people around the world who made me feel less alone.

While the internet was a lifeline in my teenage years, it unexpectedly became one again in my late twenties after a series of disruptive events flipped my sense of self upside down. As almost everything that had propped up my identity for years—many of the things I posted about on social media, that I thought gave my life meaning—disappeared or ended, I once again found myself turning to the internet for reassurance and support. Even as I did so, however, I noticed that despite how much I was struggling through change, I continued to publicly project a digital image of confidence and calm. I wanted to understand why I was simultaneously turning to social media for reassurance and trying to post like everything was just fine. I felt like a person divided. Though the internet had helped me build a career at the beginning of my twenties, by the decade's end I was feeling disaffected by my digital life.

Much like when I first left Christianity in early adulthood and wanted to disavow it altogether, when I first began exploring questions about the digital aspects of our lives, I wanted to throw out the baby, the bathwater, and the tub, too. I read the words of the internet's heretics, people who say the web makes us faker and less connected. But I wasn't totally satisfied by what I was reading. I kept asking questions, talking to people, trying to learn more. Just as religion has often felt fraught and complicated—and determining what I think about it hasn't come easily—I followed my curiosity about the tension I felt in the digital pieces of my life. The stuff that doesn't come easily to me, that's complicated and fraught, is often what teaches me most about what it means to be human.

I first learned this in high school, when my mom said I had to go out for a sport. Initially I protested; to that point I'd largely stuck to the activities at which I naturally excelled. Finally I relented and joined the cross-country team. I was far from athletic, and training my body to run previously incomprehensible distances was one of the most difficult challenges I'd ever undertaken. But I kept at it, eventually earning the Most Improved award two years in a row. (I was *really* bad when I started.) The greatest reward, however, was twofold: I discovered a love of running, and I learned that you encounter fundamentally new things about who you are through trying something that doesn't come easily.

When you try something unfamiliar, something you're not good at, you have a chance to figure out who you are. There is something in that risk, in the vulnerability of the leap. An opportunity to see yourself in a new way. Something that disrupts the story you've told yourself about who you are and who you are not. Who you can be and who you cannot.

No matter what "brand experts" try to tell us, we're not good at social media yet. It's too new. In our often-inelegant attempts to use it, we show a lot of the things we're really bad at, like knowing and being honest about who we are. Which makes it the perfect lens through which to view ourselves. In its newness and risk, and in our less-than-graceful attempts to understand and share ourselves through it, we reveal ourselves. These revelations give us a chance to gain a better understanding of who we are and why we do the things we do. We might be surprised by what we discover about ourselves in the process. I was.

Shortly after this book was announced, I was having dinner with my dad and his girlfriend. They had seen the online announcement and wanted to know what "IRL" meant.

For a moment I thought they were joking. It didn't even occur to me that someone might not know what the acronym stands for, especially people who have Facebook and Twitter accounts like they do.

"It means 'in real life,'" I tried to explain between bites of pizza. "People usually use it to refer to the offline parts of their lives. Like when you connect with someone through one of the apps, but then you want to meet them off, you say, 'Wanna meet up IRL?'"

I could tell by their blank expressions this explanation hadn't clarified anything. As it turned out, my attempt to elucidate raised as many questions as it answered. They didn't know what I meant by "the apps," a term some queer people (and perhaps even some nonqueer people, what do I know?) use to refer to dating and hookup apps like Grindr or Scruff. I began to explain that, but I wasn't sure what to say, or how much. So we changed the subject, took some pictures with silly filters on them, and went our separate ways.

As I walked out of the restaurant, I found myself thinking about how, even though we keep up with each other more regularly than we did before social media, there are entire parts of my life they know nothing about—a huge range of things that contribute to my feeling of being a full, real person.

But there are also huge swaths of my own life and self, particularly in digital space, that I haven't understood, either. Media, teachers, and friends have explicitly and implicitly told me that I didn't have to, that they weren't real. A few years ago, though, I decided I wasn't comfortable with not understanding. I needed a better sense of what "in real life" even means now, in this time when so many important aspects of our lives happen online.

For most of our still-young digital lives, we've been encouraged not to question what we're doing, to just keep clicking and scrolling. It's been as true for me as for anyone. But if being an atheist studying religion taught me anything, it was to question. If growing up queer taught me anything, it was to question. If being an amateur in all the ways I now know that I am has taught me anything, it is to question. This book attempts to ask questions about what it means to be digital and to reframe our frustrating, fascinating, and fraught digital lives as a new opportunity to ask persistently difficult questions about what it means to be human.

What *does* it mean to be real? How are age-old questions of meaning, belonging, and identity—the things that make us feel alive—taking new shape in our increasingly digital lives? For those of us using digital platforms to seek out things frequently considered central to the human experience—purpose, connection, community—it's vital we ask ourselves if our technology is making these things easier or harder to find, or just changing how we find them.

This is the story of how and why I went searching for a better understanding of what makes for a "real life," online and off. Like some of the performers on amateur night or me in my earliest days on the cross-country team, I'm not entirely sure what I'm doing—but I hope my messiness, my trying to figure it out as I go, has its benefits. Just as runners and drag queens often take novices under their wings and help point them in the right direction, my search for a better understanding of how to be human in a digital world was rarely undertaken alone. A lot of people gave me pointers along the way, walked with me as I tried to figure this out. Now I invite you to join me, too, as I tentatively step out onto the stage and try to take some risks in search of a better understanding of realness.

2

ANXIETWEETS

On a sunny Monday afternoon in June 2017, after hours of walking around Minneapolis alone, I paced outside my apartment building. Unwilling to make my way back inside but having nowhere else to go, I walked from one end of the block to the other before heading back to where I started, the punishing heat irritating my already tortured skin.

I couldn't remember the last time I'd felt so alone, but I also didn't want to talk to anyone, so I pulled my phone out of my pocket and scrolled through my Twitter timeline.

I was one year removed from the end of my longest relationship, and the year that followed my breakup had been a marathon of misery: the unexpected end of the job that was supposed to be my career summit, a traumatizing encounter with bedbugs, the dismal 2016 US presidential election cycle, a difficult move across the country undertaken alone with no sense of how I would make a living on the other side, and an all-consuming itch that finally—after months of sleepless nights, puzzled doctors, painful tests, and fruitless biopsies—was identified as a severe scabies infestation.

For those fortunate enough not to know from experience, scabies are microscopic mites that burrow beneath your skin and cause an itch so extraordinary and violent that the Latin root of their name is literally "the itch." Months later an ex who works as a hospital chaplain told me he'd heard scabies was so agonizing that before it became easier to treat, it had driven many to suicide. This didn't surprise me; the last year had been one of the worst I could remember, but the three days following the diagnosis felt like the lowest point yet. I was defeated and hopeless.

My life falling apart around me, I furiously scrolled Twitter in search of any distraction—flicking anxiously past a cluster of gays posing on an inflatable flamingo at a pool party, a few hot takes about the latest inflammatory opinion piece designed to go rage-viral, and several iterations of the "the floor is . . ." meme (an image of someone contorting their body to avoid touching the floor) that was making the rounds that month. But there was no meme stupidly funny enough to pull me out of my misery.

After pacing back and forth and anxiety-scrolling outside my building until putting my phone away in frustration, I stopped and fished it back out of my pocket. I'm not sure what possessed me to do what I did next; it felt like an unthinking act of muscle memory. After turning my phone over in my right hand a few times, I opened my camera app and took six or seven pictures of myself.

When I was finished, I lowered my phone and appraised the results. I almost didn't recognize the face looking back at me. I hadn't shaved in days, my closed-mouth half smile was entirely unconvincing, and my hair was disheveled, but not at all in a good way. My eyes broadcast exhaustion and sadness. I was jarred by this alien person. Gone were the selfie smirk and Instagram angle I defaulted to in the pictures I typically posted for my modest online following (let's be clear: I'm not Chrissy Teigen). In their place was a portrait of a man who looked like he didn't want to be alive.

I can be very particular about the photos I share online. I'm not proud of it, but I'm not ashamed, either. It's just the way it is in this age of filters and Facetune—an app for smoothing out blemishes, erasing under-eye bags, and enabling truly wild edits like superimposing a smile where there wasn't one or completely reshaping your face's, well, shape—when half of the people I follow online look like they've got a professional photographer trailing them at all times. I sometimes take over a dozen pictures before I get one I deem satisfactory enough to post, and I almost always ask friends if I can review a picture they've taken of us before they upload it.

Under normal conditions, the pictures I took that day would never have passed my aesthetic standards. They weren't just unflattering—I looked exactly as I was: unkempt and unwell. I tried a couple filters. There was no hiding what a mess I was. In those photos I saw the entire year leading up to those moments.

But for reasons as indiscernible as those guiding my decision to take them in the first place, I decided to post one anyway.

Uploading this photo ran counter to the way I had treated social media for years: as a space to share curated career highlights, personal triumphs, carefully considered reflections on challenging situations after they had been resolved, edited selfies, and the occasional self-deprecating but totally safe joke.

I opened Instagram and started typing a draft. "I will not forget this time in my life and the perspective it is giving me," I wrote, not sure if my words were a cry for help or a declaration of victory. In truth they were neither. I was offering this photo as proof of life, a flare from the wilderness of my misery.

Too worn out to pretend to be okay, I wasn't thinking about impressing anyone or garnering sympathy. I didn't have it in me to consider how my post would be received. It was simply a dispatch from the brink. After years of careful, self-conscious status updates and selfies, here, in this post's muscle memory and immediacy, was something that felt a little more real.

Listening to cars pass by on a Minneapolis highway just out of sight, hundreds of lives moving past me like ephemeral tweets, I hit Post. As I watched the photo-upload progress bar fill in, I stood perfectly still, the sun shining down on the battle-ground of my skin. *I'm still here*, I thought. *I'm still here. I'm alive.*

—■—

For most of my twenties, I was what you might call Very Online—constantly plugged in and logged on. Still, among my peers, the volume of my social media output felt pretty average, sometimes even below average. I mostly stopped using Face-book in my midtwenties, quit Snapchat (a platform for images and videos that supposedly vanish within twenty-four hours, so a lot of people use it to share nudes) shortly after signing up, and totally failed at Tumblr (even my abiding love of sad lyrics wasn't enough to help me navigate the microblogging site). But even with these gaps, there were few windows in my twenties where I let more than twenty-four hours go completely undocu-mented online.

This digital comprehensiveness makes the fact that entire swaths of my life—significant struggles and fears, projects and celebrations—remain unrecorded and unshared all the more glaring. It's almost as though those things never happened.

For some time, one of the gaps in my Very Onlineness was Instagram. If you were viewing my life solely through the lens of my Instagram footprint, I'd only be a few years old. I resisted joining for years, thinking it somehow signaled that I wasn't *truly* glued to social media, but finally signed up a few months after my relationship ended. Posting on Instagram quickly became a way of saying *EVERYTHING IS FINE*, even though it very obviously wasn't; my feed was all pictures of me smiling, carefully posed photos of food I was eating (why do so many of us do this?), and cute shots of Tuna, my dog. I was trying to prove to myself that I was okay, that my life still had happiness in it, by showing it to the world. But it wasn't really about the world; it was about me, and for me.

Since my adolescence the social internet has been a space where I've shared some of my greatest hopes and fears, reached out for help and consolation, and gone to get information and process evolving thoughts. Once on the edge of my life, over time it moved ever closer to the center. Eventually it was no longer just a place where I sometimes shared things that happened elsewhere in my life. It became a place where life happened.

By and large, though, our "real world" norms haven't caught up with how we behave on social media. Some of us tweet about things we couldn't imagine sharing with our parents or have "alt" accounts where we disclose secrets we can't even bring ourselves to tell our therapists. Conversely, as demonstrated by how many "Wait, you have a boyfriend?" comments I see gays tweet at one another each year in response to Valentine's Day posts, we often leave big and important parts of our lives out of what we share online.

This isn't a totally new phenomenon. In so many other areas of our lives, we fear being perceived as incompetent or unsuccessful or unkind, and we strive to present a more polished version of ourselves. This takes many forms—like not mentioning your seasonal depression to coworkers because you don't want to be judged or telling a first date about your track-and-field trophies but leaving out your student loan debt.

But even if it isn't exclusive to the internet, the pressure to perform and calibrate—to make your life look more appealing or put together—can feel especially acute online. Because of the seduction of editing, depending on the day and who appears at the top of our newsfeed, social media sometimes seems like a culture of extremes: the highly curated and overly safe "personal brands" that feel so pristine they're sterile, the joke or "irony" accounts that traffic in barbed memes and sarcasm, and the compulsively performative oversharers in search of constant validation. Many have come to regard all of these types as equally fake, and, because of this, social media is frequently castigated as an authenticity-killer.

As a result, we often look for our suspicions to be confirmed: we hunger for the latest person to contradict their online identity and prove themselves fraudulent or insincere while simultaneously living in fear that we might be next to slip up. Put another way, we are waiting for everyone to become exposed. Which is why, pushed to what felt like a breaking point, I decided it was time to stop worrying so much and expose some of my struggles myself.

A few weeks before posting that selfie, I jolted awake one night. It was just days before Tuna and I would begin a three-day drive across the country in a tiny stick-shift orange Ford packed to the roof. I was in the middle of packing up my life in Connecticut; my job had ended, and with it the near-decade I'd spent on the East Coast. I was moving back to my home state of Minnesota, and to a future that felt wildly uncertain. But that wasn't why I couldn't sleep.

After several hours lying awake in the dark, I had finally slipped into a weary slumber, but now I was up again. I reached down to the floor, feeling around in the dust between moving boxes for my phone. When I finally found it, the screen revealed that I'd barely slept an hour. I couldn't get back to sleep, so I pulled up Twitter and started scrolling.

Many recent nights had gone like this. I would lie in bed squirming, miserable, desperately wishing to pass out. But after just one or two fitful hours of sleep my hands would twist behind my back to dig into my itching flesh, staining my short fingernails with blood and jerking me awake again. I was plagued by a mysterious malady that I didn't yet know was mites. But I did know that it was slowly marching me toward a madness from which I feared I might never return.

The insufferable itch had started on my right shin, then migrated. Soon I was breaking out in hive-like blushes of blistering pink. By the time I was packing up my car to move they had marched from the crowns of my ears to the creases of my feet, spotted rashes interspersed with red scratch lines that bloomed into purple bruises.

My drive across the country—something that had originally sounded fun, an opportunity to be alone with Tuna and my thoughts after a rough year—was torturous. The weather was hot and humid, the car seats sticky. I was itching from head to toe, sitting in the car for nine hours at a time with a nervous dog by my side. Having to keep my eyes on the road meant I couldn't even use Twitter to distract myself from the fact that I was digging my fingernails into the steering wheel in order to abstain from scratching.

By the time I got to Minnesota I could barely function. I hadn't had a full night's sleep in ages. Finally, in late June—several months after seeing the first of four doctors about this mysterious itch—I got the diagnosis that I had been exposed to scabies. As I began the first of my four rounds of treatment—putting all the clothing I had just unpacked from my move into garbage bags for quarantine purposes, furiously cleaning my apartment, and covering my body in insecticide—the prolonged lack of sleep made it difficult to think straight. I couldn't tell what was a rational thought and what was an unnecessary worry (exacerbated by the trauma I'd sustained from staying somewhere infested with bedbugs just months earlier). So soon after moving, I hadn't had an opportunity to organically develop a support network, and my apartment felt tainted and unsafe, so I spent hours each day walking around Minneapolis alone, trying to tire myself out.

I had imagined arriving in my new city and hitting the ground running, charming new friends and posting Instagram updates about my next chapter. Instead, I navigated my scabies treatments and associated anxieties in those first months back in Minneapolis. In every conversation with a cute stranger ("Hi! You might not want to shake my hand because I'm only two rounds into my scabies treatments"), in every introduction, and—as in the selfie I posted a few days after my diagnosis—at times even online, I was forced into honesty. I was broken open before friends and strangers alike.

Though I would never wish scabies on my worst enemy, there was a kind of helpful, even beautiful, irony in its impact. It came at a pivotal moment, at the beginning of a chapter, when I was trying to start over after a difficult year and dive headfirst into a new life. The impulse to start over as someone new when things get hard runs deep in me (and is a big part of social media's appeal). It's an old habit I developed so that I could flee from the uglier or messier parts of myself. It was reinforced with each move—when I could start over with people who didn't know who I once was—and each social media platform I joined in my twenties. It was a way to feel charming and new. But having scabies prevented me from being able to do that. I couldn't reenter the world shiny and fresh, online or off. I had to show up as the real person, frayed and flawed, that I had become.

Initially after my diagnosis I went quiet online. The shift in my social media output immediately elicited worry from those who know me best; two days after my diagnosis, I awoke to a text from my sister: "Are you still sleeping? What are you doing? I'm concerned. You're not tweeting."

I wasn't tweeting because I didn't know what to say. As with so many of my experiences from the previous year, it felt too vulnerable to share. But three days after my scabies diagnosis, I couldn't keep quiet anymore. I didn't have the words to describe what I was going through or how I was feeling, but looking at that selfie, I didn't need them—my misery was all over my face. And I could share it in real time, instead of safely from a distance, after the fact, in service of a lesson.

Now in my thirties, on the other side of those difficult few years, I'm still Pretty Online. Gaps remain, to be sure; I don't fully understand what's up with WhatsApp, and the only TikTok I acknowledge is Kesha's. (Actually, I take that back. Somehow, over the course of writing this book, we all decided some Tik-Toks are pretty funny.) But I continue to tweet most days, and the pink circle alerting users that there's content on my Instagram story—where temporary photos and videos are stored for twenty-four hours, so basically it's Snapchat but embedded in your Instagram—is generally active, pointing the way to videos of Tuna stretching and screenshots of what I'm listening to on Spotify. (Just the cool stuff, of course. Relient K, the Christian pop-punk band I loved as a teenager and still secretly listen to, doesn't make the story.)

But I am, at least in some key ways, differently online. The erosion of many of the things that I thought made me who I am, the stuff I would so often crow about on Twitter, invited me to reassess my relationship with social media—not just how much I use it but *how* I use it. It's not that I'd never questioned it before, but mostly I'd been all or nothing about it, feeling like I needed to go all in or recuse myself entirely. But it turns out neither approach is viable for me. I like it too much to quit, and I dislike it too much to let it run my life. If I'm going to be online as much as I am, though, I want to feel more like myself there.

As I've reflected these last few years on what keeps me online, despite it being a complicated and fraught space for me, I've come to wonder if social media is actually the problem. I now suspect that, rather than being this entirely or even largely destructive force, social media is instead a new tool for expressing ourselves and connecting with others, as susceptible to abuse or misuse as any other. Yes, it presents immense new challenges. But it also offers profound new opportunities to see things about ourselves: chances, in our amateurish attempts to be human online, to learn more about our impulse to broadcast an edited image of ourselves. We can come to better know ourselves by looking at how we use the internet.

If being online feels difficult, it is, in no small part, because *being* is difficult. After all, social media hasn't necessarily made us express anything that wasn't already inside of us and previously expressed in other, offline ways. Sure, our new outlets for connecting with others and expressing ourselves may exacerbate some of our preexisting anxieties, and some genuinely new behaviors have emerged as a result. But I'm not sure many of our social media habits reflect brand-new impulses. Before I was ever on social media, I still often felt partitioned into an interior "true" self and an exterior "curated" self. I still compared my life against other people's and tried to present a more polished version of myself to the world. I still felt pressure to appear charming and accomplished. These aren't products of the internet; if anything, my social media use has helped me recognize this split between public and private self, and the fears and inclinations that underscore and bolster it, by making it more obvious to me.

As applied anthropologist Sophie Goodman points out in a piece for *SAPIENS*, "in face-to-face settings, we often have more control over our identity because we can tailor how we present ourselves in a given social situation." But online we lose some of that control, like when an acquaintance tagged a photo of me partying on Facebook in college, putting it in the newsfeeds of several members of my family. Before social media, they would never have seen such a photo, because neither I nor my acquaintance would have shown it to them. But these moments when we lose control can help us notice the ways we partition. "The digital equivalent of 'a slip of the tongue,'" says Goodman—like when a college buddy revealed my underage drinking to my younger cousins—"happens easily and often. And it's less likely to go unnoticed in a format where everything is written down and broadcasted to a converged network."

That hot summer day when muscle memory kicked in and told me to post a picture, I began to confront the divide between my online and offline selves. In that grimacing selfie—taken in a moment so miserable that even social media, for many years a pretty reliable tool for distracting me from the things I struggled with, couldn't pull me out of it—I saw reflected back at me not the curated self but an honest depiction of how terrible I felt.

In retrospect, it is less the misery of that moment that I find jarring and more how alien its depiction was, how out of place it seemed alongside my otherwise considered and careful posts. But it was my own digital slip of the tongue.

If I'm going to spend as much of my life online as I do—as so many of us increasingly do, for things we would very much consider "real"—I don't want to continue to feel so split. I'm not always sure how to go about getting more integrated, but I do know that as the internet becomes more ingrained in all aspects of our lives, figuring out how to carve out a bit more space for realness in the venues we use to document our lives, express ourselves, learn more, and build connections with one another feels vital.

—■—

When I look back at that photo from three days after my scabies diagnosis, it rustles up old ghosts of how alone I felt at that time, how devastating and hopeless everything seemed. They are ghosts I don't care to remember. But they are accompanied by lessons I don't want to forget.

Here was proof that all my efforts were for naught: carefully managing my online identity didn't prevent my life from falling apart. That photo is a kind of portal or bookmark, a stamp in time that provides a direct line to the recognitions I made during that period.

On some level, I knew that if I didn't post it, it could eventually seem like it never happened. I didn't want to scroll back through my Instagram history months later and see an invisible gap between highlights.

This book attempts to look at what falls into this kind of gap. Instead of an in-depth analysis of online behaviors, I seek a better understanding of the whys—what our social media habits, the things we do and don't show, reveal about what it means to be human and what it means to be in relationship with others. What our online presentations say about how we see ourselves and other people, and how the ways we narrate our lives digitally mirror ancient habits and express deeper human impulses and struggles that predate social media. Because while the desire to tell certain kinds of stories about ourselves and others isn't new, the ways we do it today can teach us about what it means to be real.

On that sleepless night, tormented by undiagnosed scabies just days before my move, I took a break from scrolling through my Twitter feed to read *The Velveteen Rabbit*. It was my favorite story as a child, the one my mom would read to me when I couldn't sleep. In the year after my breakup, I found myself returning to it as the life I thought I knew—a life I once thought would go on like that for a long time, if not forever—disintegrated.

In my favorite part, the rabbit asks an old toy horse about realness.

"Real isn't how you are made," the horse replies. "It's a thing that happens to you."

The rabbit then asks if it's painful or uncomfortable to become real. Sometimes, the horse explains, but "when you are real you don't mind being hurt."

To be more real online—to become worn and ragged, but also soft like velveteen itself—we may have to let go of our desire to be seen as strong and stitched together and let the stuffing spill out. To embrace the discomfort of sharing not just the flattering or neutral parts of our lives but also the seams. To be works in progress, to be wounded, and to be real. At times this will be painful and uncomfortable, but today it feels essential.

But how do we do it? In a world that so often draws a sharp line between our "fake" online lives and our "real" offline ones, I picked up my phone and went searching for answers.

3

IN THE STARS

On a beautiful day during the terrible summer when at least two-thirds of the things in my life fell apart, I walked into a "spiritual resource center" in Ohio. I was there for a tarot reading, which was not like me for several reasons.

Reason one: I don't believe in tarot. Reason two: I was in Ohio that weekend to speak at a conference on *atheism*. Reason three: the friend who brought me to the reading was someone I knew because at one point we'd both worked for atheist nonprofits. If you were brainstorming a list of pairs most likely to go get their cards read together, "friends who met as professional atheists" would probably be near the bottom alongside "married fundamentalists who vacation at the Creation Museum." And if I'd told the atheist conference attendees about our plans, I would have been met with uncomfortable laughter, possibly boos.

Yet there we were, just a couple of atheists surrounded by sleeves of nag champa sticks and what appeared to be the exact tapestries my college friends and I had used to cover our dorm room walls, looking for something "cleansing" to burn and someone to read my cards. We'd laughed at the irony on the way over—two of only a handful of professional atheists (sorry, it's just so fun to say) in the US en route to a tarot reading—but as I watched the reader shuffle her deck and draw the first card, I couldn't even summon a smile. The shop went quiet, my friend left the room, and, alone with the reader, it hit me all at once that I wasn't joking. That I wouldn't be fine if she laid out bad news on the table before us. I had told myself I was going as a joke, but as she began dealing the cards I knew the truth: I was there because I needed to hear that things were going to be okay.

I wanted help understanding who I was now, this new person in a newly tattered life. I wanted someone to tell me how to find a way forward, to give me some hope.

That same month, on another gorgeous but miserable summer day, after wading through a glut of selfies and shitposts (ironic, sarcastic, and heavily layered jokes that are often impenetrable to those who aren't extremely online), I opened a web browser and typed a question: *What does it mean to be real?* I couldn't believe I was doing something so obvious, so stupidly on the nose, but the truth was I'd been going online to seek answers for most of my adulthood. That summer, when nothing felt right, I was reaching out in all directions. In many moments, not only during that summer but for years before it, it seemed like the internet was the easiest, best, or sometimes only place I could turn for meaning or connection—even though, as with my tarot reading, I've sometimes suspected it couldn't give me what I was looking for.

I scrolled through the search results, past conservative Christian blog posts, a life-coach directory, and a series of truly wild Urban Dictionary definitions. It wasn't even a start. If I wanted answers to my questions about what it means to be real in the digital age, it was going to take more than an impulsive tarot reading or internet search.

———■———

Whenever I have a question, my first instinct is almost always to reach for my phone. What's causing this weird pain in my arm? Let me Google it. (Typically a terrible idea.) What's the name of that one song I loved in seventh grade? The internet will know. (It does, but I'm not telling you because it's mortifying.) Is it normal for my dog to cough like that? I bet there's some helpful information online! (Nope, just a bunch of strangers on a forum saying either it's nothing or she's about to die.)

The first time I went searching for answers to questions I couldn't shake, I was an adolescent—a time in my life when things were even more tumultuous than that awful summer, and I was far less equipped to handle tumult. My parents had just divorced, my mom was working multiple jobs to keep us afloat, and I was queer, closeted, and ashamed. I was desperate for stability and answers, and I didn't have regular internet access. Unfortunately, like many American adolescents before me, my search led me to a fundamentalist Christian church.

It's not all that surprising that I sought refuge in the certainty and security of born-again beliefs. I'd spent the entire year before my conversion immersing myself in stories of immense suffering, as depicted in books like Alex Haley's *Roots*, John Hersey's *Hiroshima*, and Anne Frank's *The Diary of a Young*

Girl. Although I was learning about the events detailed in these books in school, they were largely treated as historical fact—merely as things that had happened—and as a white person growing up in a society built on white supremacy, I had been ignorant of many of its consequences. But these stories gave me some understanding of what the people who'd experienced such inconceivable cruelties had endured, and that limited perspective was more than enough to fill me with rage and despair. Being human didn't make sense if it included such inhumanity. (Not that I would've articulated it in this way at that time, obviously. I was, like, ten.)

As much as any preteen can become consumed by moral, philosophical, and metaphysical questions, I was. I found myself looking for answers everywhere. At the fundamentalist Christian church, I was told that God could help me make sense of my questions. So I decided to give God a try.

Believing in God wasn't the most natural fit for me, which isn't surprising because God wasn't really what had brought me to church. I wasn't searching for God but for a way to be more human. Church appealed to me because it was a space oriented around the project of trying to make sense of an unjust world and where I fit in it. *What is my responsibility to others? Can I do anything about the suffering of my fellow human beings?*

Today, with a better understanding of what appealed to me about church and how it functioned in my life, it's hard to say how much I *really* believed in God as an adolescent. But in church I found a community that gave me so many of the things I'd been looking for—stability in the wake of my parents' divorce, food in a time of limited resources, acceptance during a period of social alienation (except for the whole gay thing, but I kept that to myself), and answers to some of my big questions about injustice and identity. Everyone at church said God was responsible for these things—for community, for abundance in times of need, for acceptance, for answers. That it was God who had brought us all together and provided a way of making sense of the things that troubled me. So I accepted the idea of God's existence along with the rest like a package deal.

Years later, while studying religion at a Lutheran college, I was challenged by my Christian religious studies professors to interrogate my faith and investigate why I believed the things I did. With the encouragement to ask myself difficult questions and the permission to answer them honestly, I could no longer deny that I didn't actually have my own reasons for believing in God. Since leaving church, much of my life has been a series of attempts to make meaning and find community outside of religion.

That move, from searching for meaning and belonging within a religious tradition to venturing beyond its boundaries into unincorporated territory, is far from unique today. Americans are leaving religious institutions in droves, and the "nones"—those who do not claim a religious affiliation, a group that includes atheists, agnostics, and "nothing in particulars" (those who, when asked about their religious preference, say that theirs is, well, you can figure it out)—are now the fastest-growing segment of America's religious landscape. According to a study by New York University's Michael Hout and University of California, Berkeley's, Claude S. Fischer, 7 percent of Americans were nones in 1987, the year I was born. By the 2018 General Social Survey, however, the nones made up 23 percent of the general population and 34 percent of those under the age of thirty. They numbered about equal to evangelicals, and they outnumbered Catholics. In some parts of the country the nones are now the largest plurality, surpassing any individual religious category.

Most nones aren't atheists like me—according to Pew, a majority still say they believe in a God or universal spirit. (Though what they mean by that remains unclear. The Public Religion Research Institute found that about two-thirds of nones say God is either a person or an impersonal force, which doesn't really clarify things.) So people may be leaving religion, but that doesn't mean they're not still believers in some sense.

The relative persistence of belief in God and practices like prayer, along with the resurgent popularity of spiritual exercises like tarot and astrology, suggests that the causes behind this massive demographic shift are less theological than practical. People are leaving religious institutions not necessarily or exclusively because of their beliefs about God but rather because they have issues with the institutions themselves.

My sense of this is informed not just by demographic trends but by my experiences serving as a chaplain to the nones at Harvard and Yale for the better part of a decade. Many of the students I worked with were atheist or agnostic, but even more students I encountered didn't seem to chart themselves on the a/theistic spectrum at all. They weren't sure what they believed, exactly, but they knew they weren't religious. Additionally, surveys show that even those who *do* identify as religious are now attending their houses of worship at markedly decreased levels. Overall the issue seems to be one of approach more than content.

Many atheists I've met credit "New Atheism"—the antireligious atheist movement spearheaded by Richard Dawkins, Sam Harris, and the late Christopher Hitchens—for the rise of the nones. If that were true, though, we would expect the turning point in religious disaffiliation—the moment when their number began to rise dramatically—to be in the 2000s, when New Atheist titles were published in the aftermath of the 9/11 terrorist attacks. But it was not in 2001, 2002, or even 2007, by which time Dawkins, Harris, and Hitchens had all released anti-religious bestsellers. The turning point was not New Atheism. It was actually much earlier: in 1990.

Sure enough, some studies suggest that America's dramatic decline in religious affiliation has been caused at least in part by an increase in internet usage beginning in the early '90s. Perhaps it's because people are now able to access domains over which religion once had a near monopoly on their own and thus feel less need to belong to a religious community—especially if that community doesn't help them feel real.

At one point in American life, houses of worship were, for many, *the* place to go to connect with others, learn more about what was going on in the world, and reflect on life. In many small towns like those peppering the Upper Midwest where I grew up, they were the only option available to people searching for connection and reflection. And if people didn't end up in a house of worship, they could turn to some other political, civic, or social institution to find community and learn more about the world. But today, as long as you have a smartphone, you can do all of those things without ever leaving your bed. Why get up on a Sunday morning when you can log on at any time?

And instead of having just one option available to you— like the church in my town with a popular after-school youth group, which *also* came along with conservative politics—you're able to see a multiplicity of options. Which may be making us more resistant to choosing a single box, be it religious, political, or something else. In a 2016 paper in *Sociological Perspectives*, University of Lynchburg's Paul McClure says that young adults who use social networking sites are more likely to adopt a syncretic approach to religion, or "to think it is acceptable to pick and choose their religious beliefs, and practice multiple religions independent of what their religious tradition teaches." Online, we have a world of options at our fingertips—which can make the idea of limiting yourself to a single set of ideas in the search for realness less appealing.

The same goes for community. Today, instead of being restricted by circumstance or geography, we can find belonging based on shared interests—using digital tools instead of traditional institutions to build our commitments and sense of belonging. "Many young adults treat their religiosity like they do their other 'likes' and preferences on social media," nonreligion scholar Jacqui Frost writes of McClure's research on the Society Pages, "and religion functions as a malleable and often inconsistent expression of their personality, morality, and spirituality."

Even though social media enables young adults to be more syncretic in their beliefs, incorporating ideas from across the religious spectrum, "social media use does not make young adults any more or less pluralistic" when it comes to other people's beliefs, says Frost. This ability to be "both pluralistic and exclusivist" may arise from the fact that social media makes it easier to choose our own communities instead of having to negotiate our way through our communities of origin.

With this syncretic exclusivism (try saying that five times fast), a lot of religiously unaffiliated Americans now turn to the internet in search of the things many people once got from religion—not just community but also meaning, purpose, and a sense of realness. Whether we are religious or nonreligious, today we can go online to meet the needs once served in religious spaces: to connect, but also to confess our secrets, seek out information, process tragedies, and pursue a more just world. All of the things that make us feel real. If our institutions don't serve us, we can piece together our own meaning and community online. And even if they do, we still might prefer to log on instead anyway.

Has social media become our new church—the place we turn to in search of answers about where we fit in and what makes us who we are? It can certainly feel like it. As author Bri-allen Hopper says in a conversation with the Revealer, there are countless ways for "forms of media to become religion: ecstatic consumption, collective textual study, cultural edicts about what is or is not permissible to consume, the instinctive clutch of your phone in your pocket as if it were a handful of beads." Instead of moving our fingers from prayer bead to prayer bead in times of trouble, many of us—as I did time and again during that nightmare of a summer—now flip from app to app to find consolation.

Like the evangelical Christian church I ended up in as an adolescent and its unquestionable beliefs, sometimes it feels like the internet demands an almost dogmatic kind of faith. One that urges us not to interrogate what we're seeing and doing and to just adopt the practices and ideas we encounter online—the memes, the callout posts, and, worst of all, #ThrowbackThursday—like the religious beliefs and rituals I took on in adolescence because of all the good that came along with them.

But there's reason to question. Religious rituals and communities offer people regular, structured, and often effective opportunities to reflect on their lives and the needs of others. Yes, someone can approach tarot or religion dogmatically, but these frameworks for understanding the self can also open people up and prompt them to see things in a new way.

When I was a teen, my mom found a journal (today it would probably be a "finsta," or secret Instagram account, instead of a notebook) where I expressed in excruciating detail the struggle I was experiencing between my fundamentalist faith and sexual orientation. Because she wasn't a Christian herself and didn't know how to support me best, she went to the phone book and called up local churches. She reached a Lutheran church, where she found an LGBTQ-affirming minister, and took me there the next day.

This minister did something revolutionary. While he was forthright about his own perspective, above all else he pointed me toward resources and urged me to make up my own mind. Instead of saying there was just one path, he gave me books that showed me Christians understand sexuality and gender in a variety of ways, and invited me to enter into spiritual practices— prayer and reflection—so that I could listen to what my heart was saying instead of to the voices that were drowning it out. In doing so, he helped me understand new things about myself, including that I could be Christian and queer if that's what I wanted. I ended up moving into progressive Lutheran churches, where I found a community that grounded me in reflective practices and a sense of belonging that gave me the courage to come out as queer in a homophobic public high school. Those Lutheran communities were religion at its best—forums for support and spaces that invited me to look both inward and outward for a better understanding of what made me real.

Can the internet provide these same kinds of insights? If it doesn't, this may explain why the quickly growing number of nones has some social scientists concerned. In a piece for Religion News Service, Eastern Illinois University's Ryan Burge points out that the nones have the lowest levels of education and civic engagement of any religious category. While atheists and agnostics are as involved in political, social, and educational activities as their religious counterparts, it's the "nothing in particulars"—again, those who don't offer a particular identity or label when asked what they believe—that lag behind. "Nothing in particulars," according to Burge, "appear to be a growing segment of society that is 'checked out.'"

Because they are opting out of education, the political process, and many forms of community, he suggests that "they are adrift in modern society, refusing to be labeled by a religious group or a political party." This apathy could hurt all of us, not just the nones. Not only because our world needs people who are reflecting on their lives and values, but also because religious traditions have built strong support networks to aid people in times of crisis and need, like the Lutherans who helped me plug back in to the world as a teenager after years of withdrawal and isolation. As these religious traditions decline, unless the nones check back in, many of those resources could disappear.

Of course, effective as religious resources and rituals can often be, that doesn't mean religious institutions don't fail people. Looking at the reasons many of the nones give for rejecting religious affiliation—that they think religious institutions are too bound up in money and politics, that they're hypocritical, that they divide and alienate people—I see a phenomenon reflected across society. People are leaving institutions, like political parties or civic groups, that they see as being more interested in self-preservation than honesty, in easy answers than messiness.

In her essay collection *Interior States*, writer Meghan O'Gieblyn (a none herself) cautions that we shouldn't just look at why the nones are leaving institutions of old but must also consider what happens after they do. "Even when a person outwardly denounces a long-standing belief," she says, "the architecture of the idea persists and can come to be inhabited by other things." Looking at my own life, I see it: the search for meaning, the desire for connection and community, the quest for a sense of realness—all the things that brought me into religion—didn't just dissipate when I left Christianity. They found new homes. As the internet became a place where I spent more of my life, it became host to more of these needs.

But if many of us are now turning to social media for the things we once got from the institutions we're leaving—meaning, belonging, a sense of real connection—that requires putting trust in something new and largely untested. Long-standing institutions are on the decline not just because we have new options and don't want to limit ourselves to one thing but because of "the lack of trust in elites and gatekeepers," writes University of North Carolina at Chapel Hill's Zeynep Tufekci in *Twitter and Tear Gas*.

"As trust drops in institutions, it doesn't go away entirely," internet researcher and artist An Xiao Mina adds in *Memes to Movements*. "Trust just moves elsewhere." Much of that trust has moved online. One obvious example is the privacy policies and terms of use we never read for all the apps, social media platforms, and online services we use. We just click Accept and assume it'll be fine. Call it laziness or apathy, but what it really is is trust. Trust that there's nothing *too* bad in there, nothing we couldn't accept in order to enjoy this new home for our needs and desires. As media design professor David Carroll says in the beginning of the Netflix documentary *The Great Hack*:

> It began with a dream of a connected world. A space where everyone could share each other's experiences and

feel less alone. It wasn't long before this world became our matchmaker, instant fact checker, personal entertainer, guardian of our memories, even our therapist . . . We were so in love with the gift of this free connectivity that no one bothered to read the terms and conditions.

But it's not that we didn't bother. It's that we trusted we didn't have to.

We put our trust online because we need to put it *somewhere* in order to function. But what happens when we put our trust in the internet instead of in traditional institutions, when we opt out of spaces that were designed and refined to induce regular reflection and personal development? When we try searching for meaning, belonging, and realness on our own, in the chaotic minefield of the internet?

When I asked Google what it means to be real, I was far from the first person to turn to the internet in search of answers. Because many of us, religious and nonreligious alike, are searching for meaning online today, much of the internet is in the business of advice-giving. Social media in particular is full of inspiration bloggers, life coaches, astrology memes, wellness accounts hashtagging every other word, inspiring Instagram captions that mostly inspire eyerolls, and lots and lots of posts about #SelfCare.

There is also, at least in some social media circles, a growing interest in the pursuit of "authenticity"—a "more real" way of being in the world. Beyond inspiration and wellness accounts, much of online culture more broadly is attempting to move in the direction of authenticity. As internet culture writer Taylor Lorenz notes in "The Instagram Aesthetic Is Over" for the *Atlantic*, even Instagram influencers—long thought of as among the *least* authentic people online—are now trying to pivot toward content that makes them seem more real.

In a piece for *Jacobin*, the University of Pennsylvania's Kristen R. Ghodsee reflects that today many people aspire to be "authentic in a world overflowing with fakes," and as a result authenticity is now considered culturally valuable. Because of this, it has also become a commodity. But the sometimes desperate pursuit of authenticity comes at a cost. "Because young people today learn that realness has economic value," Ghodsee writes, "they spend so much time perfecting their performances of authenticity that we may be on the cusp of producing a generation of Americans that can't distinguish a faked emotion from a real one."

If that worries you, you're not alone. Most blogs, essays, and selfies celebrating authenticity feel deeply dissatisfying, full of phrases that at first feel true, but a second glance reveals that they could mean *anything*, so they actually mean *nothing*. (This is what philosopher Daniel Dennett calls a "deepity.")

Ultimately, this is the irony of digital authenticity culture: so much of it feels, well, fake. Like it's been focus-grouped to appeal to the widest possible number of people. If authenticity sells, its proponents are trying to make it as sellable as possible. Perhaps this is why, while often intentionally vague, much of online authenticity culture also feels highly and narrowly prescriptive, even polemical—like there's a right way to be real, and lots of ways to be wrong. As if the secret to being your true self can be revealed in ten simple steps. (Like and subscribe to get steps four through ten!) As if everyone else has been getting it so wrong, but here, at last, is how to get it right.

This doesn't mean, of course, that social media can't *ever* be a vehicle for authenticity. We may just have to stop trying so hard to force it. For example, I once had a genuine personal breakthrough while writing an Instagram caption. It was late April, a year after my ex-boyfriend Alex and I had started breaking up, and I was beginning the long process of packing up my apartment ahead of my move back to Minnesota. I still hadn't fully processed our breakup and I'd hardly said a word about it online. But one day, between filling boxes with books, I took a picture of the living room fireplace. I sat down on the floor, loaded the photo into Instagram, and began drafting a caption:

> We were so excited to move into an apartment with a working fireplace. It made us feel like adults. That first winter we used it constantly, up until April, when things began to end. The second winter, when I was here alone, I tried to start the fireplace a few times, but I could never get it to work. (It wasn't something wrong with the fireplace; I had it inspected. It was that it was touchy, and he had always been the one to turn it on, and I just didn't have the touch.) It's April again and I'm moving next month, to a place that I'm sure won't have a fireplace, and I'm not sure what it means to be an adult, really. I'm pretty sure it isn't having a fireplace, or even knowing how to operate one, but I'm still figuring out the rest. I do know that I'm never going to use this fireplace again, and while I wish I could have made it work, I will always remember how warm it made me feel that first winter.

By the time I finished writing it, I was crying. I'd told myself it was just a dumb picture of a fireplace. However, prompted to create a caption for it, I unexpectedly extracted the immense sense of loss I'd spent a year trying to hide in order to tell the world that I was okay.

That post stands out as much more real than most of the times I've *tried* to be authentic online. It helps me see, with a beginner's mind, things in myself that I need to understand.

The questions that brought me into the church as an adolescent—*Who am I? How do I live a life of meaning and purpose? What are my responsibilities to the world?*—are now questions I and many others engage online. In those online conversations, polemics often win out. The simplest, easiest, least complicated answer often feels safest (and most sellable).

So many of the ways we think and talk on social media—and, in particular, *about* social media—are highly polarized. In most discussions about the impact social media is having on society, self-appointed experts lead with strong opinions. And like the polemicists of authenticity, when it comes to helping us make sense of our digital lives more broadly, these experts often speak in generalized extremes.

Most of us recognize the split between these experts' polarized groups: cheerleaders and doomsday prophets. Social media's champions argue the internet is bringing us closer together and making our world smaller and vaster all at once, in all the best ways. These technological utopians believe the internet is enhancing our quality of life to a previously unimaginable degree, opening up endless possibilities for authentic self-expression and the dissemination of information.

This side of the conversation speaks of social media with the wide-eyed wonder of an astronaut, the affection of a poet, sometimes even the fervor of a prophet, and it's hard not to get swept up in their conviction that our digital platforms are making us more efficient, more interconnected, and more able to express ideas in striking new ways. That these new avenues for building relationships are helping us become fuller, better versions of ourselves. More real.

Looking at how social media has aided in boosting and cohering social movements like the Arab Spring, or how it's helped transgender people and those with disabilities render their lives and identities more visible than ever before, it's easy to see why people get excited about social media's potential to transform the world. Its power to help people connect, learn, and effect change is staggering.

But then there are naysayers. They suggest that social media is making us more isolated, lonelier, a generation of raging narcissists, and, perhaps most concerning of all, that it's making us deeply inauthentic. Their picture of the digital age—one in which everyone is getting more calculated, in which engagement and likes and influence are valued above all else, in which people are rewarded for being fake and punished for being real—is deeply worrying. For them, it is a world where we are becoming less human.

Surveying some of the research out there, it's easy to see why their outlook is so grim. Every day another disquieting tweet crosses my timeline akin to this one from NPR: "A recent study finds that people who checked social media the most frequently had almost three times the risk of depression, compared with people who checked less often." Of course, just because two things are correlated doesn't mean one caused the other, but that's far from the only study suggesting that excessive social media use is negatively correlated with well-being (in other words, that increased social media use hurts us).

That NPR tweet certainly feels true when I look at the tweets that surround it and consider how difficult it is to know which ones to believe. How hard it is to see through the pristine Instagram posts of those seemingly living picture-perfect lives or the Reddit account of someone whose layers of irony you can't quite decipher. The way people hide their failures and trumpet their successes or even the way the internet lets us try on different affects, aesthetics, and identities like they're costumes.

As a result, on social media, we're equally suspicious and credulous. We don't know who to trust. Disoriented by the challenge of determining what's real and what's not, we trust no one and everyone all at once, including ourselves. We alternate between the optimism of the cheerleaders and the defeatism of the doomsday prophets, sometimes even maintaining both at the same time.

"One feels like a person who has one foot in an ice bucket and the other in boiling water," writes University of Illinois at Urbana–Champaign's Robert W. McChesney of this back-and-forth in *Digital Disconnect*. The celebrants offer us optimism we need, he says, but often at the expense of an honest assessment of the challenges our digital lives present. Social media's critics, however, offer realism and point to concerning red flags. But, McChesney adds, "like the original skeptics in ancient Greece"—or the skeptics of contemporary movement atheism, I might add—"their values are unclear and they generally offer no credible alternative course."

But perhaps we need one side's questions *and* the other's optimism. Because despite all that's novel about social media, the impulses we use it to satiate largely aren't new ones. Long before the internet, we sought ways to document our lives, express ourselves, forge connections, find communities of belonging, and access and share information with others. What's changed isn't what we're doing, necessarily, but how we're doing it (and how often). As Tufekci writes in *Twitter and Tear Gas*, "the emergence of the digitally networked public sphere has not necessarily introduced new fundamental social mechanisms—humans still behave like humans." But, she continues, it *has* "drastically altered the conditions under which these mechanisms operate." (This is true for all of us, she notes, whether we're online or not. For example, while only 25 percent of Egyptians were online in January 2011, as Egypt's digitally driven political uprising that began that month demonstrated, "only a segment of the population needs to be connected digitally to affect the entire environment.") We need to take stock of these new conditions.

If I have to choose between the digital utopians and the digital alarmists, I often find myself sympathizing more with the latter group, even if I think some of their nostalgia for a predigital time incorrectly relies on a rewritten history that obscures the good changes the internet has brought about. I err in their direction because I think we should apply this kind of questioning instinct to all aspects of our lives—particularly for the pieces we don't have a long history of studying, as is the case with our digital tools. Especially since we use them for ever more important functions, like the central questions of what it means to be human.

Technological alarmism, however, is nothing new. As many others have pointed out, it's a tale as old as time. Technology has always had its champions but also its critics—from Socrates in Plato's *Phaedrus* critiquing the technology of writing to my grandma telling seven-year-old me that television literally rots your brain. Early on in her book *The People's Platform*, Astra Taylor cites a defense of technological progress written by Timothy Walker in 1831. Responding to critics of his day who figured that technological advances—which, in the 1830s, included a steel plow for farming, a type of sewing machine, and a more sophisticated bicycle—would harm our "spiritual nature" and turn us into machines, Walker argued instead that "machines would free our minds by freeing our bodies from tedious labor," writes Taylor. Thus liberated, Walker suggested, we can all become artists, philosophers, and poets. (I'm sure my grandpa will be thrilled.)

This refrain continues today, with techno-utopians arguing that technology will free us up to do the things that *truly matter*. In theory this ought to be true. In *This Life*, Yale University's Martin Hägglund explains that through technological innovation, we should be able to "decrease our realm of necessity (the time required to keep ourselves alive) and increase our realm of freedom (the time available for activities that we count as ends in themselves, which includes time for engaging the *question* of what matters to us and which activities we *should* count as ends in themselves)." So why does it sometimes feel like instead of making us all philosophers—or, at the very least, making us more authentic—technological advances have made many of us feel less thoughtful and less productive, swamped in the small things instead of free of them?

I'm certain technology makes some people productive, thoughtful, and balanced; I just don't know those people. As I mentioned, many studies seem to suggest there's a negative relationship between technology and well-being. But, as it turns out, it might really just be who I know and who I don't. In an article for the journal *Nature Human Behavior*, "The Association between Adolescent Well-Being and Digital Technology Use," researchers Amy Orben and Andrew K. Przybylski argue that the relationship between technology and well-being actually varies a great deal depending on how you set up the statistical model. When they test many of these different approaches, they conclude that the negative relationship between technology and well-being is really quite small and probably negligible.

Yes, our digital tools make some of us unhappy, but it's not correct to say that they always do, or that they *must*. Which suggests that the fault lies not in the tools themselves but rather somewhere in human nature. This feels monumentally daunting—it would be much simpler to identify a problem in our technology and patch it—which is why I understand the draw of easy answers, of polemicists who can say "this is good" or "this is bad" when it comes to our digital lives.

Still, in a time when we hear the word "fake" a lot—fake news, deepfakes, fake followers—we're not wrong to be skeptical. It's unwise to put your complete trust in the internet. I was reminded of this when, not long after that terrible summer, someone reached out to me through social media and said my work had caught his interest. We began chatting, and while there wasn't a great deal of substance to our conversations, I found him attractive. So attractive, in fact, that if we had met offline I would've been suspicious—like, why is this person talking to *me*? (I don't mean this in a self-critical way. Well, maybe I do a little. But I'll save that for therapy.)

In hindsight, there were red flags I ignored; some of his pictures didn't quite match up, he was vague about personal details, and he once proposed FaceTiming only to say his phone broke. I didn't see what I didn't want to—I was bored, lonely, and at the time actively working in therapy to change the story of who could or couldn't be attracted to me. My therapist (who is great—don't blame him for my obliviousness!) encouraged me to treat it as an opportunity to stretch my own understanding of who might possibly find me attractive or interesting. Which is why it was crushing when, one day, I went to look for the profile he'd used to reach out to me and found comments from people saying he was a catfish. Our interactions were brief and infrequent, and I never sent him money or anything—but I still felt taken advantage of and humiliated.

Some part of me, even if it was unconscious, knew not to trust what I was seeing. I held myself back in ways I don't usually when getting to know someone. And this shines a light on some of the limitations of the digital search for realness under our current conditions. Because even though I was using our interactions to try to stretch myself (and attempted to ignore the warning signs), on some level a piece of me still wasn't sure I could trust this person. And I think many of us are on guard like this online. Whenever a new digital fraud is exposed—and it seems like every other day on Twitter a popular account is revealed to be run by someone with racist views or to have stolen content, so they delete their account and then try to come back later with a new one, hoping people won't figure it out—it feels like evidence that our trust was misplaced, that we should continue to hold back. All the more, it seems to prove the split between our online and offline lives; that who we are online is fake, or at best less real, than who we can be offline, and that we should regard every piece of our digital lives with suspicion.

But there's another way to look at our digital selves, sociologist Nathan Jurgenson argues in a piece for the Society Pages' *Cyborgology* blog. Instead of thinking of our lives as split between online and off, or "digital dualism"—the perspective that our online and offline lives are fundamentally different, with our offline lives being more real than our online ones—he suggests that we can see the digital and nondigital pieces of our lives as "enmesh[ed] into an *augmented reality*." That is, our modern reality is new and different from what came before; it's still reality, just altered. But augmentation isn't unfamiliar. Our new reality is sometimes skewed or heightened, yes—but it is nonetheless real like the lives we previously skewed or heightened in offline ways, whether by compiling a scrapbook that only shows the highlights, writing a family Christmas letter that makes no mention of Dad's DUI, or buying a new outfit before a first date.

Under this view—one that sees our lives as not newly augmented, just differently so—our online and offline lives aren't separate, but rather increasingly entangled. After all, we created the internet; everything in it is a product of human invention. "The politics, structures and inequalities of the physical world are part of the very essence of the digital domain; a domain built by human beings with histories, standpoints, interests, morals and biases," Jurgenson writes. Of course, it shapes us in return, and as we change, so does it.

Still, whether or not we accept the idea that in the current digital order it's sometimes easier to be less real online than off, at least in certain respects, it's something many of us certainly *feel.* For the last few years I've been working with a group of researchers—Evan Stewart, a sociology professor and researcher at the University of Massachusetts, Boston, and the aforementioned Jacqui Frost, along with support from University of Minnesota professor of sociology Penny Edgell and a group of volunteers—to better understand the nones, including a survey we ran in 2019 for a mix of religiously affiliated and unaffiliated individuals.

At the end of this survey, we asked how often respondents find community online and offline, and how often they find meaning online and off. We expected people who were meaning-oriented would find meaning both online and off, and likewise, those who were geared toward seeking community would report experiencing it both places. Not so. Instead, those who reported finding a sense of meaning online also reported finding community online, and those who said they find meaning offline also said they find community offline.

While most people ultimately report a mixture of both, these correlations between online community and meaning and offline community and meaning suggest that instead of seeing the digital and analog as intertwined and augmenting one another, people tend to see them as separate vehicles for finding connection and meaning.

Nearly my whole life I've searched for community and meaning, and I've done so both online and off, seeing digital platforms as just another set of tools to do what I'd done before I had regular access to them. I didn't necessarily assume my experience was the norm, but I figured those who seek meaning and belonging generally, like me, do so both online and off.

As it turns out, I may be in the minority in this regard. It seems that, at least in this respect, the digital dualists have a point: when it comes to seeking community and meaning, people may just view their online and offline lives as separate. They may *feel* they are split even if they do mix them in practice. Whatever the reason, it's important to look at this split. Because as people move more of their lives online and trust traditional institutions less and less, many will look to the internet to meet their needs for community and realness *more* than the offline pieces of their lives.

Even as technology advances, what we're grappling with has stayed the same—we're deciding who to be intimate with and who to keep at arm's length; we're charting and transcribing our lives as a means of remembering and understanding; we're figuring out who we are and broadcasting who we'd like to be; we are trying, perhaps more than anything else, to find a place within a community that accepts us. That we do these things digitally means we need to find ways to feel real online. It also means something else, something hopeful: there's an unprecedented opportunity to use social media to better understand the deeper human questions and impulses we often use it to explore. To maybe get a little closer to figuring out what realness even means. To address the kinds of questions that brought me into Christianity as an adolescent and that have guided my life since.

In fact, the rise of social media may be the best opportunity humans have yet had to do so. Because, as a friend once said to me, social media is a kind of fun-house mirror of society, in that it warps some things and reveals others, which makes it confusing to navigate but also fertile ground for the work of trying to better understand ourselves and the world around us. Because we are trying to do something new—because, in our digital search for meaning and realness, we are all amateurs—we have the opportunity to see things in a new way. So even though I sometimes feel tempted to look away from social media, I can't shake that feeling that jumping ship is not the best way to answer the questions I've been wrestling with for almost my entire life.

—■—

As a teenager, I got really involved in an organization called MMLTEC, or Minnesota Metro Lutheran Teens Encounter Christ. The main thing it did was put on deeply sincere weekend retreats where Lutheran teens from Minnesota's metro area (the greater Minneapolis–Saint Paul region) came together to, well, "encounter Christ." But while I'm sure some participants went first and foremost to spend time with Jesus, what we *mostly* did was encounter one another. Through the intense bonds we developed over these short weekends, we came not only to cherish one another but also to better understand ourselves so that we could commit, together, to living more intentionally.

While people still want to understand who they are and become the best version of themselves that they can, in an increasingly digital and deinstitutionalized age, many people have internalized the idea that this is something that should be done on one's own. Instead of rooting their identity in being a member of a tribe, a community, or a family, people want to be *individuals*. Which concerns some cultural critics, because the search for individual authenticity has long been associated with a narcissistic fixation on the self at the expense of others.

This anxiety is coming to a head today because we are living in what Christian philosopher Charles Taylor describes as an "age of authenticity." As people move out of long-standing institutions and abandon larger unifying stories, instead seeking their own particular identities—using the internet to construct and reconstruct these identities—it feels as if we are in an age when authenticity is valued more than ever. Some argue that the search for realness often comes at the expense of our responsibilities to community and a shared life. But in *The Ethics of Authenticity*, Taylor says we shouldn't be arguing about whether the quest for authenticity is good or bad but rather over what authenticity *means*. At its best, he says, the search for realness can tie us together rather than rend us apart.

There's an in-kind sense of change that can happen. If the motivating ideal of authenticity—and of the ways we use the internet to seek it—is a deeper understanding of the self that leads us to a stronger connection to others, we should figure out how to move it in that direction. "We ought to be trying to lift the culture [of authenticity] back up," Taylor says, "closer to its motivating ideal."

How can realness lead us to this higher ideal—to considering others, not just ourselves? At its best, the search for authenticity "points us towards a more self-responsible form of life," Taylor writes, because it challenges us to work through our own beliefs and ideas instead of taking what we've been taught at face value. This is what, on my better days, I hope for our digital lives, too. If, according to Taylor, we find balance, our technology can be more than what he calls "an insistent, unreflected imperative."

Still, some people suggest this isn't possible. At its very core, they say, the search for authenticity—the move to seeking meaning, purpose, and connection outside of traditional institutions, as individuals—represents something inherently individualistic and narcissistic (not in the clinical, diagnostic sense, but as a synonym for self-preoccupation). Instead of seeing our digital attempts to understand ourselves as self-reflection, a number of critics suggest they are just self-obsession. Online, they argue, we are all islands unto ourselves.

Others take the conversation in a different direction— suggesting that rather than making us focus on the self at the expense of others, the internet has in fact made us *too* reliant on one another. They propose that it feeds "a kind of compensatory self-obsession that requires the approval of others and is thereby pathologically beholden to them," explains Wesleyan University's Greg Goldberg in an article for *Social Media + Society*. According to these critics, even as the internet drives us apart, it makes us less able to be selves independent of others; we can't even go to the beach without posting a photo to make sure others know we were there, critics will say. The kinds of connections we forge online are ultimately not just more shallow than offline ones, these critics argue, but make us less ourselves, because who we are becomes fully dependent on the approval of others.

But what if they're all wrong about narcissism? Self-love does not have to come at the expense of loving others, nor does it require us to be fully reliant on people to prop us up. We have room to love both ourselves and others, and loving ourselves may make us feel more grounded and self-assured. It may actually be that self-love makes it *easier* for us to love others, or to at least not be hostile toward them. Ironically, I've noticed that some of the people who argue that self-love is narcissistic are the same ones who only seem to love others insecurely, based on the ways in which those people are similar to themselves.

Sure enough, Goldberg suggests that, often, embraces of difference are actually attempts to eliminate it. By trying to identify with and relate to difference, we are sometimes—knowingly or not—trying to turn it into a kind of sameness, so that we can feel more comfortable with it. *We're not so different after all*, the saying goes.

While selfie haters scold people "for not attending to the 'real world' or our 'real lives,'" says Goldberg, selfies may in fact present an opportunity for us to reassess our narrow understanding of realness. Like drag—which subverts the real by exaggerating it, then invites us to question our own understanding of who we are in light of the norms we've inherited— the selfie functions as a provocation to our notions of the self. It both challenges us to see people in the ways they want to be seen (even if we think those ways are superficial) and invites us to become like them—"not just in terms of resemblance," Goldberg says, "but also in finding pleasure in similar modes" of being and relating.

This, he suspects, is what *really* bothers critics of the selfie. Not the narcissism they claim it exemplifies but rather the individual focus it communicates and even promotes and inspires:

> Perhaps, then, what so rankles critics about the selfie is its invitation to reflect others' "types of being" and little else: no relations of responsibility, accountability, or sacrifice; no knowledge of the other's illicit desires or innermost psychological truths; no ugly interior to expose in exchange for love or redemption; and no threatening difference to be assimilated, deported, or otherwise annihilated. In the selfie, critics see not only a vehicle for our superficiality but also, alongside this, a mechanism for our detachment from social bonds. Far from being anti-relational, though, the selfie disturbs in the kinds of perverse attachments it solicits: irresponsible, unaccountable, fickle, and fleeting,

where social bonds are responsible, accountable, dedicated, and sustained.

The ways in which we now seek connection and self-expression don't always look like the ways of old—they are, as Goldberg suggests, often fleeting and fickle, sometimes irresponsible and unaccountable. But are not the fickle, the fleeting, and the irresponsible all ways of being human, too? Is it better to repress and refuse them or to find healthier, more honest ways of engaging them?

For all that critics pan the selfie as inauthentic, or the search for authenticity as narcissistic, both are often more honest than denying that the desire to understand and love ourselves and to love others in a multitude of ways, including ephemerally, are important pieces of who we are. Through selfies, we can engage these aspects of ourselves—the fickle, the self-directed, the detached—in ways that don't have to harm ourselves or others. It is when we are not honest about our fickleness that we hurt ourselves or one another.

Lasting connections are meaningful, of course, but not every connection is lifelong. Andrew Haigh's 2011 film *Weekend* tells the story of two men who meet and develop an immediate connection just days before one of them is set to move to the other side of the Atlantic Ocean. But what differentiates it from just about every other movie in which two people meet and quickly fall for each other is that the movie doesn't end with one of them cancelling his move or both of them committing to pursue a long-distance relationship. Instead, they acknowledge their short time together for what it was—a special, transformative weekend.

Something can be both meaningful and fleeting. Sometimes the fact that something is fleeting is part of what *makes* it meaningful. No matter how long something lasts, its brevity doesn't erase its meaning; that everything must at some point end offers a horizon against which we can understand why something matters to us. Our lives, relationships, work—we care about them and try not to take them for granted because we might (and someday, in some way, will) lose them.

When social media's critics claim that it is self-oriented rather than other-oriented, or that it is focused on the fleeting rather than the lasting, they are operating with the assumption that these are bad things. But it is better to identify the value of the fickle and fleeting: what they have to teach us, what it is they offer. And to find healthier ways of expressing them.

Ultimately, it's worth examining not only the assumption that a focus on the self is a bad thing but also the normative ideas we have about *how* we should connect with one another—for example, the idea that soul baring is a requirement for intimacy, which Goldberg digs into. Social media has shown me more clearly the importance of keeping some things private—that privacy and mystery are just as necessary when it comes to feeling real as sharing and revealing are. It has helped me make sense of the fact that, even with family and friends, I need to have some things that are just for me.

If wanting to know yourself is narcissistic (again, not in the clinical sense!), so what? What if self-love, instead of causing us to turn our backs on others, can help us better understand one another? As we move away from old institutions and toward what we might call a more individual form of living, new elements of our humanity may emerge. Perhaps becoming more rooted in an understanding of ourselves will also make us more able to recognize that we are part of a larger whole.

At first I looked at this new digital frontier with despair, as a shift from community to isolation, from neighborliness to narcissism. But then I considered another possibility: that my culture was crying out for self-expression, and the internet came to answer the call. Perhaps the challenges that arise in our digital lives aren't a product of a shift in value for the worse but rather a tension born of the fact that this ideal—of authenticity, of realness—is currently not being realized. But if there's tension, it means things can still go either way. Many of us aren't going back to the old forms of community, connection, and self-expression. But we can do *this* new digital form better.

As many of us leave long-standing institutions and search for meaning and belonging online, we're doing something new and untested, something we're not yet good at. And like the queens on amateur night who seek a mentor to help them refine their craft, we often look to others online for insights into how to be human. The kinds of insights many of us once got from belonging to a religious community but for which we now turn to astrology apps and online advice columns instead.

Writing for the *Columbia Journalism Review*, online advice columnist (and my good friend) John Paul Brammer (or "JP" as I call him) talks about how people email him looking for someone who can help affirm their desire to live out their values—how his readers "want an authority figure to affirm their worldview and authorize them to live in accordance with it." When I asked JP to say more about this while we drove across Oklahoma together one summer scarfing "everything bagel"–flavored cashews (what is this world we now live in?), he said that even when we leave moral systems and traditions, we still want someone to help us figure out how to live.

Like a religion, the advice columnist or personal guru can sometimes allow you to see what you already wanted to see. Which isn't always bad; it can be immensely validating to find something that affirms your worldview and gives you the courage to act on it. In an interview with the *New York Times*, Dorothea Lasky—one-half of the popular Twitter account Astro Poets and coauthor of its eponymous book, alongside fellow poet Alex Dimitrov—says that every poem has an infinite set of meanings, and "anybody's star chart is like that too." Within those infinite meanings, we can find what we need to act.

In his *Columbia Journalism Review* piece, JP asks a reader, Charlotte de Anda, to explain why she turned to him for insight. "I think people trust advice columns generally for the same reason they trust horoscopes," de Anda told him. "They're specific enough to be relatable, but broad enough to apply to most people. They're a voice of comfort."

It's true that people have found words of comfort in religious communities, too. But in many religious communities, people *also* hear things that challenge them—that ask them to consider if they are living in line with the values they profess. Are we challenged by the online systems we establish, by our digital voices of comfort, or is it easier to hit Unfollow when we can't find the meaning in something we thought we wanted to hear? When someone makes us uncomfortable—when they shine a light on a truth we'd perhaps prefer not to acknowledge—is it simpler to walk away online than it is to leave a religious community that provokes and pushes you but also holds you in the conversation? It's much easier to abandon the latest person we idolize on Twitter when they say something offensive or challenging, or to reject our horoscope if it isn't telling us what we want to hear, than it is to leave a church or political group. These institutions can wield this power in ways that trap and harm people, of course, but one of their strengths is that they lock us in to uncomfortable relationships and urge us to stay the course.

I'm not convinced the decline of certain kinds of institutions is a bad thing. They have major problems, and more egalitarian forms of meaning-based systems would be preferable in many ways. Outside of these institutions, we can attempt more collectivist forms of community and meaning. We have the opportunity to reimagine these forms and how they function.

But it's also difficult to navigate a world less rooted in institutions, a world bound together not by time-tested practices but instead by shifting webs of people. Which is part of what makes navigating accountability deeply challenging in an age when institutions wield less influence. As Hilton Als writes in an essay for the *New Yorker*, "We are living at a time when nuance and all the confused intentions, desires, and beliefs that go along with it are considered less a way of understanding human frailty than a failure of 'accountability.'" Churches, mosques, and synagogues certainly haven't always done accountability well— one only needs to look at the scandals plaguing the Catholic Church for an egregious example—but that doesn't mean our disorganized online efforts don't have problems of their own.

As Astra Taylor writes in *The People's Platform*, many of our old institutions "relieved some of the burdens now borne solely by individuals." The idea of trying to satisfy on our own all of the needs traditional institutions have helped us meet over the years can feel overwhelming. Which may be a big part of why people write into advice columnists like JP in search of dating advice—in trying to navigate life's trials on our own, we eventually hit a point where we recognize we need input outside of ourselves.

Writing for the *Atlantic*, Derek Thompson explains that for much of human history, individuals relied on people they knew to introduce them to a prospective significant other; our romantic relationships were largely what sociologists call "mediated." But dating has changed more in the last twenty years than in the two thousand that preceded them, he explains, thanks to the internet. According to a paper coauthored by sociologists Michael Rosenfeld of Stanford University and Reuben J. Thomas of the University of New Mexico, the number of straight couples who met online went from around 0 percent in the mid-1990s to around 20 percent in 2009; for same-sex couples, that number is now almost 70 percent. As Rosenfeld and Thomas write in another paper co-authored with Stanford's Sonia Hausen, "Internet dating has displaced friends and family . . . as key intermediaries." While we used to have help in dating, the burden of screening potential partners has moved to the individual.

Simultaneously, given that you can swipe through dozens of potential dates in seconds on Tinder, it's easy to expect a partner to be a perfect match (because if they're not, you can just go right back to swiping). The result is a crisis in dating: an unsustainable level of responsibility as individuals, and an unreasonable set of expectations. And this is not just a dating problem. Thompson continues:

> Gone are the days when young generations inherited religions and occupations and life paths from their parents as if these were unalterable strands of DNA. This is the age of DIY-everything, in which individuals are charged with the full-service construction of their careers, lives, faiths, and public identities. When in the early 1800s the

Danish philosopher Søren Kierkegaard called anxiety "the dizziness of freedom," he wasn't slamming the door on modernity so much as foreseeing its existential contradiction: All the forces of maximal freedom are also forces of anxiety, because anybody who feels obligated to select the ingredients of a perfect life from an infinite menu of options may feel lost in the infinitude.

I was feeling this anxiety when, shortly after finishing my master's in religion, I got my largest tattoo. It's a giant fig tree, inspired by the passage in *The Bell Jar* by Sylvia Plath in which the protagonist imagines herself sitting in the crotch of a fig tree, surveying the fruit above her head. In each fruit she imagines a possible future for herself: different careers, lovers, lives. Recognizing that choosing one means not choosing the others, she becomes frozen with indecision. Of course, not choosing is a choice, too, and all of the fruit fall to the ground and die. Cheery story, I know. But choosing isn't always cheery when you believe, per the medieval dictum, that "every choice is a renunciation."

Instead of different jobs or lovers, though, the figs in my tattoo contain symbols of the world's religions. Before I studied systems of meaning, I thought I had to choose a path and renounce the others. But instead I learned that I could draw from the insights of each tradition while also standing firm in my own nonreligious understanding of the world. Still, this path has been challenging because I often have to do the work myself instead of being supported by a community.

There's reason to be concerned about the solitude of these journeys even beyond the burden they place on the individual and the kinds of expectations they engender. In *The War for Kindness*, director of Stanford University's Social Neuroscience Lab Jamil Zaki highlights the fact that humans live closer together than ever before in history: in 2007 we learned that, "for the first time, more people lived in cities than outside of them." At this rate, two-thirds of humans will live in cities by 2050. And yet, despite our increased proximity, in some essential ways we live further apart than before. As an increasing number of us live in cities but also live alone, we see more people than ever but know fewer of them, says Zaki. Meanwhile, rituals that once brought people together—church, yes, but also things like grocery shopping—are being replaced by activities we do online.

In August 2019, there was a short period of time in which a bizarre exercise spread online: people started sending text messages to their "number neighbor," or someone with a phone number that differed from their own by just one digit. It took the internet by storm, and for a short period I saw screenshots from these text conversations between strangers all over my Twitter timeline. Before long, I got a text from a number neighbor myself. It was amusing, but after we finished exchanging messages, I realized I'd had a more meaningful conversation with my number neighbor than I've had with my literal neighbors in my apartment building, whom I almost never see, but sometimes pass in the hallway while we each stare at our phones.

Still, even as we lament our losses, we've gained things in the transition to individuality, too. Outright dismissals of digital community ignore how it helps people connect in ways they couldn't before, particularly people with physical disabilities, those living in geographically remote areas, and members of marginalized communities who are isolated or would face significant risk if they revealed their identities. Yes, the internet has made life more convenient for many of us, but "for some people—those who've long lacked access to media and voice in society—the internet has been so much more," writes An Xiao Mina in *Memes to Movements.* In their examples, we see ways to move toward an internet that makes us feel more human, not less.

———■———

There was something else that propelled my entrée into Christianity as an adolescent, besides my desire to figure out how to connect with others and make sense of an unjust world. Like my questions about the suffering of others, about human cruelty and injustice, this thing ate away at me. It simmered just below the surface, whispering to me that, like many of the people I was reading about, there was something about me that was . . . different. Something dangerous. Something that made me vulnerable to human cruelty, too.

That something was that I was queer. On some level, it's why I devoured those narratives about suffering and injustice. Even though the experiences I read about were hugely different from anything I'd ever face, I knew that I, too, was "other," and that it put me at risk.

My early fixation on questions of personhood, injustice, and suffering was rooted in my own suffering, in my internal conflicts over my emerging sexuality. *Who am I? How can I know who I really am? Maybe I don't really understand myself. Maybe I'm not really gay. And if I am, and I don't like who I am, maybe the only way to change that is through something as apparently powerful as God.*

After converting I embarked on an immensely private struggle, an inner war waged over my sexuality and faith that largely consisted of begging the God I newly believed in to change me into another person entirely. I hid this struggle from everyone around me, which was ultimately the grand irony of my conversion: I'd become a Christian because I was seeking a sense of community, trying to connect with others, and looking for answers to questions about suffering and injustice. Instead I went inward, isolating myself from everyone around me, and my own suffering increased tenfold.

Eventually, with my mother's help, I made my way into LGBTQ-affirming Lutheran communities. But those years in fundamentalist Christianity had a consequence that I didn't anticipate, which left a deep imprint on me. They taught me that the key to finding belonging was to constantly edit myself. To monitor my behavior and filter every word, every decision, through a risk assessment. *How will others react to what I want to say? To who I am? Will they reject me if they see it all?*

I started coming out in early adolescence, and by my twenties I was confident that I had worked through my adolescent struggles and accepted my sexuality. But after my breakup, I realized that I had unknowingly held back. I was compartmentalizing, in my relationship and elsewhere. I was editing. This is sometimes referred to as "splitting," and it's a challenge for many LGBTQ people. Even after many of us accept our identities, clinical psychologist Alan Downs writes in *The Velvet Rage*, "we continue to split off unacceptable parts of ourselves." Anything that might make us unworthy in the eyes of others gets cleaved off and hidden away.

On the surface, this may simply sound like lying, but Downs says it is a much deeper psychological issue. "It's about living dishonestly, faking an entire segment of our lives for the benefit of getting along in life," he writes. "Even more troubling, when we are actively splitting we generally don't think of ourselves as being dishonest." In other words, for many LGBTQ people, splitting is first a survival technique, and then it becomes learned behavior, so ingrained we're not aware that we're doing it. Which is why some of us struggle to be honest with ourselves about the less pleasant parts of our lives—the problems in our relationships, at work, or in our own sense of self—until we can't deny them anymore. That's what happened in my late twenties when the end of my relationship completely snuck up on me.

It's hard not to feel like our digital lives are an act of constant splitting. Not in the sense that we're being intentionally dishonest, as Downs writes, but rather that being online can teach us to split off the messier, more unkempt parts of our lives, and not even be aware that we're doing it. Digital technologies didn't invent this impulse, but at times they may reinforce it by showing us a constant stream of others doing it.

As people who often struggle with splitting, it's no surprise to me that a lot of my fellow queer people, many of whom have been burned by institutional religion, are deeply into astrology, tarot, and similar ways of trying to know yourself. Because society taught us to disengage with pieces of ourselves—to split— we want to find a way to get back in touch with ourselves, to trust ourselves, to put ourselves back together. We want to know who we are, why we feel the things we feel. *Who am I* really? *How much of me is my* true *self, and how much of it is rooted in trauma? How much is a pose, a mask I learned to wear to survive, and how much of it is real?*

It's also, I suspect, a large part of why so many queer people are so online, existing in a space that lends itself to searching, editing, and broadcasting. Social media can be the perfect place for curation, for adjusting and fine-tuning yourself based on others' reactions. And we were perfectly, brokenly, designed to live under those conditions.

It's something we all do at times, though—present a self that adheres to social norms. At the end of the second season of Dan Perrault and Tony Yacenda's crudely brilliant Netflix mockumentary series *American Vandal*, the closing monologue tackles this issue—building to a kind of defense of the digital posturing we do, the masks we hide behind online:

> We're living in a constant state of feedback—and judgment. So maybe the masks are a tool to survive the time. Maybe they provide a thin layer of protection. A place to grow, discover, reinvent. The important part is having people who know you without the mask, and being happy with who you are beneath it.

The mask, of course, isn't a new phenomenon—before the internet, people still created different versions of themselves, public selves and private selves. And yes, sometimes that split can protect us. But today the lines between public and private are so blurred. I'm not always sure how to take the mask off, what I will find underneath, and if I will be happy with what I see.

The most important question about our digital efforts to find meaning and belonging doesn't necessarily concern what's literally real or fake online but rather what *feels true*—what we are trying to express about who we are and what we value through our digital presentations. When we get mired in the debate over real versus fake, stuck in the pundit cycle of the polemicists who ask again and again if social media is good or bad, we are cut off from having conversations about specifics. About etiquette and norms. About what social media can teach us about how to live. We miss the opportunity to look at what's animating our online actions. We might spend less time picking apart the fruits and more time digging down to the roots.

In the end, blaming social media and the internet for the ways we edit and split may be just another means of hiding from ourselves—a way of denying truths about who we are, about things we struggled with long before Twitter or Instagram. To assign the blame elsewhere and say the fault lies outside of us, with something out there beyond our control. Something in the algorithms, or in the stars.

When I was a kid, my mom excelled at making magic from the mundane. Our house was a small single-story stucco block completely devoid of personality, but she made it feel hospitable, warm, and utterly *us*. The bedroom my brothers and I shared, for example, was transformed by paintings on its walls depicting a rainforest scene, meticulously crafted by my mother because all three of us loved animals. Later, when I got a room of my own for a couple years, she painted something more tailored to my individual interests on the walls and ceiling—constellations.

For as long as I can remember I've loved constellations. I think it's because they represent one of our greatest capacities as humans: the ability to create something out of nothing. To build meaning and order out of things that don't obviously have it. To see a bigger story that connects smaller pieces. To, as we do with tarot cards, religion, or the individual search for authenticity, put words to things.

Which is also a big part of why I love the internet. I love forging connections between things, ideas, and people. Ties that make each component bigger than itself. Finding or creating the thread that binds things together and builds meaning out of them is one of my favorite exercises, especially when the connections are surprising or unexpected. (I mean, I wrote an entire book on the power of seeking common ground between people with different worldviews.) Because it is at the intersections where my greatest learning happens. And it is at the points of connection that we can name things; where roads come together, a town is born, and it's given a name.

Part of the appeal of things like astrology and tarot—religion, too—is that they can help us name things, often as the first step toward addressing a specific reality. One thing I love about irony, often regarded as the language of the perpetually online, is that it sometimes enables me to articulate hard truths by couching them in humor. In the sense that engaging something ironically helps me get comfortable enough with it to start engaging it sincerely, irony can be a bridge from enjoyment to enrichment. A friend of mine once tweeted, "Everything annoying about my personality started out as irony. Let me be a lesson." And I do see a lesson there, but not a cautionary tale. Maybe irony is a safe way to test the waters, to ask yourself, "Am I allowed to like this for real?" Putting words to something, even if we initially articulate it as a joke, is often the first step toward integration.

Over the last few years, new acquaintances and I have used Co—Star, an astrology app that shows your apparent astrological compatibility with friends, to see how aligned it says we are. It's always fun, and while we dismiss it if it says we're not compatible, it feels affirming when it says we are. Sure enough, I once met someone who the app said was essentially a perfect match, and we've since become friends and writing companions. (Funny enough, unlike some of the others I've done this with, they also don't believe astrology is literally true. Guess we really are a good match.) Like irony, astrology can help us name and accept things about ourselves and others. "Couching characteristics in the language of astrology seems to make it easier for many people to hear, or admit, unpleasant things about their personalities," Christine Smallwood writes of astrology in a 2019 piece entitled "Astrology in the Age of Uncertainty" for the *New Yorker,* "and to accept those traits in others. (The friend who comes over and never leaves? She can't help it. She's a Taurus.)"

Perhaps best of all, though, is how astrology places you in a larger story. For me, that means the Aries story, which says that I am supposedly passionate, driven, and impulsive. (Aries is a fire sign, which, as those adjectives and the word itself all suggest, is intense. In fact, I'm a *triple fire* sign—Aries, Aries rising, and Leo moon—and while I can't really tell you all that much about what that means, I do know that it's a *very* fun thing to say.)

Growing up nonreligious, I'll never forget when I learned about my childhood friend's Judaism—specifically about how her tradition invited her to situate herself in its larger story. I remember going home, looking at my own life, and wondering what my family's story was. Some of this was the result of growing up white in a culture in which whiteness is considered the default—when your story is the dominant story, it's easy to feel like you don't have one—but it's also a common experience among the irreligious. Much of my life since has been looking for that story, the broader narrative in which I can locate myself, and a great deal of that searching, particularly over the last decade, has happened online.

The constellations situate us within the universe. And connect us to it. Astrology, one of humanity's older ways of making meaning, looks within a smaller segment of the constellations to place us in a larger cosmic story. It is a way of looking up to look in. But why do we look to the stars for meaning when there's already so much around us that we don't understand? Perhaps for the same reason I sometimes log on seeking to forge new connections even when I already have offline connections around me: because I can project my hopes and aspirations onto the empty spaces between the lines of digital text, like the meaning some of us project onto the spaces between stars. Or because my digital connections feel farther away, like the stars, and thus there's both a safety and a mystery that pull me toward them. But I suspect more than anything it is because I can build a story out of distant stars—finding my place in a larger narrative, connected to things beyond myself.

It's a story in which I began to search for my place as an adolescent, and it's what led me to study religion. If the richest information is found in these bigger stories, in connection— which may not feel true for everyone but certainly does for me— what happens when we become less able to forge connections? It is an irony, and not the good kind, that the internet, which is inherently about connecting people and ideas, can sometimes make it feel harder to connect to others.

As with religion or constellations, the organizing and naming powers of social media can help us learn more about what it means to be human—and what kind of humans we will be—by helping us develop practices for better understanding ourselves and the world around us. If some of the greatest insights are born of the places where things intersect, then it stands to reason that the internet should be one of our greatest tools for insight. Just because social media can make us feel disconnected at times doesn't mean it has to. The outcome isn't yet set.

Rather than return to some nostalgic (and, as such, unreal) past, we need to figure out our present and our future. The answer is not to try to go back to our lives before by rejecting technology. The door has already been opened, and we've gone through it. The internet can help us make meaning, connect with others, and give order to our lives and the world around us in ways that are often profoundly real.

What is real is found in the questions: why (why we use it) and what (what needs we're trying to meet). One afternoon, scrolling through Twitter as I started and finished a bag of pretzels, I saw a tweet about tarot. I went back a little later to read the thread, but it was gone. So I emailed the person who had posted the tweet—Kaya Oakes, author of *The Nones Are Alright: A New Generation of Believers, Seekers, and Those in Between*—and asked her to tell me a bit more about what she had posted. The current vogue for tarot and the like "is an example of how capitalism devours folk religions and sends them into the mainstream," she replied. "The fact that these practices are also being primarily adapted by anxiety-prone Millennials demonstrates that traditional religion is not meeting their needs, so they are turning to DIY alternatives." But whether this results in lasting community or is merely a passing commodified trend is still unknown. Either way, she continued, "traditional religious practice in America is not going back to what it used to be, and capitalism will move on from tarot cards." What will remain, however, is "the baseline anxiety and sense of a lack of central identity and control that drove people to them."

That anxiety and lack of central identity are what drove me to Christianity, and while I thought I left them behind when I left the faith, they have surfaced in my social media rites and rituals. Just as I wasn't sure what drove me to that tarot reading, I wasn't entirely sure of my motivations when I started writing this book. I didn't realize that I was trying to understand some of the same anxieties I've wrestled with my whole life and how they've taken on new DIY digital forms: *Where do I find meaning? How should I connect? And who exactly am I?* Only once we ask ourselves the questions, honestly and curiously—putting words to the needs we're trying to meet when we log on—can we begin to understand our digital habits.

—■—

My friend Carrie Poppy often tells a story about a time she thought her apartment was haunted. She'd just moved in, and while she'd initially loved her new place, she soon began experiencing an overwhelming sense of dread, feeling an ominous pressure on her chest, and hearing a whooshing sound, like something was flying past her, whenever she went home. All signs pointed to a haunting.

Carrie tried to address the issue over the course of several days—burning sage (as I did with a friend during my own terrible summer), picturing herself surrounded by a bright white light that expanded to push the evil out (I do have limits), and telling the spirit to vacate the premises in a commanding voice (I don't think I have one of those)—before discovering the truth. A valve in her water heater was leaking carbon monoxide, exposure to which can cause symptoms consistent with what she was experiencing: an inexplicable sense of dread, chest pressure, and auditory hallucinations.

Today, in part because of that experience, Carrie is an investigative journalist who explores extraordinary claims—things that sometimes fall into the same category as tarot and astrology. But when telling that story and talking about her work investigating the paranormal or supernatural, she explains that she tries to meet every claim she encounters—whether it's a haunting, a UFO, a psychic reading, or some wellness trend or alleged miracle drug—with open-mindedness, taking them seriously. Even with her skepticism, she goes into these encounters with wonder, curiosity, and even a degree of hope that maybe *this* one is actually real.

When I sat down at the tarot table that summer afternoon, I didn't believe it was real. But on some level I hoped it might be. I felt so lost, so sad, so completely despondent that I was willing to give something different a chance. I went in for a tarot reading that day because I felt like I had nowhere else to turn, no resources or guidance, so why not try this? Why not try, as my friend Vanessa Zoltan says, to go into the experience *as if* it could be true—to approach something with faith instead of my usual skepticism? To, as philosopher Simone Weil would say, approach something with an "experimental certainty" that it can offer some insight I might not have expected?

And here's the thing: that day, when I got my cards read, I didn't leave thinking that things would get better just because my cards said so. But I did leave feeling like things would get better. That approach—treating an experience I normally wouldn't pursue *as if* it might have something to offer me—drove me to that tarot reading. And it also drove me to type "what does it mean to be real?" into a web search even though it felt stupid. In both cases this experimental certainty led to a hope I needed.

Even if we feel on some level that the internet isn't real—considering how often we're told it's fake, and how new it is—so many of us still go into our digital search for authenticity with the hope that it *might* be. And so, inspired by Carrie, I decided to go in with wonder. To treat our digital lives *as if* they have important things to teach us about what it means to be human.

To bring an honest assessment of how our digital lives can help us begin to see what's behind our tweets, our posts, and our likes—the needs we're trying to meet digitally.

"To discover the direction of your own thinking in the course of mining the past—this is a practice historical ecologists and essayists share," writer and Brown University professor Elizabeth Rush says in *Rising*. "The conclusion arrived at not in advance but through the process, by unearthing whatever is buried in the strata." Now, as amateur digital ecologists, I suggest we dig through our digital strata and see what we can unearth about what it means to be real—to discover the hopes and anxieties that drive us to the internet in search of belonging and connection. To look at what the ways we use it reveal about how we are trying to become more real.

Digging through this kind of strata, it helps to have a map. Which means looking for the order in our digital lives, the well-worn paths, the signposts and thoroughfares. If religion has helped many people organize their lives and create a feeling of order so that they can develop a sense of central identity, does the internet do the same? In what ways does the internet assist us in creating order and meaning? Are there unintended consequences to the ways we use social media to order our lives? To find out, I went looking for insight in a perhaps unexpected place, a place I first turned to in order to make sense of my world as a child: the field of cartography.

4

MAPPING THE TERRITORY

The first time I took in a map as a child, I felt something stir deep in my gut. It was a hot summer afternoon, and, after listening to me lament that I was bored, my mom told me to go to the living room shelf and pick out something to read. Tucked between storybooks was a collection of free educational volumes that our local library had put out for the taking after getting newer editions—one about the animals of the world, another about rocks and crystals, a third on machines and technology. Intrigued, but not enchanted, I kept looking at the set. I pulled the one about maps from the shelf. Its cover was unexciting, but it contained the world.

Growing up, my world—school, library, grocery store, all mere miles apart—felt small. But as I opened this atlas, the world expanded into near infinity: a dazzling array of cities and coastlines, plains and plateaus, topographies and territories stretching far beyond the flat midwestern river town I called home.

Before long my favorite books were atlases, and I pleaded with my mom to take me to the library so I could check out more. I stayed up late and read them by night-light or flashlight, memorizing statistics about the highest mountains and longest rivers and tallest buildings. Before I knew my blood type or shoe size, I knew the capital of Burkina Faso and the lowest point in Australia. Eventually my walls were covered in maps, and a desk globe was my most treasured possession. Reading atlases beneath my sheets, exploring an unfamiliar world, was sometimes escapism—but it was also a world-building exercise that showed me I was part of something bigger than myself and my small town. That I was connected to people and places far beyond the ones I could see with my eyes.

Soon, I was drawing my own maps, filling entire notebooks with them. I explored my neighborhood, charting the marsh behind my house, a nearby apple orchard, and the woods at the end of my street. Sometimes these maps would use existing names of things; where a name didn't exist, I'd make one up. The liberties compounded: in some maps I added new roads, and in others I reimagined the topography completely. When I was creating maps, I was no longer the kid wearing worn-out and too-small hand-me-downs, the kid who had never traveled anywhere, the kid whose stomach was grumbling because the grocery store didn't honor an expired coupon, or the kid who couldn't catch a football to save his life. I was able to escape into worlds of my own design.

In middle school my love of maps—which had been a mostly solitary hobby—resulted in a surprising achievement: I won my class's geography bee, then my grade's, and then the entire school's. Eventually I got all the way to the finals, the top ten in the state. I made it to the final five but lost on a history question, which at the time felt very unfair.

But my family was so proud. My grandparents even taped a news broadcast that included footage of me answering a question. I felt good, too, especially because they did, but I kept my pride private. The next day, though, a crackling voice announced my win over the loudspeaker to the whole school, and the teacher made me stand up and asked my peers to applaud. Some congratulated me, but others laughed. I sat frozen in my desk after the bell signaling the end of class rang, wishing it had been the one announcing the end of the school day instead. When I finally made my way out into the hall, cruel whispers echoed behind me.

It wasn't the end of the world—I had been teased before—but my love for geography was never the same. What had once been a way of branching out beyond the confines of my small world became tainted by the world I was trying to reach beyond. It wasn't long before the cartographer hung up his compass and retired.

By the end of middle school, I had traveled a little more—like the time my family crammed into a minivan and drove to visit relatives in Virginia, sleeping overnight in Walmart parking lots along the way, or when we stayed in a small-town motel a couple hours north of the city over spring break just so we could use its pool—but my world felt smaller than ever. Other people had taught me that my love of geography was strange and shouldn't be advertised, but that was just an appetizer. Gripped daily by fear that the world couldn't, wouldn't understand my queerness, I retreated within myself entirely, putting up borders thicker than the dark lines separating nations in my beloved atlas.

But one summer day, unable to bear my loneliness anymore, I biked to the library. After passing the atlases, I took a seat at one of the large desktop computers and worked up the nerve to type "gay" into a search engine. Crouching close to the computer to shield the screen from onlookers, I inched down the page, my heart racing and palms sweating as I moved the mouse. The search results charted a territory I had never explored; there was an entire queer planet out there beyond the borders of my world.

I had no map, but, as it turned out, I wasn't the first to visit this territory. Other people had worn in paths and left digital signposts pointing the way. Sometimes these arrows pointed in different, and even occasionally opposing, directions—there were many different ways of being gay, and I couldn't tell which map to follow. But I kept scrolling and searching, and, eventually, I set about charting a course for myself.

———▪———

The creation and increased availability of maps had a transformative effect on the world they attempted to document. As maps became more readily accessible, people became more able to travel far from the places where they'd previously been confined, to share information and resources with other populations.

But there was a dark side. Not only were maps tools of colonialism, making it easier for groups to go to war and conquest, but they in fact shaped the world by how they showed it. When the British government sent Sir Cyril Radcliffe to India in 1947 to create a boundary separating Muslim and Hindu populations, the outcome was devastating: ten to twelve million people had to move across the newly established borders of Punjab and Bengal, and an estimated one million people died.

Maps are not just tools for takeover and division but also creators of it. Those who colonize an already inhabited land or win a battle with a warring group get to draw the borders. These borders, which have historically been created through colonization, establish the framework for future exploration. They build the world people have to live in. Maps have always privileged particular understandings of the world, certain stories and lives, while ignoring and even erasing others. Despite what I thought as a child, that atlas I picked off the shelf didn't contain the whole world. It barely captured a sliver of it, telling only the stories its creators thought mattered.

This power—enlivening, erasing, and destructive—probably sounds familiar. Transforming our world in many ways, the internet has been a democratizing force for the disempowered and marginalized. Many social movements have used the internet to organize and signal-boost. And individuals who previously felt isolated, like LGBTQ people living in environments where they didn't see any openly queer people (like me as an adolescent) or religious minorities living in totalitarian and ultraconservative climates where it isn't safe to be open about their beliefs and identities, are now more able to access information and connect with others.

Yet, while more democratic than an atlas, the internet can be similarly misleading. It feels like the entire world, but it's just a piece of it, where only certain stories are told. Conversations online are often driven by those with power—outlets and influencers backed by the wealthy shape our online discussions, and certain kinds of content are rewarded over others. Invisible algorithms chart courses for us, and we're often swept right along. So often unseen or unacknowledged, they warp our sense of proportion, making some stories and lives feel bigger and more influential than they are.

These forces can be traced all the way back to the internet's roots. A large chunk of the first internet users were members of the United States military and American academics, and as a result American telephone wires were used to develop much of the internet's early infrastructure. This physical history, of course, shaped the direction of the internet that followed, and it's why the parallels between maps and the internet are more literal than you might think. "'The information superhighway' is a dated metaphor that obscures the ways people use the internet for affirmation and other emotional benefits, but the comparison with a road system is apt for the actual physical structure of the internet," writes An Xiao Mina in Memes to Movements. The US highway system consists of tiered roads, she explains, with major highways linking bigger cities, while more rural and lower-income communities have to rely on smaller roads with fewer lanes. That is true of the internet, too.

Drawing on the work of author Andrew Blum, Mina explains that "the earliest infrastructure of the internet emerged in urban areas in Western countries, frequently accessible to people from middle-class backgrounds and doing information work." It was only later that the internet reached other parts of the world: first coastal cities, connected by cables that crossed oceans, and from there smaller and smaller inland communities could become connected. Thus, people in more geographically isolated areas, as well as those who were (and continue to be) unable to afford internet access, have had far less of an impact on what the internet does and doesn't enable us to do. In short, the system so many of us now use to connect and express ourselves was structured to respond to the needs and interests of a particular population in power in a particular part of the world.

And this, of course, is not a past-tense problem. Not even half of the world's population was online as of 2019 (compared to the US, where internet users made up more than 80 percent of the public), which means there's still a very large percentage of the world that has had little influence on shaping the internet—and those who aren't online come from many different backgrounds. We ought to think long and hard about the perspectives our collective map is missing. If we don't do so now, these disparities will be starker in the future.

At the same time, the internet has long been a space where alienated individuals have connected and built community. It's similar to how many of the physical places where marginalized groups have found and built community in the US over the years—black Americans, Indigenous communities, low-income individuals and families—have been on largely unoccupied land that was considered less than desirable. (For example, in my state of Minnesota, the Prairie Island Indian Community, a Mdewakanton Sioux reservation, is the closest population to a nuclear plant anywhere in the US, according to tribal council president Shelley Buck.) Undesired land often becomes home to people that society has deemed undesirable.

In its early years, this was also true of the social internet. Digital spaces were once regarded as the realm of "losers" who couldn't connect in any other way—less-real spaces for less-real connections. In a sense, the internet became a place where a number of marginalized groups could move into unoccupied, seemingly undesired territory and make a home for themselves.

Yet today, like the gentrification sweeping through low-income neighborhoods across American cities, dominant groups are coming into the digital territories that were once a home for socially excluded people.

Almost all of the people who once dismissed the internet have now moved in. In *Rising*, Elizabeth Rush points out that a great deal of America's undesirable land has existed along its shores. Thus, the often-marshy land found on America's coasts was once home to various groups of people who couldn't live elsewhere, a place where boundaries faded and people mixed. She gives Pensacola, Florida as an example—what was formerly a swamp became "one of the most racially mixed cities in the South." Until, of course, it became segregated as more privileged people began to see the appeal of coastal living. And the internet, too—once a place where people could mix—has in some respects become more segregated as more people have moved in.

Today, the presence of the privileged brings attention to problems on the internet that have been ignored for years, like online harassment. But when these problems are addressed, the changes still tend to benefit the already advantaged. Meanwhile, marginalized people are largely left hugging the coastline, as it were.

None of this means that maps, or the internet, don't tell a story of their landscapes. Their representation may be partial and skewed, but it's still real and powerful. As a closeted adolescent I used the internet to create spaces where I could be myself, fully, for the first time ever. The internet, like atlases, hinted at a world that was so much larger than the one I knew—and helped me imagine myself someday living in it.

One of the first things many of us do when encountering a map is check to see if we're on it. As a child I felt almost personally offended if one didn't include Minneapolis–Saint Paul, the Twin Cities, on it—and if I came across such a map, I would immediately begin assembling a mental list of reasons I felt my hometown deserved to be marked. Without being asked, I started building a case for why that map was wrong.

I didn't know it then, but I wanted these maps to include the places that mattered to me because I wanted them to validate that where I was from mattered. That I mattered. That I did in fact exist.

As more of us map our lives online, this desire to affirm that we matter, that we exist, has taken on new shape. As Taylor Lorenz writes in "When Kids Google Themselves" for the *Atlantic*, an increasing number of toddlers have distinct online identities moulded by their parents. Eventually these children get older and discover that there's a public story of their lives online, written by someone else. Some find this invasive and violating, a record that may trouble them well into adulthood. For other teens, though, the discovery is thrilling. Natalie, a thirteen-year-old, tells Lorenz that she and her friends were delighted to find pictures of themselves online: "We were like, 'Whoa, we're real people.'"

We all have, in one way or another, this desire to be visible and charted. But that's not all maps and the internet do. Maps also give us a feeling of coherence—the sense not just that we're visible to the world around us but that this world has order, that it makes sense. It can place us in the world and then help us understand that world and how to navigate it. In the digital age, we are invited to become a kind of self-cartographer, using our new digital tools to map out our own lives—to give our lives order, to make ourselves visible, to help us understand the world around us, and to make ourselves more understandable to others.

These tools are susceptible to the same nefarious forces that show up in mapmaking, though. And just as I didn't understand, as a child, the reasons a mapmaker might leave my hometown off of a map, most of us haven't the slightest clue about how our digital platforms encourage us to chart certain things and leave others off the map as we attempt to render ourselves visible.

In the wake of my breakup, I told myself that I should try dating again. So I began hanging out with a guy who was a bit of a puzzle, and courting him felt like a game of tug-of-war. In moments he would be soft and warm, but then he would turn unemotional and distant. (Fresh off my breakup, I was doing the same.) For a while I felt pulled toward the challenge of it; attempting to map the territory between us gave me a sense of agency and security during a time when my world felt uncharted.

One of our biggest differences was evident in his aversion to social media—a stance he made so well known that his friends created an Instagram hashtag about how he didn't have an account. He did, however, share my love of maps. We talked at length about them, and about how nice it felt to return to an abandoned childhood interest. During one such conversation, he rose from his couch, pushed off the blanket he'd draped over his legs, and walked to one of his bookshelves. Sandwiched between academic textbooks was a copy of *The Mapmakers*, a book on the history of cartography. He extracted it and placed it in my hands.

Early in the book, author John Noble Wilford explains how cartographers attempt to capture and communicate what's real but have to simplify what they document in order to fit it on a map—how the need to "choose what to show and how to show it, and what not to show," requires them to deconstruct the world (or part of it) and then reassemble some of the pieces. "The most conscientious mapmaker perforce falls short of telling the whole truth. Some things are left out: a map of waterways subtracts highways," he writes. "Space is much reduced: cities become mere dots or squares."

In nearly every book about maps I've read since *The Mapmakers*, the same point is made. In Denis Wood's *The Power of Maps* he discusses at length *A Clear Day*—a "portrait map" (photograph) of the world created with satellites by artist Tom Van Sant and scientist Lloyd Van Warren. Wood concludes the discussion with a warning to those who regard this satellite composite view of the earth as literally documenting reality. Though it is an "acme of cartographic perfection," he acknowledges, it emerges in the context of a community of mapmakers with "a certain vision of what it means to live."

While you might look at Van Sant's satellite map of the world as a neutral depiction of Earth, it, too, has an agenda. And it's not just expressing the vision of its creators—it's also a record of what colonialism has done to the planet, through its borders and highways and environmental devastation. Informed by the interests of those who hold power, both maps and the internet have shown and reinforced colonialism and moulded the people who used them. We bring all of our cultural biases to both, whether it's the kinds of information we share online or how we understand a satellite record of the way previous maps have divided the planet. The forces that shape both our maps and the internet are ever present, whether we acknowledge them or not.

My childhood cartography games had agendas I couldn't see at the time, too. So often even our own motives are hidden from us. Just as I couldn't see what I was getting out of hanging out with my fellow map lover until after the fact—years later, once I had moved back to Minnesota and accidentally taken his copy of *The Mapmakers* with me—we won't understand the maps we make of ourselves until we can be honest about the underlying reasons we share certain things while leaving others off the map.

On a cold day in January 2018, I walked into the University of Minnesota's John R. Borchert Map Library to meet with Ryan Mattke, who oversees it. I had noticed that the ways I was using the internet weren't dissimilar to the ways I'd used maps as a kid—like how posting pictures of a put-together life on Instagram in the year after my breakup allowed me to feel like a mapmaker taking control of a confusing and complicated world. I wanted to explore the connection, and Mattke invited me to come talk with him—and explore their archives for as long as I'd like, an idea that filled me with a flush of childlike wonder.

Buried within the university's O. Meredith Wilson Library, the Borchert Library is a hidden treasure trove of maps. It has around 365,000 aerial photos that capture the entire state of Minnesota beginning in the 1930s, nautical charts, National Park and Forest maps, and block-level atlases for Minneapolis and Saint Paul dating back to the 1880s. But it also has collections of strange and unusual works that push the definition of what constitutes a map, from maps that chart Nintendo's Mushroom Kingdom and reports of paranormal activity in the US to a wall-sized map of joy and pain created by artists and community members in Minneapolis and Saint Paul.

Sitting across from me in a cluttered office, Mattke explained from behind a pronounced red mustache that maps are "a grand exercise in hierarchy" in which what you choose to show and emphasize profoundly impacts how a map is used—and how what it documents is understood.

"People view maps as factual information," he said, "but that's not true." He talked about teaching students about a map of Germany in 1880. Looking at the map, he explained, students initially assume that this is how Germany literally appeared in 1880. But then he informs them that this map was made for a king, and it emphasized his view of the nation. It was the king's Germany, not the peasant's.

Maps are inherently edited works, the outcome of a process of culling and curation strikingly similar to the one we apply to ourselves. No matter how unfiltered and honest we may feel, the self we present to the world is fundamentally constructed. Like a cartographer, we both knowingly and unconsciously select what to share and what to leave out. This is true in our everyday presentation, from the clothing we choose to wear to the things we choose to say (or not). But the development of online personas may actually intensify this selection process. We are given filters and character limits. Algorithms prioritize particular kinds of content, and if we pay attention, we may—again, intentionally or unknowingly—find ourselves tailoring our output to what we know will be rewarded with retweets and likes. Online, we all exist within a framework that someone else had the power to draw.

As in maps, certain points of view and personality types are privileged above others online. While the number of people with regular access to the internet is growing—the 2018 Global Digital suite of reports from We Are Social and Hootsuite found that more than four billion people were using the internet in 2017, and a quarter of a million of those people were first-time users—there are, as I mentioned, still many who cannot afford the technology to get online, even as it becomes more accessible. Those who can get online are often still limited; people or brands with expendable income who can afford to promote their Facebook posts or tweets are more likely to gain followers than those who cannot. The same is true of people who have more time available to dedicate to social media, whereas people working long hours at jobs that don't allow them to be on their phones or computers are less able to log on. The "rewards" for content also tend to skew toward the privileged, from viral outrage tweets posted by people who don't have to worry about possibly losing their jobs over them to photos taken by those who can afford more technologically advanced cameras and editing software. More broadly, as social media has become more and more central to the ways we live our lives, those who cannot afford to access it are moved toward the margins of society.

But the privileging of certain perspectives in both social media and maps runs much deeper than that. In *Maps Are Territories*, David Turnbull draws on Martin Rudwick's *The Emergence of a Visual Language for Geological Science* to explain how maps are documents presented in a "visual language"—and, like any language, it comprises a complex set of rules and conventions learned through practice and maintained by a community that accepts them. Social media platforms, too, have their own languages, each with their own rules and conventions that one must learn and that are upheld and transformed by a community of users.

Just as maps are shaped by the conventions of cartography as much as by the territory they're conveying, the self we construct online is in part based on received assumptions of how we should present ourselves. I can't begin to tell you how many times a friend of mine has signed up for Twitter after hearing me talk about it constantly, only to report a few days later that they don't really get it. It took me years to learn how to tweet properly, though the truth is that I'm very much still learning, especially because the rules keep changing, and there's always some new SpongeBob meme I don't understand until everyone has already moved on to the next one. Those who learn how to abide by these rules and modify quickly when they shift seem much more likely to build a successful online platform than those who can't or refuse to do so.

Some of the unwritten rules and norms of social media are almost universally agreed to be unreasonable or stupid, yet so many of us feel pressure to practice them anyway. One such norm is the idea that someone is more worthy of following if they have a larger following. Sure enough, there's someone who follows me on Twitter, where I have a lot of followers, and interacts with me often; but on Instagram, where I have something like one-eighth as many followers as I do on Twitter, they never followed me back. And they're far from the only one. But before you get offended on my behalf, you should know: I follow them on Instagram, where they have more followers, but not on Twitter. These "rules," we know, are ridiculous—we mock them, roll our eyes at others who talk about them like they're sacrosanct—yet so many of us still practice them anyway.

Adapting ourselves to these norms and rules changes the ways we communicate and move through the world more broadly. One of my favorite things about Twitter, for example, is that using it daily for nearly a decade has made me a more concise writer (which is why I was among the many disappointed when Twitter doubled the character limit for tweets). Similarly, after I joined Instagram, I started taking more photos, documenting experiences and moments I previously might not have—creating a visual map of my life from which I could venture more easily into memory. Slang from social media has wormed its way into everyday conversation, too. I noticed it the first time I accidentally said "L-O-L" out loud and felt my mortification grow as everyone gave me a strange look, but even more so when I said it again a year later and no one blinked. Just as maps don't just convey the world but also change it, the ways we use social media to document the world around us end up altering the world we're documenting.

The unseen structural lines of these platforms can end up warping how we see ourselves and others. I remember reading my first atlas as a child and imagining Greenland as this frozen behemoth far larger than Australia. It was only later that I learned that, while large, Greenland is nowhere near as large as it appears on projected maps, which often stretch the parts of the world appearing closest to the poles. Sometimes the distorted version is all we get to see; barring a midlife-crisis career change to astronaut, a map is probably the only way I'll ever view Greenland from above. Likewise, one bad, out-of-context tweet from a stranger, retweeted into our timeline, may be all that person ever is to us.

But what is "real" in the worlds of maps and social media, anyway—especially when whether something is real or not is almost beside the point when the projections hold this much power? The truth is that the lines between "real" and "online" are much more blurred than we often think. As Turnbull writes: "Our experience of the world and our representations of it are mutually interdependent, so there is a sense in which the two are inseparable. Or, to put it in its most contentious form, 'the map is the territory.'"

Just as we construct ourselves via social media, social media constructs us in return. To paraphrase Ralph Waldo Emerson, we become what we worship. The more we see ourselves in a certain way, and are seen by others in this way, the truer it feels. When I'm told online that I'm a good writer, it feels closer to being true; on the other hand, the more I'm inundated by trolls calling me weak or stupid, the more true that can feel. As we construct ourselves online, others are able to participate in that construction, changing or reinforcing it, for better or for worse.

There's an element of this that can be beautifully aspirational and world-making. At its best, social media can be a place to practice better, more authentic versions of ourselves that don't yet exist. Sometimes, like the maps of imaginary towns and cities that I made as a child, these things will never come to be. But other times, like blueprints of a house or a map of a planned development, once it's sketched out, we can slowly build toward becoming the person we present online.

In *A History of the World in Twelve Maps*, Queen Mary University of London's Jerry Brotton describes the first known map of the world, a clay tablet found in the ruins of the ancient city of Sippar. Beyond the landmass and the sea surrounding it, this map also included "uncharted spaces, the mythical, far-away places beyond the circular limits of the known Babylonian world." As Wilford explains in *The Mapmakers*, for centuries before the rise of mapmaking, "people satisfied themselves with outrageous tales, told as fact, of lands where there existed fierce griffons and men without heads, dog-headed simians and birds that glowed in the dark."

While social media can be a place to imagine positive futures for ourselves, the things unseen on the social media landscape can similarly inspire fear. We forecast dread, asking ourselves what lies beyond our current technological borders, often imagining the worst in those empty spaces. Instead of monsters or men without heads, we dream of dystopias like those depicted in the Netflix techno-drama *Black Mirror*. The future of mapping can feel scary, too. Every now and then a screenshot of someone who was captured in an embarrassing position by Google Maps cameras makes the rounds on social media—something I now think about whenever I'm bent over in pajamas digging my dog's excrement out of a snowbank and feel my waistband begin to slip below my waistline. And in the map library, Mattke showed me lidar (light detection and ranging) mapping, in which a plane or drone shoots down a laser and gives multilevel returns with almost perfect precision. As he navigated through a three-dimensional lidar point-cloud map of Saint Paul, I was slightly terrified by how easy it now is to map every inch of our world.

The increasing reach of social media into all spaces of our lives, which feel more public and less private than ever, can be scary as well. And yet, alongside those fears, many of us still experience social media as a space where we can chart new territory. Many ideas are first spoken as a concept online and then later turned into reality. A song uploaded by a relative unknown goes viral and soon becomes the longest-running number-one song in the history of the Billboard Hot 100 chart (Lil Nas X's "Old Town Road"), or someone tweets out a goal and forgets they ever posted about it until that goal has been reached. Crowdfunding websites, like Kickstarter and Indiegogo, exist for the very purpose of making people's dreams a reality.

Still, this constructive process is often less overt or intentional. When I got my first cell phone, it had the option of creating nine speed-dial shortcuts. I had to choose my nine people, and if I wanted to add one, I had to take someone else out. I suspect this implicitly impacted the way I thought about my capacity for close friendship. (And don't get me started on how Myspace's top eight feature *explicitly* fractured friendships in high school.) Similarly, if space and style constraints limit a map to its nine "most important" features, how do the things shown—and those left out—impact the way we think about that place?

I continue to navigate these dynamics today. A couple years ago, I decided to unfollow some accounts on Twitter to cut down on the number of tweets in my timeline. One person I unfollowed—someone I'd never met off Twitter, and with whom I didn't seem to share many interests—sent me a message within hours: "Why unfollow me?" It was our first interaction in over a year. I hadn't meant anything by the unfollow, I told him; I was just trying to make my timeline a little less overwhelming. "I don't think it's good to cut people who support you," he responded.

I could tell he was hurt, that he interpreted the unfollow as a rejection. His hurt shouldn't have surprised me, given my own reaction when I'm unfollowed. While we act as if we're playing the same game in the same way, the truth is that we are all interpreting these often arbitrarily drawn lines differently. We're all projecting ourselves onto a map—but just as different mapmakers use different projection styles, we abide by radically different understandings of what's significant. Turnbull explains that "no curved surface like that of the Earth can be projected in two dimensions without some distortion." Likewise, some distortion is necessary to capture and describe the realities of our lives online.

Yes, the lies of maps are built right in. "To portray meaningful relationships for a complex, three-dimensional world on a flat sheet of paper or video screen," Syracuse University's Mark Monmonier writes in *How to Lie with Maps*, "a map must distort reality." Yet the power of maps to deceive goes deeper than that. We willingly abide a map's necessary white lies, so it's easy for mapmakers to lie in more egregious ways, too, Monmonier argues. We trust cartographers to know "where to draw the line, figuratively as well as literally," just as we so often trust the privacy policies of the platforms we use. As we rarely question their authority, we "often fail to appreciate the map's power as a tool of deliberate falsification or subtle propaganda."

Because of the trust we place in our platforms, social media has been weaponized in the service of both subtle and overt propaganda, too—from platforms knowingly sharing users' personal data with bad actors to allowing trending topics to be rife with misinformation. On Twitter, breaking stories frequently turn out to be wrong. Living in Boston, Massachusetts, at the time of the 2013 marathon bombing, I remember the rapidity with which conspiracy theories and false information spread in the wake of the attack. There is a danger in the amount of credibility we give to information shared online, and we would do well to be skeptical, especially when information comes from a source we're more inclined to unquestioningly believe.

Even beyond overt propaganda, digital distortion sometimes changes how we see ourselves due to how we see others. Online, we witness other people's highlights and unfairly compare them to our own life, of which we have a fuller picture. I spent many nights after my breakup scrolling past smiling couples and seemingly carefree single friends, wondering why life seemed so easy for everyone else when everything felt so difficult for me. Instead of finding comfort in others' happiness, I compared their highs to my lows, and this contrast pushed me deeper down into the dirt.

In *A Circle of Quiet*, author Madeleine L'Engle explains that because it's hard to see our "inner, essential" selves, we seek "glimpses" of it in others' eyes. But she warns that we need to be "careful of our mirrors." Looking in the wrong ones can hurt us; she writes of feeling like a failure as a writer after comparing herself to others, of how looking "for an image in someone else's mirror" prevents her from seeing herself clearly.

It's not just comparison, either. The digital maps we create of our own lives can contain distortions we're not aware of. In *The Memory Illusion*, psychologist and science writer Julia Shaw argues that you "aren't as attractive as you think." Which, first of all, rude. She argues there are two reasons for this: "basic memory processes and the way we use technology."

"Unless you are currently looking in a mirror," she explains, "your perception of what you look like is a type of memory." Not just a memory of how you appeared the last time you looked in a mirror—a composite of how you've looked pretty much every time you've ever caught your reflection or taken in a photo of yourself. "The problem," she continues, "is that this patchwork memory of what you look like never stood a chance because it can never exist in reality. You cannot look today like you did every day until today." This is why, if we see a photo of ourselves that we don't like, we say it's a bad picture. "Often what makes it a bad picture is simply that it is at odds with what we *think* we look like, at odds with our memory of ourselves." Our reality doesn't match up with the map we've constructed.

To drive this home, Shaw cites a study by Nicholas Epley at the University of Chicago and Erin Whitchurch at the University of Virginia in which researchers digitally altered photos of participants and then, several weeks later, asked them to identify the original. Participants selected photos of themselves that were 13 percent better looking for themselves, 10 percent for their friends, but only 2.3 percent for strangers. (Poor strangers.) While Shaw says we could chalk this phenomenon up to the fact that most people generally think they're above average, she suggests it's actually that we have distorted our self-perception, as well how we see those closest to us, over time. We can see strangers more objectively, but our understanding of ourselves and those we love is warped as we go back again and again to the representations we've created. Over time, the distortions become how we see ourselves and those closest to us. It's like my childhood image of Greenland, influenced more by a representation than an actual image.

It's not surprising that digital technology may exacerbate this problem. Instead of waiting a week to get your photos developed and praying there would be one good one in the bunch, like I did growing up, you can now take a hundred photos, instantly review them, select your favorite and delete the "bad ones," digitally alter the winner to make it look even better, upload it for online engagement, and return again and again to the images that get the most likes and comments, seeking the dopamine boost of engagement. These hyperreal versions of our faces loom ever larger in our imaginations, shaping how we see ourselves. And when we are confronted with a self that contradicts this image, it can feel crushing.

With this in mind, we ought to be careful about the ways in which we map ourselves online and how that can alter our understanding of ourselves. (I'm trying! A year ago I stopped putting filters on my photos, though I do still adjust the lighting. Baby steps.) Just as a map is only a representation of how a place looked at one particular moment in time, and treating it as gospel truth can warp our perspective of that place, the maps we create of ourselves online can cause us to see ourselves in distorted ways if we don't chart with care.

If we are to use social media in a way that feels remotely authentic, we must first recognize its conventions. You can't play a game if you don't know the rules. (Well, I mean, you *can*, but there's a reason I don't let myself get dragged into playing Risk with people who can't be bothered to explain the rules anymore.)

Still, a lot of the norms and rules that we use to present ourselves to the world aren't arbitrary but rather serve a specific purpose—and that purpose is worth digging into. For example, most maps put north at the top and south at the bottom, "the result of a historical process closely connected with the global rise and economic dominance of northern Europe," writes Turnbull. As Alexis Bhagat and Lize Mogel explain in the introduction to *An Atlas of Radical Cartography*, the ubiquitous mapping of the world with a northern orientation reinforces ideas of a Global South and Global North.

Just as that mapping norm has centered and benefited a particular part of the world, the norms and rules of social media frequently advantage certain groups over others. People in positions of power are much more likely to be verified on Twitter (indicated by a checkmark next to their name, verified accounts are described by Twitter as a way of letting "people know that an account of public interest is authentic"), which helps protect them, while others are much more vulnerable to harassment. And among the verified are people who absolutely do not need protection, including a number of notorious white supremacists.

Certain styles of communicating—those used by these outlets' creators—are often privileged online, making some people feel more welcome on these platforms than others. Frequently those norms change because users transform the platform themselves through regular use, but even then, creators often ignore the petitions of users. (One of the most regular, and controversial, user requests on Twitter is for an edit function that would allow people to change their tweets after the fact. As much as I hate typos—I once fired off a petty tweet about Gwen Stefani so quickly I accidentally wrote "Gwent," and of course, unlike so many of my tweets without typos, it went viral—this is one request I'm glad Twitter has ignored so far.)

As Turnbull writes, "conventions often follow cultural, political and even ideological interests, [and] if conventions are to function properly they must be so well accepted as to be almost invisible." In maps, these near-imperceptible conventions have very visible consequences. One of the most profound examples is the practice of redlining. In 1935, the Federal Home Loan Bank Board initiated the creation of "residential security maps" of American cities. These maps ranked neighborhoods from "best" to "still desirable" to "definitely declining" to "hazardous," with the last category highlighted in red. "Hazardous" neighborhoods were frequently low-income communities of color. The impact of these categorizations was ruinous: it became profoundly difficult for those who lived in red neighborhoods to get bank loans or sell their properties.

During my tour of the Borchert Map Library, Mattke showed me old redlining maps of Minneapolis and Saint Paul. Big chunks of "hazardous" neighborhoods were decimated when the interstate highways were built; put a redlining map over a contemporary highway map and the alignment is stunning. But the legacy of that redlining persists in all kinds of ways not visible on a map. In most cities, like Minneapolis, redlining maps are ingrained. Residents and financial and political institutions continue to talk about redlined neighborhoods in troubling, racialized terms, and systemic neglect and abuse occur accordingly.

Maps have historically been made by those with resources, and they have shaped the course of history. Maps made by the powerful reinforce power. As Brotton explains in A History of the World in Twelve Maps, a survey of twentieth-century atlases by geographer Jeremy Crampton revealed that Africa, which covers 20 percent of the earth's land, is often represented on a smaller, less detailed scale than the United Kingdom, which makes up only 0.16 percent of land on earth.

But efforts are underway to address this, including websites like The Decolonial Atlas, a collection of maps intended to "challenge our relationships with the land, people, and state . . . based on the premise that cartography is not as objective as we're made to believe." And these efforts are leading to concrete changes: in Minneapolis, grassroots movements have led to the changing of place names, like Lake Calhoun—named after proslavery politician John C. Calhoun—being restored to the Dakota name Bde Maka Ska, meaning Lake White Earth.

Six months after my first of numerous visits to the Borchert Map Library, I returned to the University of Minnesota's campus—but this time I had another destination, just one building over. I stepped into the office of Kirsten Delegard, cofounder and codirector of the Mapping Prejudice Project, to meet with her and her team.

As we sat together, she explained that Mapping Prejudice is a community effort to map private contracts written by real estate developers called racial covenants—clauses in property deeds that barred nonwhite residents. Between 1910 and 1940 they spread like wildfire across Minneapolis and other American cities. During the New Deal, the federal government folded covenants into the new practice of redlining, which determined where the federal government would underwrite mortgages.

Covenants and redlining worked in tandem, Delegard explained. Covenants first segregated cities, including Minneapolis, concentrating black people into discrete neighborhoods with hard boundaries. Then redlining was imposed, enabling federal officials and local banks to withhold loans from people in areas deemed "hazardous," devastating black-majority neighborhoods by draining them of capital. While the federal government made racial covenants illegal in 1968 with the Fair Housing Act, their impact is still evident in the demographic makeup of Minneapolis neighborhoods today. By segregating cities like Minneapolis and ensuring resources were pooled in white-majority areas, redlining and racial covenants codified inequity. In an already colonized country, they allowed people to use maps to continue colonizing.

More of us are becoming aware of how people from privileged backgrounds often move into digital landscapes created by the disenfranchised and colonize them, consciously or otherwise, redrawing the map and renaming things in their own image. So often we (this absolutely includes me) do it without realizing, so ingrained are some of the practices. We borrow pieces of other people's digital maps without even knowing where those pieces came from. But the fact that this often happens without intention doesn't make it okay. It makes it all the more pernicious. Like mapmakers and the people who have commissioned their work, social media creators and users often act in ways that feel colonial. From a growing recognition of how memes and slang are co-opted from marginalized groups (white people co-opting from people of color, nonqueer people co-opting from the LGBTQ community, and so on) to emerging conversations about the use of "digital blackface"—when nonblack social media users frequently or exclusively employ reaction GIFs of black people. Many of the practices and conventions we accept as artless or "neutral" in fact represent the interests of those in power.

And yet even as its conventions are stacked against the disenfranchised, the internet has created unprecedented opportunities for those organizing and asserting their existence. Social media often helps communities that have historically been rendered invisible document their lives. As poet Alejandro de Acosta writes in "Latino/a America: A Geophilosophy for Wanderers" in *An Atlas of Radical Cartography*:

> My wish (or slogan) is: that the marginalization of peoples become something other than the source of reactive identities and new nationalisms; or: that marginality be increasingly revealed as a space, as an array of places, for a particularly free kind of thinking. This revelation requires a physical form for its emergence: a map. A philosophical map, then, would chart the ephemeral events of everyday life and invest them with new significance,

documenting experiences and increasing the possibility of their communication.

That sounds a lot like social networks at their best, right? Marginalized communities are more able than ever before to map their lives online and document the things people in power wish to deny or erase. Platforms like Twitter have been critical to the growth of movements like Black Lives Matter. In the wake of the death of Michael Brown, an unarmed teenager shot by a police officer in Ferguson, Missouri, people used Twitter to organize on the ground, share their locations with one another, and broadcast evidence of systemic injustice to the nation. Similarly, hashtags like #DisabledAndCute and #BlackGirlMagic empower members of disenfranchised communities to do more than just document their trauma and pain—they are ways of mapping and sharing their joys with a world that is less inclined to tell those kinds of stories. If mapping is an act of power, social media at its best can enable communities that have been disempowered to take control of their own narratives and assert their agency.

Maps and the internet can allow us to recast the world, for good and for ill. In *GeNtry!fication: Or the Scene of the Crime*, Minneapolis poet Chaun Webster notes that in the 1930s, University of Washington sociology professor Calvin Schmid produced a report about Minneapolis and Saint Paul entitled *Social Saga of Two Cities* (I was able to find a digitized copy of it online, thanks to Mattke), which identified a portion of North Minneapolis as a "Negro slum." This designation forever changed how people outside the neighborhood thought of and related to it. At Mapping Prejudice, I mentioned Schmid's map. In response, Delegard told me about a memory map of Minneapolis's Near Northside that Clarence Miller created with neighborhood residents in the 1950s to document an area that had been razed by urban renewal. While Schmid's map was geographically accurate and the memory map was not, the latter captured things about the neighborhood that the former didn't think of as important, as worth communicating. Rather than streets or the ages of buildings, Miller's map conveyed relationships and social infrastructure. These are the qualities that bind a neighborhood together, that create meaning for a place that goes beyond property values to recognize the value of human connection.

Delegard pointed out that these two maps show a profound difference between how residents conceptualize space and how, for example, urban planners do. Urban planning, she said, requires boundaries and clear delineations. But residents are more interested in how a neighborhood *feels* than how it's zoned. When community members are given the opportunity to create a map of the place they call home, they create something *differently* accurate.

We have a long way to go to address the inherent disparities of maps, both digital and cartographic platforms. "Cartography is about representation," writes Penn State's Alan M. MacEachren in the first chapter of *How Maps Work*, and social media is, too. And as Kaitlin Ugolik Phillips explains in *The Future of Feeling*, the lack of representation in the companies that developed our social technology has had a tremendous impact on how much different communities' needs are met—or not.

Even as we consider the organizing power of social media, it's important to continue asking how those in power are adapting their tactics to use it to their advantage. "The appearance of a more level playing field is not the fact of it, and everything that happens on the internet bounces and refracts," writes Jia Tolentino in *Trick Mirror*. "At the same time that ideologies that lead toward equality and freedom have gained power through the internet's open discourse, existing power structures have solidified."

Sure enough, in *Twitter and Tear Gas* Zeynep Tufekci reflects on how her sense of optimism about the internet's ability to empower dissidents shifted in a short period of time. Within just a couple of years, she became far less optimistic about the internet's potential because of the advantage that existing power structures have. "Whereas a social movement has to persuade people to act," writes Tufekci, "a government or a powerful group defending the status quo only has to create enough confusion to paralyze people into inaction. The internet's relatively chaotic nature, with too much information and weak gatekeepers, can asymmetrically empower governments by allowing them to develop new forms of censorship based not on blocking information, but on making available information unusable." While grassroots movements must completely overhaul societal conventions in order to organize, those in power have been able to adapt more quickly.

But it's more than just the advantages those in power already have. Part of the issue also lies in our inability to use the internet to organize well and sustain that organization. Challenges exist in tandem with opportunities. Yes, the internet allows movements to develop quickly, Tufekci acknowledges, but it does so without requiring "prior building of formal or informal organizational and other collective capacities that could prepare them for the inevitable challenges they will face and give them the ability to respond to what comes next."

Just as movements can grow swiftly online, as an untrained cartographer I can quickly make my own map of my city without input from anyone else. Both might bring fresh perspectives, and, as Tufekci says, there is real value there. But she offers an important caveat. "The tedious work performed during the pre-internet era served other purposes as well," she writes. "Perhaps most importantly, it acclimated people to the process of collective decision making and helped create the resilience all movements need to survive and thrive in the long term."

In some respects we once publicly mapped our lives in more collaborative ways. By participating in a church, for example, I could stand up and share a message one Sunday, thus rendering myself and my concerns visible to the community. But belonging to that community would also require me to engage in all the negotiation and cooperation that comes with being a member. If I wanted to map my life in the predigital age, most of the time I would be forced to work with other people in order to relay the self I wanted to share with the world. Now that process is more individual, and just as in movement organizing, perhaps something is lost when we aren't required to go through the slow and sometimes sticky process of cooperating with others.

Of course, there are huge positives about this shift. The opportunities we now have to find and make these connections, says Tufecki, "are thoroughly intertwined with the online architectures of interaction and visibility and the design of online platforms." But, she cautions, it's not the same for every person on every platform: "These factors—the affordances of digital spaces—shape who can find and see whom, and under what conditions; not all platforms create identical environments and opportunities for connection. Rather, online platforms have architectures just as our cities, roads, and buildings do, and those architectures affect how we navigate them."

Still, digital networks can be more democratizing than those enabled by technologies that came before. Social media is the new town square, Tufekci says. And if connecting is essential to what makes us human—not just having access to the same information but also being together, being able to interact with and learn from one another—then the internet, while far from perfect, can certainly feel like a marked improvement over the less expansive networks of the past.

Ultimately, just as mapmaking has shaped the world, the digital maps we create—of ourselves and also of the networks we build between ourselves and others—will shape the future. Once upon a time the various societies of the world were much more disconnected, but gradually, thanks in part to maps—cartographic and digital—we have grown to see ourselves as part of something bigger.

—■—

As a child, I was mesmerized by different maps of the same place. Looking at a highway map of Minnesota gave me one understanding of my state, but a topographic map imparted an entirely different view. These maps didn't contradict; they complemented, relaying distinct information about the same place.

Just as there are many kinds of maps, each with its own purpose, the various online platforms we use convey different aspects of the same personal terrain. For many, Twitter is for short and often more impulsive thoughts, for testing out ideas and getting news as it breaks. Instagram is for aesthetics, for creating a visual collage of our lives. Tumblr and Facebook are for sharing memes, expressing longer thoughts, and getting into more in-depth conversations. And even within these platforms, subsections like "Gay Twitter" and "Stan Tumblr" (where pop music fans gather to shower their musical icons in adoration while roasting other people's) allow us to comport ourselves slightly differently within separate spaces on the same platform.

While in an ideal world you would have multiple maps of the same place—highway, topographic, and so on—you usually just have one with you at any given moment, and that limits your ability to fully navigate that place. This can fragment your perception of the terrain you're trying to understand. For instance, on Instagram, I mostly just post smiling pictures of myself and my dog and *not* the more sarcastic or cynical thoughts that I share on Twitter. I happen to know that many family members and friends from high school follow me on Instagram, and that probably affects what I post there.

On Twitter, however, having a much larger following, I strangely feel more anonymous and thus more free to be myself. Which is why I end up not only sharing intimate admissions about personal struggles but also tweeting out stupid jokes about tops and bottoms. (And—to paraphrase a comment Katy Perry made to an American Idol contestant that quickly turned into a Gay Twitter meme in 2018 before being just as quickly forgotten—if you don't know what that means, it's not for you.)

Despite the many different kinds of maps we now have access to, sometimes we're left with no map at all, which can seem almost unimaginable. Opening a map app has become so automatic and instinctual for many of us that it hardly registers that we're using a map at all. Years ago, if I got lost I could usually figure out where I needed to go with a little thinking. Now, if my phone dies—well, you know the feeling.

What happens when you're offline? If there's no map? If there's no documentation? If we didn't capture it, did it happen? If no map shows on your phone, is this even a place?

Those questions can quickly turn to fear. As Chet Van Duzer explains in *"With Savage Pictures Fill Their Gaps": On Cartographers' Fears of Blank Spaces*, cartography historians sometimes use the term *horror vacui* (a concept utilized within art history more broadly) to describe the hesitance some mapmakers have to leave a space on a map blank instead of filling it with decorations. "A fear of empty spaces on maps, or at least a fondness for filling every available space, was indeed an important factor in the design of maps" in previous centuries, writes Van Duzer. In the twenty-first century, *horror vacui* has gone digital.

Social media can seem like it's inherently designed to address our fear of empty spaces; when I'm bored or restless, I feel the urge to go on Twitter. Of course, many of these platforms' algorithms *are* designed to get us to post and like more, but the fear of blank spaces looms large on social media itself, too. Sometimes, when I haven't tweeted all day, I feel like I *should*. I'm afraid to leave the space blank. We often talk of FOMO, or fear of missing out, but what about FOOMO: fear of others missing out (on seeing the things we're doing)? Instead of just existing on the smaller scale of our friends, our neighbors, or the family two pews back, this fear is now often intensified by the feeling that we also need to consider the opinions of distant internet observers.

In an interview in Hulu's *Fyre Fraud* documentary, which chronicles the now infamously disastrous Fyre Festival, writer Jia Tolentino makes a poignant point: "FOMO is . . . this underlying anxiety where if you don't continue to escalate your visibility, your identity will start to crumble in pieces." Driven by this anxiety, people stay online.

If we don't post, if we don't add every little thing to our digital map, it's like we don't exist. But the days or events that we choose not to document have their own power, too. We may even be doing ourselves a disservice by charting every inch of our lives. Perhaps we need pieces of our lives that we don't put on our public maps, the off-the-map things that are just for us—places where we can still explore and discover new aspects of ourselves.

Sometimes, instead of beasts unknown, the empty spaces on our maps hold hidden treasure. Deep in the woods of the Chippewa National Forest, nearly five hours north of Minneapolis, lies an anomaly: 144 acres of "virgin" timber, including rare red pines thought to be 250 years old. This patch of land, referred to as the Lost Forty, houses trees towering more than one hundred feet in the air. These trees weren't left alone to grow tall due to some kind-hearted, environmentally thoughtful steward. They survived due to a mapping error. During the 1882 Public Land Survey, surveyors accidentally mapped the Lost Forty as part of a nearby lake. So loggers never came for its trees, and they were allowed to grow old undisturbed. They are truly a sight to behold— one Tuna and I have enjoyed, walking together among these magnificent giants in silence. Beautiful things may grow and develop in quiet solitude if we leave them off our maps, and we might discover them if we're willing to wander into uncharted territory.

On the other hand, if we think our digital maps already contain everything we need to know about ourselves and our experiences, it's easy to become as reliant on them as we are our map apps. In *The War for Kindness*, Jamil Zaki writes of an experiment he conducted with colleagues in which he had people take a tour of Stanford's Memorial Church, with some posting online about their experience and others going without their phones. As it turned out, people who shared their experiences about the tour online actually remembered *less* than those who didn't. Sometimes, going into something without a map—or without the intention of mapping—makes us more attentive to it, even if it means we have to risk getting lost.

Constantly allowing the internet to chart our courses affects more than just travel. Many of the books I read these days are based on recommendations from people I follow online, which has reduced the amount of bookstore ambling I do, meaning that the art and thought I'm consuming has changed as well. Today, algorithms determine so much of the content we take in. In *How to Do Nothing*, writer Jenny Odell takes issue with Spotify playlists. Yes, Spotify might develop a personalized series of songs tailored to introduce her to more of the kind of music she tends to listen to already. And yes, she might really like what she finds in that playlist. But when she's listening to the radio instead, she has the chance to be exposed to something more left field, more outside of her norm.

"To acknowledge that there's something I didn't know I liked is to be surprised not only by the song but by myself," she writes. If we put ourselves in situations in which we can be surprised by ourselves, we will continue to grow and change—a core aspect of what it means to be human. "By contrast," she continues, "at its most successful, an algorithmic 'honing in' would seem to incrementally entomb me as an ever more stable image of what I like and why." If we always choose efficiency, we lose the chance to stumble upon something new and unexpected.

Of course, it's a trade-off. Just as I hear people proudly express all the things they gain by not being online—and I'm certain they're right—I also find myself thinking of all the things I've learned and discovered by being online that I probably wouldn't have otherwise. What's important is an openness to surprise and to things uncharted, or we become unable to navigate life without a map.

After leaving the Borchert Map Library on the day of my first visit, I pulled out my phone and posted a dozen or so photos from my visit to my Instagram story. A couple hours later, someone responded asking if I was there doing research.

I said I was, and he commented that it seemed like a radical departure from my work in atheism and religion. In my eyes, though, the shift isn't actually all that severe. Much of my work in religion and atheism has revolved around the use of storytelling to break down barriers across lines of religious difference. I've always been drawn to maps for the same reason I've always been drawn to stories, the subject of my master's in religion thesis. Maps tell the story of a place. As Daniel Tuzzeo writes in *Religious Cartography and the Cosmological Imagination*, "in addition to aiding in geographic navigation, scientific observation, and political demarcation, maps serve a narrative, almost novelistic, function." Maps attempt to order the world around us—to give it structure and meaning, to make sense of something that is inherently complicated in order to make it navigable. Where our understanding falls short, stories step in, which is why they feature prominently in the world's major religious texts.

Building maps and building storied systems of meaning share common impulses: the desire to give order to a chaotic and changing world, to establish signposts and routes that help us traverse the tumultuous inner and outer journeys we undertake, and to develop structures and tools that help others along the way so their journeys won't be as hard as ours were. At their best, maps are a gateway—taking you to a destination so that you can see it for yourself. In religion those maps look like rituals, practices, and communities that allow you to connect more fully with yourself and the world around you. But religion has its limitations—its power plays, its fear of empty spaces, its harm to the most vulnerable.

If social media maps our lives, these same opportunities and problems are present. As in religion or maps, the danger lies in not acknowledging their limitations, or thinking that they can completely capture reality in its entirety rather than point the way toward it.

It feels particularly important to recognize that danger at this moment in human history, in the still-early years of the social media age. "We live in a time of rapid change and uncertainty," Mina writes in *Memes to Movements*, "and as we look to history, we see that it's during times of great tumult that new symbols and narratives take hold in society." Just as the stories embodied in the maps of history have shaped our past and present, the narratives we build with our digital tools will shape our future. There's reason to be concerned about what narratives will emerge out of this age, out of the maps we're making, if we're not intentional about attending to them.

The best way to be careful about the digital narratives we develop is to recognize the inherent limitations of any narrative we develop with such a tool. I spent time as an undergrad in religion studying the Mahayana Buddhist concept of Indra's Net. Said to have been created by the Vedic god Indra, this net contains a multifaceted jewel at each vertex; the jewels are connected to one another by the strings of the net, like cities connected by roadways on a map. Or think of those imaginary lines between stars or constellations. The net stretches into infinity, each jewel reflecting every other jewel. The image is meant to underscore the intimate interconnectedness of all phenomena.

As I studied the image of the net, I thought of its value for some Christians, who could benefit from seeing the ways in which their underlying hopes and questions are reflected in other traditions like Buddhism and how studying another tradition could improve one's understanding of their own.

Ultimately, I was attempting to suggest a move away from a rigid literalism that insists that every single word of the Bible, and only the Bible, is true. I had come to see sacred texts in light of the Buddhist idea of the finger and the moon, which argues that we often mistake the finger for the thing it is actually pointing to. The Bible, I wrote in my thesis, was a finger pointing at deeper truths about life—a signpost that one could use in the quest to understand the meaning and purpose of life, but not a literal representation of ultimate truth.

I could have put it this way: the Bible is a map. It was created by people who had particular interests, and those interests are represented in the text. It contains some very useful and valuable information about the world, but it is not—and could never be—the entire world. While its 31,102 verses are thorough, there is no book long enough to address all of life's questions. "If the map were identical with the territory it would literally be the territory," writes Turnbull in *Maps Are Territories*. "It would have a scale of an inch to the inch and, apart from anything else, it would be unworkable as a map since you would have to be standing on it or in it." No map, book, or social media platform is large enough to capture all of reality.

We need maps, but we also need to understand their limitations. "There will always be maps of the world," Brotton concludes in *A History of the World in Twelve Maps*, "and their technology and appearance at some point in the future will make the world map in a modern atlas, and even Google

Earth's home page, seem as quaint and unfamiliar as the Babylonian world map." Social media, too, is making our old ways of documenting and sharing the self seem quaint, and surely in the future we will look back on Twitter and Instagram and laugh at them like we do with Myspace today. (Some people, mostly those younger than me, are already there.)

But, as Brotton continues, the future maps "will also inevitably pursue a particular agenda, insist on a certain geographical interpretation at the expense of possible alternatives, and ultimately define the earth in one way rather than another. But they certainly will not show the world 'as it really is,' because that cannot be represented. There is simply no such thing as an accurate map of the world, and there never will be. The paradox is that we can never know the world without a map, nor definitely represent it with one."

Instead of boxing us in and flattening us out, perhaps our digital maps can function more like the concept of Indra's Net. If we use it with care, social media can surprise us, helping us forge connections and constellations that make us more visible than any map ever could. After all, our digital cartography isn't just a tool—it is a revealer, showing what we value about ourselves and the world around us. "The map is a sensitive indicator" of shifts in culture, writes University of California, Los Angeles's, Norman J. W. Thrower in *Maps and Man*. It may be the case that the mapping we do on social media is an even better indicator. If we step back and really take it in, it may inspire a similar gut stirring to that induced by my childhood map gazing—a recognition of how broad and complex we really are.

Stepping back for perspective isn't so simple in a world where distance is the norm, though. When it's easy to hold other people at arm's length through the internet, how do we map the spaces between ourselves and others? If maps help us think about how we see ourselves, perhaps they might also point the way to a better understanding of how we use social media to both close and establish distance.

5

DRAFTING DISTANCE

As far back as I can remember, my thoughts turned to running away.

The impulse to leave first expressed itself through my love of maps, which was about both the places I might go and *not* being where I was. Growing up queer in the Midwest, I felt out of place, like I was born where I shouldn't have been. My thoughts were forever shifting to how I might put distance between myself and my surroundings.

By the time I was out of the closet in a largely homophobic high school, I would use maps to chart a course into the city. Whenever I could, I'd flee the suburbs for LGBTQ drop-in centers, antiwar rallies, and coffee shops full of city dwellers I imagined were light-years more enlightened than the suburban bros shoving past me between classes. When I couldn't get into the city, I'd bike to the library and look for those enlightened people online. All throughout my teen years, online and off, I was always in motion—because if I stayed still for too long I might be seen for what I was, and being seen for what I was would open me up to danger.

Though the internet was designed to close distances—between us and information and between one another—that's not always how we use it. While our digital tools sometimes help us forge connections and close distances, they can also be a means of putting distance between ourselves and our fears, or between one another. Online we have the power to see and be seen but also to hide from ourselves and others. We can reveal, and we can run away. Both have value sometimes—but are we aware of when we're doing which, and why?

—■—

The distance we establish online isn't always intentional; sometimes it's a product of the ways we're encouraged to simplify. In our online profiles, we're asked to describe ourselves in fewer characters than you'll find on the side of a cereal box.

When I think about our social media bios, I'm reminded of Nick White's *Sweet and Low*. "Summing up a person's life is a tough business," he writes of a woman trying to think of how to describe her late husband. "You're bound up by simple nouns and verbs. 'He was a doctor,' she says. 'A father, an amateur golfer.' She pauses to think. 'He recycled.'" This is frequently how we describe ourselves online. "Writer. Activist. Beyoncé fan."

The words we use to describe ourselves can come to make us feel smaller instead of more fully human. I've learned this firsthand from years of involvement in interfaith work. Interfaith dialogues aim to provide an opportunity for participants to better understand people with different beliefs, which is why the people organizing them often work to ensure that there are representatives from many different communities present. But what happens when you don't get to be Steven, or Samir, or Sara, and instead have to be Muslim, Hindu, or humanist?

The goal of interfaith dialogue is to help us see the humanity in one another, and when done well it is immensely valuable. But if organizers aren't careful, participants can feel an unspoken expectation to be good representatives of their respective communities. This is especially true for members of less understood communities, including my own, both atheist and LGBTQ. This can result in an implicit pressure to not be messy or complicated, to not be fully human, to show people only the part of yourself you think they can handle or accept. To reduce yourself down to your comprehensible identity.

Some people are able to navigate this pressure gracefully and still show up as themselves, but for me it has occasionally proven too great. I've long wanted to give people the version of myself I believe they want or can handle. It's not entirely a desire to be liked, though that's part of it. It's also this sense it's the most compassionate thing to do—to meet someone where they are and give them a version of myself that isn't a lie but is more palatable and accommodating. Toned down, smoothed out, quieter. As a result, I have sometimes felt a sense of distance at interfaith events—between me and others and between the self I'm showing up as and the self I feel like on the inside—even though this flies fully in the face of their very purpose.

There's nothing wrong with our desire to please others, but when it causes us to self-censor, it can easily impede people getting to know us. And we see evidence of a desire to please others, or at least not incur their ire, all over our social media platforms. Which is why I've come to believe that one of the largest shared goals of interfaith dialogue and the internet—forging connections between people so that they can better understand one another—is hampered by the ways they have sometimes encouraged people to simplify themselves.

One of the biggest ironies of simplifying ourselves—of boxing ourselves in and boiling ourselves down to just a handful of words—is that it can actually *complicate* our lives. When we simplify, putting who we are into the simplest terms depending on the context, we then have to shift between different versions of ourselves and keep track of who knows which version.

If we aren't careful, attempts to close distance, online and off, can instead increase the distance between us. As Greg Goldberg suggests, efforts to close distance between different people are sometimes *actually* expressions of discomfort with the very fact of difference and easily morph into attempts to eliminate it by transforming it into sameness. But closing distance doesn't need to be contingent on simplifying ourselves, or on pretending our differences aren't real. When navigated well, interfaith dialogues and the internet can close distance in ways that don't demand conformity. As Audre Lorde said, "Difference must be not merely tolerated, but seen as a fund of necessary polarities between which our creativity can spark like a dialectic. Only then does the necessity for interdependency become unthreatening."

The problem of digital simplification isn't just in how we share and then also compare our full lives—the highs *and* the lows—to the highlight reels others post, though we all know that's a problem online. There's also the gap that can develop between what we *think* and what we *say*. Just like comparing our lives to other people's highlight reels, this isn't a new phenomenon emerging from social media, but it can be exacerbated in our increasingly digital lives.

It can sometimes seem as if we're walking a tightrope when expressing an opinion online—especially one we're actively trying to sift through in real time. As a result, there's often a distance between what we want to say and what we think we *can* say without putting ourselves at risk. When I've spoken out about systemic racism or homophobia online, for example, I've been inundated by harassment. That harassment has occasionally made me hesitant to express things important to me, and I don't want to feel reluctant to speak out about things that matter.

In Jon Ronson's *So You've Been Publicly Shamed*, he recounts something monologist Mike Daisey—who was revealed to have fabricated details in a story, for which he received harsh online criticism—once said to him: "I'd never had the opportunity to be the object of hate before. The hard part isn't the hate. It's the object." People we agree with, and especially those we don't, can easily become objects instead of people online. This is in part a product of the ways we simplify and expect others to do the same.

Seeing one another as objects online can lead to a distortion of scale. When thousands of people publicly shame someone over an often comparably small thing, the person being shamed can sincerely feel as if the whole world has turned against them, even though it is really only a small subset.

Sure enough, while Twitter can feel like the entire world, it's far from it. A 2019 Pew study found that American Twitter users are statistically younger, wealthier, and more politically progressive than the general public. Because of this, Twitter users' reactions to things aren't necessarily a barometer for the general public (which may also explain why some Very Online pundits were so completely taken aback by the results of the 2016 US presidential election). Even within Twitter there are further distortions of scale. In the *Atlantic*, Alexis C. Madrigal points out that Pew split its Twitter users into two categories: the top 10 percent most active users and the bottom 90 percent. While the median user from the latter group had only tweeted twice and had fewer than twenty followers, the former group tweeted on average nearly 150 times a month.

This split between the more and less active users calcifies over time. "As the platforms age," Madrigal writes, "their devotees become more and more distinct from the regular person." He continues:

> For more than a decade now, many people in media and technology have been feeding an hour or two of Twitter into our brains every single day. Because we're surrounded by people who live their lives like this—and, crucially, because so many of the journalists who write about the internet *experience* the internet in this way—it might *feel* like this is just how Twitter is, that a representative sample of America is plugged into the machine in this way. But it's not. Twitter is not America.

Frequent social media use can put distance between the most online among us and an accurate perception of the world. A common refrain that began on Twitter in 2016 and saw another spike in the run-up to the 2020 election was that supporters of politician Bernie Sanders were largely white, aggressive, male "Bernie bros"—a narrative that erases that in the 2020 Democratic primary season Sanders had a broader range of support from young, working-class people of color than any of the other candidates, who largely had whiter, wealthier bases.

Yet the "Bernie bro" perception itself is a result of the internet's problem of proportion. Yes, there are over-the-top and abusive tweets from some white male Sanders supporters. But they're not representative; computational social scientist Jeff Winchell looked at tweets from the supporters of each 2020 Democratic candidate, using sentiment analysis to determine how many of them were positive or negative, and told Salon's Keith A. Spencer that "Bernie followers act pretty much the same on Twitter as any other follower." Yet while by all available evidence they only represent a sliver of his base, the image of toxic Bernie bros has come to form the basis of how many people understand Sanders's support more broadly. His in fact highly diverse working-class coalition has struggled against Twitter pundits with massive followings to combat this narrative.

It's not that harassment from Sanders supporters doesn't exist; it's that the story took hold and became a defining narrative about who supports him, eclipsing the voices of many of his other, less online supporters. As *New York Times* political reporter Astead W. Herndon pointed out in a tweet about the aforementioned Pew study, the poorest, most marginalized, and least educated people (a population who most heavily supported Sanders in 2020) are also the least represented online. "Certainly journalism via Twitter misses them," says Herndon. But, he adds, "let's be clear: they were being missed long before that, too." Again, this isn't exclusively an internet problem, but our social media platforms may exacerbate it.

In *Trick Mirror*, Jia Tolentino argues that social media's distortions of scale are perhaps the "most psychologically destructive" of the various ways the internet can warp how we understand the world, because social media platforms train us to think that things matter because of our relationship to them. This, then, is the irony of our digital tools as they currently exist: what is supposed to make the world bigger can in fact make it smaller, placing us at the center of our own digital universe.

And herein lies what might be the biggest problem of the distortion of scale. By enabling us to put ourselves at the center of things and filter out whatever isn't on our radar, we distance ourselves from other people's realities. That distance has always been there, of course, but it's all the more startling now because the digital ability to maintain distance between us can sometimes equal and even exceed the physical distance between us.

I was reminded of this when, just before moving back to Minnesota and leaving the East Coast behind, I had a going-away party with friends at Nowhere Bar in New York City. I remember friend after friend—most of whom I had met through the internet and many of whom were involved in NYC media Twitter circles—joking that I was going back to the middle of nowhere to die. They were teasing, but between the lines there was this sense I really was moving to a place that was culturally irrelevant. But once I was back in Minnesota, I found myself doing all kinds of things that mattered. The fact that Minnesota felt almost nonexistent to those in certain social media circles—even though the world is so digitally connected now— shows that the internet can in some ways make us feel all the more removed from people who aren't a part of the communities we engage with online.

In theory, the distance-diminishing power of our digital tools should be able to transform our world for the better. By closing the distance between events, and between people and ideas—making it harder for people to ignore the struggles others have, or to ignore something because it happened in the past and they happened to not see it—we should be able to navigate challenges more easily and better understand the struggles of people in very different circumstances from our own. But so far, it hasn't worked that way.

In *The War for Kindness*, Jamil Zaki explains the concept of *Einfühlung*, or "feeling into," coined by art theorist Robert Vischer. *Einfühlung* is "a state of close attention, which allows viewers to truly 'see' the emotional meaning behind sculptures and paintings." If human connection is also about seeing and being seen, Zaki says, we should celebrate the internet. After all, it gives us access to "millions of people, in every country, on their own terms," and also allows us to "broadcast our lives back to them." With the internet, we can continue expanding what philosopher Peter Singer calls our "circle of care" beyond the boundaries of our immediate communities and "finally widen this circle to embrace all of humanity."

"Human history," the late astronomer Carl Sagan once wrote, "can be viewed as a slowly dawning awareness that we are members of a larger group. Initially our loyalties were to ourselves and our immediate family, next, to bands of wandering hunter-gatherers, then to tribes, small settlements, city-states, nations. We have broadened the circle of those we love." The internet, in theory, has the power to help us expand it even further. But digital distance as we currently establish and maintain it is at odds with the internet's widening possibilities.

"Technology allows us to 'see' an unprecedented number of people, but what we get back is thin gruel compared to old-fashioned social contact," Zaki argues. Offline, we get all kinds of information—the tone of someone's voice, an expression on their face. But "online, social life is reduced to strings of texts and images." In other words, one of the biggest things we lose with digital distance is context. "Spatial and temporal context both have to do with the neighboring entities around something that helps define it. Context also helps establish the order of events," Jenny Odell writes in *How to Do Nothing*. "Obviously, the bits of information we're assailed with on Twitter and Facebook feeds are missing both these kinds of context."

"Scrolling through the feed," continues Odell, "I can't help but wonder: What am I supposed to think of all this? How am I supposed to think of all this?" Technology scholar danah boyd calls this "context collapse," and it can cause us to try to be everything for everyone, posting only stuff that feels safe. If there's no context online, we can feel compelled to post only that which can exist without it.

But could it be we just haven't spent enough time online yet to master its intricacies, that it's too new, and we're too inexperienced? It's hard to say for sure. The reasons empathy evolved among humans more so than in most species—declining testosterone levels that resulted in softer, less aggressive-looking faces; larger whites in our eyes that allowed for following one another's gazes; facial muscles that enabled us to express emotion more effectively—are extremely physical, Zaki explains. What happens as our relationships become increasingly mediated by screens?

Perhaps empathy will evolve. In *The Future of Feeling*, Kaitlin Ugolik Phillips dives deep into the various ways people are trying to use social media and virtual reality to boost empathy, but she admits that a more empathetic future is far from guaranteed. In many respects it seems the odds are stacked against us. But, to my mind, that's all the more reason to work toward one.

Of course, we're familiar with the numerous positives to the distance we establish digitally. Anonymity allows people to more easily speak truth to power and organize more safely in unsafe environments. But there's also a shadow side. "When people are accountable to one another—for instance, in small communities—cruelty becomes socially expensive," Zaki writes. But "anonymity frees people from these constraints, cutting the brake lines on social exchange. The internet is filled with the resulting wrecks."

The distance-closing power of the internet can also give us more information than we can process, the distortion of scale making it difficult to empathize with such large numbers of people. Zaki uses the example of a photo of Syrian refugees who died while seeking safety in 2015 that went viral online. Though the Syrian refugee crisis had been going on for a long time, this photo spread because it's easier to empathize with individuals than with masses. Before that photo, many people struggled to understand the immensity of the issue. That changed when they saw the photo, and donations rose dramatically. And yet their social media timelines kept moving, and before long the swell of empathy was over. To many online, Syrian refugees were once again a faceless mass after a few days.

We should feel challenged to close the distance, especially now, as people leave the religious and civic institutions that have historically helped us learn about the struggles of others and act to address them. The agendas of these institutions have been supplanted by other agendas, controlled by those running our social media platforms. The role of compassion in society is "not just one of sacrificing time and money to relieve the plight of others, but also of pushing a political agenda that recognizes everyone's dignity," Emory University's Frans de Waal writes in *The Age of Empathy*. But what happens to our agenda when our digital platforms make it harder for us to have compassion for others?

As our trust leaves institutions of old and moves to the internet, it's important to be concerned about its ability to allow us to put distance between ourselves and one another, making empathy more difficult. Our world is large and complex, de Waal says, but we don't just have to rely on our intellect to navigate it. We also have our empathy, an essential ingredient in the quest for meaning, belonging, and realness. We just need to figure out how to use it online.

How well do you know—and empathize with—the people you follow on social media? Think about that person who followed you years ago, for reasons you can't totally remember, and something inspired you to follow back. You still occasionally like each other's stuff and every once in a while even respond with a comment. You've seen their profile picture enough times over the years that you could probably pick them out of a crowd, if you really tried. And while you don't think of them often, whenever you see their posts, you're like, *Hey, that's interesting.* Interesting enough that you keep following.

What *is* that connection, exactly, and how much do you care about them? To find out, in late 2018 I reached out to someone I'd followed for about a decade and asked if we could talk for the first time, hoping it might help me better understand digital empathy and the distances we establish and close online.

Zain was among my earliest followers, one of the first who wasn't someone I already knew. We're not entirely sure how we first connected on Twitter. I suspect it had something to do with the fact that we share a favorite singer in Sufjan Stevens.

In the eight years since we started following each other, our exchanges had been pretty infrequent, though always amicable. He tweeted at me to express support for my work, offer a suggestion of somewhere to eat when I was speaking in an unfamiliar city, or laugh at a stupid joke I made. Over the course of those eight years we exchanged a couple dozen tweets and fewer than ten private messages. Zain never completely disappeared from my timeline, briefly resurfacing in my notifications when he spotted my book in a Belfast bookstore or whenever Stevens released a new record. But our relationship never deepened beyond the occasional ping between long stretches of digital silence.

From what little I gathered on Twitter, his life seemed incredibly ordinary. He posted about travel and politics. He loved Stevens—a lot. He was friendly. It all seemed very pleasant and basic. I didn't see the point in looking any closer.

I had no clue.

In fall 2018 Zain answered my Skype call, and, after some initial pleasantries, I asked him to tell me his story. As it turns out, Zain was born into a conservative Shia Muslim family in London in 1982, five years before I was born to a young secular couple in their early twenties sharing a Section 8 apartment in Minnesota. My family had resided in the US for at least a couple of generations; Zain's was far newer to their nation. His father's family, refugees from Uganda, came to London in the 1970s. His mother's family were migrants from East Africa who traced their lineage back to India.

Living in a city that largely didn't understand them—one that was at best coldly indifferent and at worst overtly hostile toward their existence—Zain's family immersed themselves in a tight-knit community of fellow immigrants. He grew up in a full house, living with his dad's brothers, grandparents, and other family members.

Family was all around. But he felt distant from them, in large part due to the fact that he was abused by a relative he believes targeted him because they suspected he was gay. Unable to tell anyone about his sexuality, or the abuse, Zain felt profoundly disconnected and different from his family—who already felt disconnected and different from everyone around them.

When his father's business became quite successful, Zain was sent to a private school, and the distance provided some relief. There, among other openly gay students and away from his family, he was able to come out and even began to flourish. Finally, he had a space where he could be himself. But after going off to college at his parents' insistence, Zain's childhood trauma caught up with him. Unable to outrun his pain, he became severely depressed, spending most of his time in his dorm room. Separated from his family and cut off from most of the people around him, Zain felt profoundly alone. The distance that had once felt like a comfort now felt crushing.

Except online. Zain created a Tumblr account where he was able to talk about being gay, and his following quickly grew. It became his primary outlet, and he found community there—especially among fans of Stevens, whose music inspired and consoled him during some of his most difficult moments. But any accounts on online platforms that his family might find, like Facebook or Twitter, were closeted spaces for Zain. His digital life became highly compartmentalized.

And so, when he and I connected on Twitter, he was in the closet, even to me—a stranger from the internet who was openly queer and working on issues of religion, sexuality, and identity. Zain had a full life as an out gay man online, but only on Tumblr. Everywhere else, online and off, he had to hide.

In 2010, he moved to the US to work with death row inmates for a year in North Carolina. He became deeply passionate about

US politics and social justice, and it was at that time he came across my Twitter feed. While working with death row inmates, he began, for the first time, to seriously reflect on his own happiness. Working with so many people whose lives had been taken from them, he found himself asking if he was truly alive.

After returning to London, Zain tried to continue shifting his priorities more toward his happiness. But that was harder to do at home. Frustrated that old demons were returning to haunt him, he slipped into an all-consuming addiction. Meanwhile, across the ocean, my long-term relationship was heading toward its end, and my life was about to fall apart, too. But, of course, neither of us had any idea what the other was going through.

In 2015 Stevens released *Carrie & Lowell*, his best and most vulnerable record. Zain and I exchanged a couple tweets about it, our first in years. Still, I had no clue that, on the day *Carrie & Lowell* was released, Zain was reaching a breaking point. His life completely consumed by addiction, he decided he had to change. So he packed a couple bags and flew to Australia to follow Stevens on tour. He needed to put some distance between himself and his problems.

As it turned out, the distance from his home not only gave him fresh clarity but also helped him to close an unexpected distance of another kind. In an airport lobby, Zain met Stevens. And then he met him again at the next airport. And again at the next. As Zain followed Stevens's tour around Australia, they continued to cross paths. Each time, Stevens was immensely kind and generous.

The kindness Stevens showed Zain was healing. Closing the distance between himself and his idol, and coming to see Stevens as human, set Zain on a different path. It was a kind of release. Having accomplished his dream of meeting Stevens,

Zain turned around, ready to look at his own reality. At the end of the tour, he decided he needed to get his life in order. So he spent a year traveling the world and getting clean before determining he could safely return home.

As I sat there absorbing everything Zain had told me, I was overwhelmed that just a few tweets and likes over the years had connected me to this person and this incredible story. It struck me then that there was another way to look at our digital distance—one that doesn't just see our online relationships as less than, as shallow versions of the "real thing." The relationships that we see as less "real" are actually just a different *kind* of relationship, not a worse or lesser version of the same thing.

In *Twitter and Tear Gas*, Zeynep Tufekci explains that people have different kinds of social ties, including strong ties, or those we're closest to. Strong ties are, of course, vital to our well-being and sense of meaning. But they are also, in some respects, easier to uphold than the social ties we have to work colleagues, acquaintances, or childhood friends. "People tend to try to keep up with those to whom they have strong ties no matter what technology is available," writes Tufekci. But that's not the case for weak ties, which easily disappear.

Thanks to social media, though, we can now keep up with even those we only briefly meet or aren't very close to. The internet, says Tufekci, enables us to maintain even our weaker connections, the relationships "that without digital assistance might have withered away or involved much less contact."

Here's why that matters, if an important part of being human is being exposed to information that can challenge us, shape us, and help us grow: "People with strong ties likely already share similar views, so such views are less likely to surprise when they are expressed on social media," writes Tufekci. "However, weaker ties may be far flung and composed of people with varying political and social ties." In other words, weak ties can help us get out of our in-groups and filter bubbles—a problem social media enables, but may also be able to help us combat, if we use it mindfully.

When we put distance between ourselves and others—something we often do to feel safer and more secure—we ironically end up hurting ourselves because we isolate ourselves from people who can help us become more fully human. Online, we sometimes create filter bubbles and echo chambers when what we need is to be surrounded by people who see the world in different ways than we do. But the same tool that can allow us to wall ourselves off can also enable us to connect with a wider range of weak ties.

There's another value in weak ties: they can serve as a bridge. Tufekci gives the example of a coworker who sees political news on your Facebook and shares it with their own social network, which includes their family and friends—people you otherwise would not have any access to. In her scenario, the coworker is what's called a "bridge tie." Our weak ties are more likely to bridge us to disparate groups, she points out. Furthermore, as Harvard University's Mario L. Small explores in *Someone to Talk To*, research on social networks finds that people are more likely to confide in weak ties. We often turn to our digital weak ties in order to cope with deep, serious problems we feel we can't bring to our strong ties.

While there's reason to be concerned about the impact social media is having on our strong ties, there's also clearly cause for celebration in light of how much more access it gives us to our network of weak ties. Weak doesn't mean less real; our weak ties can help us become more complex, informed versions of ourselves. They can bridge us to stories and perspectives we would never have encountered otherwise, like Zain's. We just have to be willing to walk across and bridge the distance.

The bridges we can build online to weak and distant ties are essential if you believe that understanding the experiences of people who are different from you is an important part of becoming more fully human.

Zain is far from the only queer person from a Muslim background that I've connected with online over the years. Because of my work at the intersection of faith and sexuality, I've met many. As I started hearing their stories, I became invested; I made friends, wrote pieces from my perspective as an ally, and began donating to LGBTQ Muslim organizations. Over time, these experiences helped close the gap between me and a community I didn't understand very well. This understanding has shaped the person I've become since.

As a marginalized community, many LGBTQ Muslims and LGBTQ people from Muslim backgrounds connect with one another and with allies online. Like Zain's online connections through his secret Tumblr, the friendships they forge are immensely valuable. And they are just one community of many harnessing the power of the internet to build meaningful, often life-saving connections across immense distances.

There are obviously reasons to be concerned about how we connect online, but it is worth listening to the perspectives of the activists who have powerfully used it to establish and sustain meaningful connections—as well as to drive and transform conversations on critical issues. In *Reclaiming Our*

Space, Feminista Jones points to the "immediacy, access, and connectivity of social media platforms like Facebook, Twitter, and Instagram." As a result of how accessible digital spaces can be, members of marginalized communities—such as LGBTQ Muslims or, as Jones writes about, black women—can develop and join "self-affirming, self-preserving" online communities. Through these communities, we can close the distances that make us feel isolated and alone.

But this happens in much less obvious ways, too. In *Memes to Movements*, An Xiao Mina discusses how cat memes connect people. "When the internet came along, social media platforms enabled cat owners to find each other and thereby break what sociologists call *pluralistic ignorance*—the mistaken belief that their beliefs are not shared by their peers," writes Mina. Before the internet, most people had limited outlets for self-expression. While dog owners could find one another out walking their pets, cats usually stay inside. Before the internet, many cat owners kept quiet about their love of cats and couldn't find one another by happenstance, not even realizing their neighbors across the street had several.

So while it may feel like the internet is full of cat memes today, Mina reveals that it only *seems* like cats took over the internet, a phenomenon she calls the "Internet Cat Fallacy." In fact, cat memes are no more common than dog memes. "It's not that no one loved cats before the internet—far from it, in fact," she writes. "Americans have owned more cats than dogs, making them the number two pet in the country after fish." The fallacy lies in the sense that cats are *suddenly* everywhere when, in fact, they always *were* quietly everywhere.

By finding others who share our interests or experiences, our connections empower and embolden us. In helping us feel less alone, the internet can allow us to become more comfortable with ourselves and to dig deeper into previously private aspects of who we are. In this way, social media can help us understand things about ourselves by our seeing them reflected in others. As Mina writes, "after pluralistic ignorance is broken, new norms of behavior can start to form through regular repetition and affirmation of messages—a process called *synchronization of opinion*." By connecting us across various barriers and helping us develop new norms, the internet allows us to join what political scientist and historian Benedict Anderson called "imagined communities," or groups of people we may never meet in person but still feel connected to. These imagined communities expand our understanding of not just one another but also ourselves. They help us come to see ourselves as part of a larger whole.

Sometimes the internet shatters pluralistic ignorance, showing that there are more people like us out there. Other times, it shatters other kinds of ignorance. In *Reclaiming Our Space*, Jones points to Tara L. Conley, creator of the website Hashtag Feminism, who talks about the discussions engendered by hashtags like #YouOKSis, #SolidarityIsForWhiteWomen, #SayHerName, and so many others. Without these hashtags, "we would likely be having very different public conversations, or worse, no conversations," Conley told Zeba Blay in HuffPost. Likewise, it seems entirely possible I would have remained largely ignorant to the particular circumstances of LGBTQ Muslims around the world without the internet. Online, I can close the distance between my life and the realities of others.

While many dismiss digital organizing as "slacktivism," there's real power in the conversations people engage online—and even the digital actions they take. A major part of the modern LGBTQ rights movement in the US, for example, was brought about by people applying a rainbow filter to their profile picture on Facebook. In *Memes to Movements*, Mina draws on the work of economist Mary Rowe, who developed the concept of "microaffirmations," small and sometimes subconscious expressions of support for someone who is marginalized—like a stranger who smiles at me when I'm walking in public with my arm around another guy. Things like changing your profile picture or posting a tweet about an issue can function like a microaffirmation. "They are often fleeting," writes Mina, but "it's the aggregate that matters." Every NOH8 badge or rainbow flag online becomes a microaffirmation, and for queer people, especially those who feel isolated and spend a good amount of time online, the effect can be life changing.

These small actions help change the story of what someone's experience can be in that moment, of what's possible and what isn't. Though I'm tempted to roll my eyes at all the Human Rights Campaign logos and rainbow-flag profile pictures, these aren't meaningless gestures. The truth is that witnessing a sea of them online years ago really did change the story I'd told myself that the world could never understand or accept me.

When done well, these digital efforts to reshape our narratives are immensely valuable. In *Invisible Man, Got the Whole World Watching*, writer Mychal Denzel Smith credits social media for helping him rewrite his story as a young black man in America and recognize its connections to others. After Trayvon Martin was killed, he writes, "social media became the primary outlet" for expressing anger about both Martin's death and systemic violence experienced by black people all across America. When Black Twitter users refused to let the story disappear and shamed cable news stations and major newspapers for not covering it, they picked it up. At the same time, "while the legacy civil rights organizations dragged their feet," Smith continues, "rallies and vigils were being planned in 140 characters or less." It's impossible to imagine Martin's story reaching as many as it did without social media.

Smith suggests that while "social media is not meant to be a replacement for direct action and civil disobedience," without it many of us "likely would have never heard of Trayvon Martin in the first place." This ability to rewrite the narrative, bringing stories that so often get ignored to light and circumventing the gatekeepers—people in power, wealthy owners of legacy media, elected officials—who have traditionally shaped it, is one of social media's most vital offerings.

Social media helps expand the Overton Window, which is the range of what's considered acceptable public discourse. Online we can see that a wider range of perspectives is available to us. "By exposing people to each other, and each other's ideas, [social media] expands the range of acceptable discourse, feeding a hungry public who wants to talk about issues that in previous eras might not have been discussed as openly," writes Mina.

This is generally positive but it can also be harmful. YouTube algorithms often push increasingly extreme content into people's recommendations, and as such they are frequently cited as a gateway into white supremacist movements. As the Overton Window expands, we need to be vigilant about which of these expansions move us in the direction of our values—such as helping people better understand the experiences of transgender people or immigrants—and which open the door to ideas that run counter to human dignity. But at its best, the internet is one of the most powerful tools available for seeing one another across immense distances.

Even as we cross vast distances and discover ways to advocate for one another, there are also important reasons we want to disappear—to put distance between ourselves and the world.

Some think of the desire to disappear as signaling some kind of deceit: if visibility is the norm, then wanting privacy must mean we have something to hide. For much of human history we have associated invisibility "with wrongdoing, degeneracy, malice, even the work of the devil," essayist Akiko Busch explains in *How to Disappear*. If someone is invisible, the logic goes, they are up to no good. Yet while invisibility can give cover to abusive behavior, it also provides opportunities for the kinds of reflection and experimentation that can perhaps only occur when we don't have an audience that might judge—exploration that can contribute greatly to feeling real.

Technology itself can make it easier for us to put this kind of distance in place when it's needed, even when we're physically close. One person I interviewed described their cell phone as a socially acceptable way of taking a moment for themselves in a group setting. Without a phone, checking out of a dinner with friends for a moment could be considered rude or, at best, bizarre. But today few people blink when someone pulls out their phone and takes a personal moment.

Over the last few years, formally and informally, I've interviewed dozens of people about their digital habits. Perhaps more than anything, people have described using social media as a way of establishing valuable boundaries. For example, one person told me of maintaining dual Twitter accounts, one personal and one professional. Sometimes this person felt torn between these accounts—but their locked (or private) personal Twitter account also provided a very necessary outlet for humor that they couldn't indulge publicly without worrying about their hireability down the road.

Another person I interviewed told me of doing something similar but with even higher stakes. Olivia (not her real name) moved to the US in her late twenties for graduate school. After she graduated, Donald Trump was elected, and with his presidency came new immigration policies. For the first time, she had visa troubles. Though the new administration terrified her, she had no desire to leave. But Olivia didn't even consider staying in the country undocumented—her mother's health was declining, and she didn't want to risk not being able to leave to see her if she needed to, knowing that if she left undocumented she wouldn't be able to return. So she packed up and moved back to the Caribbean nation where she grew up.

While living in the US, she was not just out as queer and nonreligious but outspoken. Everyone around her knew about her sexuality and her beliefs; she was opinionated and vocal in both professional spaces and as an activist. But after moving home to live with her devoutly religious and conservative family, she couldn't say anything without risking family rejection. Silencing herself wasn't just counterintuitive—it was suffocating.

But Olivia had one lifeline: her secret Twitter account. Unlike her Facebook and Instagram profiles and what she calls her "basic bitch" Twitter account, which mostly consists of posts about television shows she likes—all accounts where members of her family follow her—Olivia's secret Twitter account has never been associated with her legal name. She's never posted pictures of herself or talked about where she's lived; from the very beginning of the account's existence, she has always been intentionally vague about personal details.

She's not vague about her beliefs and her identity on Twitter, though. Through her anonymous account, Olivia is able to be as outspoken as she used to be in other areas of her life. For her and many others, coming out to family isn't possible, which makes having safe, low-risk spaces where she can be out—particularly digital spaces—that much more important. In this way, our digital tools can actually be a powerful way of going off the grid. We can, like Olivia, disappear into an anonymous account, stepping back from our offline life and into a space where we can freely express ourselves in invisibility.

For others I interviewed, digital tools help them close a kind of distance between who they are and who they want to be. One person I spoke with took and posted nude photographs online as a way to grow more confident and reclaim their sexuality after an assault left them feeling disempowered. By posting these photographs online under a pseudonym, they, too, went invisible, detaching themselves from their name and everyone who knew them, even as they were more visible than they'd ever been in another respect.

But some people I spoke with also described feeling challenged by how their digital lives inadvertently created distance between who they are and how others see them—how digital visibility made them feel more distant from the world around them instead of more connected and real. For example, one person described being in a relationship that looked picture-perfect online but was, in reality, abusive. She spoke painfully of the distance between the self people could see online and the reality, and how that sense of separation made it harder for her to seek resources and support. In almost every case, the people I interviewed spent hours weighing both the positives and challenges of digital distance. It's clear from their stories that digital tools are as capable of helping us feel seen in negative ways as in positive ways, and as able to help us disappear when we want to as they are to make us feel invisible when we don't.

It's not just the opportunities and challenges of going unseen that matter. We also need to consider what *we're* seeing and what we're missing, Jenny Odell argues in *How to Do Nothing*. We need distance from our screens sometimes in order to direct our attention elsewhere, to close the distance between ourselves and what is physically around us. "Patterns of attention—what we choose to notice and what we do not—are how we render reality for ourselves," Odell writes, "and thus have a direct bearing on what we feel is possible at any given time." What we notice is what we become attached to, what matters to us, what shapes our world. Which is why there is, Odell says, a "revolutionary potential [in] taking back our attention" from the platforms that have an interest in holding on to it. Redirecting some of our attention away from the internet can allow us to reinvest that attention in other important (and nondigital) pieces of who we are.

But in an increasingly digital world, opting out of the internet can put distance between us and others, too. For example, I interviewed a couple who, after deciding they wanted to be more intentional about their phone and social media use, abandoned their cell phones and got a landline. They didn't totally disconnect; they still used email and even some social media when on a computer or an old phone hooked up to Wi-Fi without a data plan. But they immediately noticed a huge change in their lives after they ditched their cell phones. There was relief, to be sure—they were no longer mindlessly and anxiously scrolling through their social media feeds at all times—but also a great deal of loss. Some of their friends who could no longer text them at the last minute to ask if they were free didn't adjust tactics and instead faded out of their lives; others stopped seeing them as much now that it required more effort to do so. They lost friendships of convenience, and as a result they narrowed down to relationships with people willing to put in the extra "work" to pick up the phone and call them, or send an email, or schedule plans in advance. There were positives about this narrowing: the relationships that remained deepened. But they definitely mourned those they lost. Opting out of the channels so many of us communicate through now—and the expectations many of us now have that people should be constantly reachable, that relationships should be flexible, and that plans should be evolving—meant that they were now more disconnected from some of the world.

They also acknowledged that being able to disconnect can be an expression of privilege. As Busch writes in *How to Disappear*, "unplugging, digital detox, and disconnecting are luxuries available only to certain professional, academic, or corporate elite." Likewise, the ability to *choose* to go invisible is itself an expression of privilege; for members of marginalized communities, invisibility often isn't a choice but an inescapable reality. For some of these individuals, social media is one of the few tools available to render themselves visible, and opting out of it is unthinkable. Yet many of these same people also cannot choose invisibility even when they might want to, while privileged people can; Busch gives the example of white people smoking weed in public without consequence as one way invisibility frequently benefits the advantaged. Odell, too, acknowledges the role of privilege in being able to "do nothing." But, importantly, she argues that "just because this right is denied to many people doesn't make it any less of a right or any less important." And just because some people can't unplug or disconnect doesn't mean there isn't value in doing so.

Besides, what feels like a way to control the distance between us—how much and what others can see—often reveals itself to be a mirage. "The idea was that social media would give us a fine-tuned sort of control over what we looked at," writes Jia Tolentino in *Trick Mirror*. But what we got instead was a reality in which, on both an individual and collective level, we "are essentially unable to exercise control at all." Even when we want to put distance between ourselves and our digital lives, doing so can feel almost impossible. Which is why it's hard to blame someone for deciding to take the all-or-nothing approach, like the couple I interviewed, or when I forced myself to take a three-month social media sabbatical while finishing this book. In the first few days of my break, I went through a withdrawal almost as bad as when I quit smoking cigarettes. I found myself desperately craving an experience I didn't always enjoy, even as I felt freed from certain pressures.

Online, writes Tolentino, "we exhibit classic reward-seeking lab-rat behavior, the sort that's observed when lab rats are put in front of an unpredictable food dispenser." If a lever either always dispenses food or never does, she explains, lab rats will eventually stop pressing that lever. If it dispenses food unpredictably, though, they will press it over and over again. "In other words, it is *essential* that social media is mostly unsatisfying," she continues. "That is what keeps us scrolling, scrolling, pressing our lever over and over in hopes of getting some fleeting sensation—some momentary rush of recognition, flattery, or rage."

Driven in our posting by what algorithms reward, even our digital "downtime" can sometimes leave us feeling the opposite of renewed—like life in digital space is about always *doing*, rather than existing. I am reminded of a story a friend told me about being engaged in Black Lives Matter organizing. She is also a Christian involved in a faith community, and she described friends of hers who do not have a faith or philosophical community—who are "nones" or, more specifically, "nothing in particulars"—finding their sense of community, belonging, and identity in activism instead. She told me that she has seen many of them struggle and burn out and wondered if this was because they didn't have an alternative space to reconnect and reflect before reentering the work. Their world was the work, and they didn't have a separate space to ground themselves, to feel encouraged and supported. I confess that she identified something I'd seen in others—and even felt in myself.

A church, at its best, doesn't disengage us from the issues of the world—but it *is* a space where people can find respite, put distance between themselves and the rest of the world in order to reconnect with themselves and renew their commitments. Where people can reorient back to their values, check in with themselves and a community of accountability, and make sure they understand why they're doing what they're doing.

As more of us move out of traditional institutions and bring our search for meaning and belonging to digital platforms, spaces that are streams of constant activity—that sometimes feel more like they're about *doing* than *being*—do we lose the opportunity to step back, take distance from the world, and get perspective? Without that opportunity, we can burn out and begin to feel numb, inundated by more than we can absorb.

For a time, my social media use functioned in a reward and algorithm cycle—it allowed me to feel busy, active, and totally in control of how I was seen. Invisible (in a bad way). But this numbing out online changed me. I came to see myself as my digital presentation. But after years of casting myself into stone online, in the years following my breakup, the distance I'd put in place began to fall away. To my surprise, a big part of what cracked me open was a group of semianonymous self-described Twitter weirdos.

After a dumb tweet of mine went viral in the spring of 2017, I was added to a Twitter direct message (DM) chat. All but one in the chat were strangers; the only person I knew already, the one who had added me, was someone married to a friend from my teenage church years. While I was aware that he was a Twitter user, I had no idea how involved he was in what some might call Weird Left Twitter. After the group discussed my viral tweet, I was invited to join, and I was quickly taken in by the constant stream of conversation in the chat. Pretty much any time of day, if I opened the DM, people there were talking. It wasn't a large group, but everyone was highly active.

While for years I'd treated Twitter as a space to engage with issues related to my career and identity, the people in this chat approached it very differently. Most of them didn't use their "real" names or photos for their profiles, and they spent most of their time on Twitter shitposting—cracking jokes and tweeting ironically. Yet, only a few months after I was added to the chat, I found myself needing this group of shitposters in a way I never could have imagined.

In the months after my move, when I was diagnosed with scabies and withdrew from most of the world around me, they (along with a couple other friends) were my lifeline. Because the chat was constantly going, there was pretty much always someone there to distract me with humor or listen to me lament. They were tender and gentle with me. They let me vent about how hopeless I felt and offered words of empathy and support. At a time when I self-isolated, afraid to see anyone (lest they witness what a bad state I was in or, worse still, accidentally bump my arm and make me paranoid I'd spread my scabies), this chat helped me to feel connected to the world. To not feel alone.

There was something about the relative anonymity of the chat—though it really *wasn't* anonymous, as most people in the chat shared intimate details from their lives, photos, names, and more—that freed me up to talk without fear of judgment. I felt safe and connected with them, free to be messy. And everyone treated the chat this way, really; it was a space for a kind of radical empathy and vulnerability that feels difficult to practice in other areas. At a time when I had withdrawn from most of my closest relationships, feeling ashamed of what I was struggling with, these so-called "weak ties" gave me strength.

In an unexpected freedom I experienced intimately that summer, I was able to be vulnerable with people from afar. Sharing personal things online with people who will read your words from a safe distance can feel like a kind of low-stakes vulnerability. But that doesn't mean it isn't genuine.

While online vulnerability may feel low stakes because it's often semianonymous, or done in a forum where you can more carefully choose your words and compose your thoughts, the complicated and porous nature of our digital boundaries means we are far less in control than we might think. Even low-stakes vulnerability isn't guaranteed to stay that way. No matter how much we labor over privacy settings, once something is out there, we can't always control who sees it. Though certain things about social media make opening up online feel easier than doing it face to face with a friend, many aspects of our digital lives are public in ways we still don't fully understand. And even our anonymous digital relationships become less anonymous over time, as I experienced in that chat.

Still, I could practice opening up about difficult experiences in the chat and then carry what I was sharing there into other parts of my life. And it also helped me see how deep my impulse to run, to withdraw, to put distance between myself and others so that I could safely manage our relationships from afar, actually goes. It wasn't until I had moved back to Minnesota and was in that chat that I began to understand how often I had indulged that impulse. That it had been a big part of why I'd moved to a small town in northern Minnesota after finishing college. Why I'd gone to graduate school in Chicago. Why I'd left Chicago for Boston, and then New Haven, Connecticut. Why I'd left my relationship of nearly five years. Why I'd moved back to Minnesota. And why I was seeking solace in this chat of strangers.

A little over a year after moving back, talking with my therapist, he described the dual, almost polar-opposite struggles many queer people have: a desire so strong for a sense of home that they seek it out somewhere and then don't leave even when it's unhealthy for them; and the inability to put roots down anywhere, struggling to feel satisfied with where they are. I could relate to both but especially the latter, so regularly had I run from home as soon as I found it.

Like me, like Zain—like many queer people I've talked to about the search for meaning and belonging in the digital age—there is something particularly queer about the impulse to run away. Many of us spent large chunks of our adolescence imagining other worlds—either worlds where we weren't different from everyone around us or worlds that were themselves different, where we would be accepted or where our way of being was the standard instead of a risky deviation. Ironically, this is part of drew me to a homophobic evangelical church in my youth: they painted a picture of an afterlife without suffering, an idealized elsewhere (even though they expressly said that gays weren't allowed in).

When you grow up dreaming of the day you can be somewhere better, it can become hard to plant yourself *anywhere*. You keep looking for a more perfect place, and this search brings into relief all of the ways in which your current surroundings are imperfect or unsafe. The "flight so you don't have to fight" stance—always being ready to run—is strong when you're queer. So many queer people who grow up in rural America, or other parts of the world where queerness is dangerous, relocate to safer areas if they can. This phenomenon is sometimes referred to as queer diaspora.

When I left Minnesota for Chicago, I discovered communities unlike any I had known before, radical queer spaces where I could try new things with new people. I became more myself in the process. Such a move can be incredibly liberating for queer people like me—but it often comes at a cost. We leave things we love in order to find greater comfort somewhere else. We seek becoming more ourselves by leaving, but we also risk becoming less ourselves, as we discard people who knew at least part of the person we were before.

Like so many other pieces of how we understand ourselves, the impulse to start fresh has taken on new shape in our digital lives; you don't have to pick up your entire life and move to start over. But with fewer barriers in place, we might seek out fresh starts when we don't actually need them, putting distance between ourselves and our circumstances even when it's not all that necessary.

Part of why we might feel a desire to put distance between ourselves and others is due to how reachable we are now expected to be. Years ago, my Google voicemail service lapsed, and I just never bothered to reinstate it. I soon discovered that I loved not having voicemail, and that I was able to get on fine without it. It's since felt like a (very small) act of resistance.

But indulging the impulse to put distance between ourselves and our communities and seeking a fresh start elsewhere has consequences, too. Those who have attempted to opt out of society, writes Odell in *How to Do Nothing*, are acting on "a familiar and age-old reaction to an untenable situation: leave and find a place to start over." She gives numerous examples, from 1960s American communes to Epicurus's garden school in the fourth century BCE, the goal of which was to "live in anonymity."

Odell acknowledges that while members of Epicurus's school clearly "felt deeply responsible to one another," it was also clear that "responsibility to everyone else was left out of the question. They had forsaken the world." When I feel tempted to put distance between myself and the digital spaces where more and more people seek connection and meaning, I realize it would mean, in a sense, forsaking the world, which is ever more digital. And ultimately that's not what I want. Even in my most frustrated moments, I don't want to abandon the world. I want to find a better way to be in it.

Ultimately, Odell sees a useful example in Thomas Merton, a Catholic monk whose writing I read as a religion student. Though he initially thought he would be a hermit, he ultimately realized that though contemplation is necessary in order to discern and reflect, it should always bring you back to a sense of responsibility to the world around you. Likewise, one value of logging off, of taking distance from our digital lives, is that it can give us perspective to bring back to our digital worlds. "If I had no choice about the age in which I was to live," writes Merton, "I nevertheless have a choice about the attitude I take."

If we have no choice about living in the digital age, then the best we can do is determine how to live in it, taking distance when we need to but refusing to opt out altogether. Odell suggests that this question—"of *how* versus *whether*"—can help us "distinguish what it is [we] really feel like running away from." We can't address what we want to run from if we don't identify it. Sometimes that means stepping out to see the problem, rather than confusing the solution as staying in retreat.

When I find myself wanting to disconnect altogether—or throw myself all in and find connection *only* in a digital refuge like that semianonymous DM chat—I now think of communes and their failures. I seek a middle path that enables me to both step back and return. I also remind myself that logging on can be a way of stepping back, too. Properly understood, digital distance can offer the kind of perspective Merton sought, a flip side to the distortion of scale. In Carl Sagan's famous *Pale Blue Dot*, he suggests that taking in the view of our small planet from the distance of deep space can lead us to find significance in our cosmic smallness. Online, we can see ourselves as small dots in the vastness, too. Sometimes I log on to remind myself how big the world is and how small I am. That I'm part of something much larger than myself.

Even though home sometimes felt fraught, something surprising happened as I moved around in my twenties: I increasingly found myself missing where I was from. Nowhere else felt as natural to me as Minnesota did. While my home was less exciting than somewhere new, there was an ease I felt in Minnesota that I couldn't replicate elsewhere.

After years of considering it too small and some of its people too narrow-minded, of feeling like I needed to be somewhere more cosmopolitan, I came to love it again. In a new way. The distance enabled me to recognize that imperfections don't negate the gifts of a place. The things I hated about Minnesota began to wield less power, and the things I loved became more pronounced with distance. I even began to romanticize it. From afar, it looked nearly perfect.

My twenties were defined by change, but home stayed the same. Things in Minnesota continued to change in my absence, sure, but whenever I went home there was always more that was familiar than not. It became the place I returned to no matter where I lived. Minnesota was my constant—and it began to occupy a mythical, near-magical status in my mind. My relationship with where I was from became, in a sense, the inverse of my childhood fantasies. Instead of being at home imagining myself somewhere else, I started to find myself somewhere else imagining myself home.

During the fall following my breakup, this nostalgia reached a zenith. I went home with a greater frequency than I ever had since moving away. I spent time with my mom looking through old photo albums and reading a letter a friend had sent her after her mother died, both of us crying and talking about how much we loved one another. I hung out with my siblings, my nephews and niece. I walked down streets I frequented in college, shuffling through dead leaves and remembering my youthful optimism, how possible things seemed back then. After each trip home, I would spend extended periods of time on Instagram looking at posts from Minnesota friends, or posting photos I'd taken while home, and dream about what it might be like to move back.

If we're not careful, our social media platforms can become real-time nostalgia devices. We can begin to view our lives nostalgically as they unfold, through sepia filters and clever captions, remembering things as better than they were even moments after they happen. In doing so, we begin to put distance between ourselves and the complicated realities of our lives. In the digital age, nostalgia is something we feel not only for the past but for the reimagined present and even the future. (Think about how many times you've sat and imagined your Instagram post and caption for a future event—I know I've done it. We can begin to wax nostalgic for things before they even happen.) This escapism is of course not new, but social media allows us to create self-protective nostalgia around ourselves in a range of new ways.

How many times have I scrolled through old photos and posts online when I've found myself less than satisfied with the present? "The sense that all these things are irrevocably gone can make them appear more precious than they actually were," Martin Hägglund writes of escaping into memories of past experiences in *This Life*. "Your nostalgia, then, can come to shelter you from the demands of a life that still has to be lived."

In each generation, a swath of the population experiences a reactionary nostalgia, a yearning for a "simpler" time. For my generation, this is a rose-tinted view of the time before our social media age that necessarily ignores its benefits, all the good it has ushered in, and focuses solely on its deficits. (This nostalgia also requires ignoring or downplaying the bad in the past, of course.)

I don't share this view. Though in moments I feel overwhelmed by the new challenges of the digital age, I don't think I'd *actually* want to go back to a time before the internet. That doesn't mean we should dismiss the point of view of the nostalgics altogether, though. There's something to be said for the perspective we gain from change. We learn from the things we've lost, or at least lost sight of. Perhaps we took certain things about our predigital lives for granted. But would we even have noticed what went missing if things hadn't changed?

As a queer person, I've had to forcibly reject a lot of heteronormative ideas in order to assert my queerness. That has included tearing down the norms and ideals I'd inherited. It meant running away from home and what I'd been taught there. But in adulthood, after questioning and running from these norms, I am closing the distance. I now see value in some of them and am interrogating my impulse to reject anything "normal," which was at one point necessary for my survival. It was a good impulse, but there was perhaps some overcorrection—things I rejected not because they were bad, but because my reflex was to interrogate, reject, and run.

Part of this interrogation has included reassessing my rejection of home. And so, midway through the year following my breakup—in the thralls of nostalgia, but not entirely driven by it—I decided to move back to Minnesota. I was tired of running.

During the difficult year leading up to my move, I would fantasize about how comforting and familiar it would feel to be home. I imagined getting together with my mom every week, taking my nephews and niece to museums, and settling into a life there. But instead of the move magically fixing everything, as soon as I got home, everything was worse: the scabies, the sleepless nights, the uncertainty of so much change. I was at a loss without my friends out east, and I forgot how to ask my family for help. So I spent most of my first few weeks at home miserable and hopeless. Home wasn't a fantasy anymore. It was real.

Finally home, in the state I had left ten years before and yearned to return to, I now not surprisingly found myself yearning for a different place and time—for the comforts of the life I'd built with Alex, the energy of larger cities, the friendships there.

Ultimately, this period was useful. It helped me see that going home had been just another form of leaving. And that by returning, I had killed the fantasy. It was never going to be everything I'd built it up to be, but I couldn't see that until I was home.

Closing the distance online can help with fantasy deflation, too. Online, we can get perspective, see the projecting we do and the fantasies we build, and perhaps even work to kill the ones that aren't serving us, just as I did when I moved home. That won't just happen on its own, though. It takes effort, and sometimes, as it was for me that summer, it will be painful. But through this pain, we can come to see what we run from and why.

I don't know if I'll ever kill the instinct to run, but killing the fantasy of home—a place I first denigrated, then idealized, and now, finally, can see as just a place like any other—and closing the distance between me and the people who have known me longest feels like a good place to start. That doesn't mean *removing* distance altogether; there's still plenty they don't know about me, including things I'm sure they don't want to. But sometimes we need less distance than we think. In an increasingly digital world, when our digital platforms often instill habits that move us in the direction of separation, that feels more important than ever to remember.

You might be wondering what happened when Zain decided to stop running and returned home, too.

When I joined Instagram in 2016, Zain was one of the first people to follow me, and I followed back right away. It was then that I began to suspect he was queer, though he didn't explicitly say so. I noticed someone's arm with a rainbow-heart temporary tattoo. A rainbow sidewalk. A drag queen. A series of pictures taken at a wedding with two grooms. (Look, I wasn't doing impressive detective work.)

While I didn't know it, Zain was intentionally chipping away at the distance he'd put between himself and his circumstances—motivated in part by falling in love. But even as he pulled back the curtain online, having to keep his relationship a secret from his family weighed on Zain. Compartmentalizing began to take a toll not only on him but also on the relationship.

Zain and I exchanged only a few tweets in 2016 and 2017. For most of 2018—the year Sufjan Stevens contributed to the soundtrack for *Call Me by Your Name*, a film about a same-sex couple struggling with a secret relationship—he was just there in my feed. While we occasionally liked each other's posts, we didn't interact. But, in the fall, a couple of Zain's posts caught my attention: first a tweet, then an Instagram post, both about coming out. It was then that I reached out and asked if he would be willing to speak with me. He filled me in on his life—his backstory and the fact that he had just come out to his family and had been fully embraced. How closing that distance between himself and his family saved not only him but also his relationship.

That someone on my social media periphery, someone I barely interacted with, had an entire life beyond what I could see online isn't particularly noteworthy. What caught me off guard was how *surprised* I was by this fact. I'd always assumed his life was simple, maybe even mundane, but his story stunned me. I'd understood that he was a human being with a full life. But I had no idea what the full story was.

We're all living incredibly complex lives, and we share what we can, what we want to, of them online. Yet, when surveying the filtered lives of others in our social media feeds, it's difficult not to fill in the gaps with simple assumptions, or to imagine that there's nothing in the gaps at all—that what you're seeing from someone online is pretty much all there is. All the important stuff, anyway. Sometimes it's easier to see people online as objects.

In 2012, Stevens released *Silver & Gold*, his second box set of Christmas music, about a week after my first book was published. On the day of its release, I tweeted, "Just purchased 'Silver & Gold' by Sufjan Stevens. Can't wait to listen to this!" It was a profoundly boring tweet, and, appropriately, almost no one cared. It got two likes, one retweet, and one reply. The retweet, one of the likes, and the reply all came from Zain.

In Zain's response he directed me to the delicate "Justice Delivers Its Death," one of the final tracks in the collection, a Stevens original. In a collection packed with ambling, zany, and twee odes to cheer, it stands out in its spareness, sadness, and beauty. It was one of my immediate favorites, too.

"Silver and gold / silver and gold," Stevens begins, leading you to believe you're about to get a familiar Christmas classic.

But it's a fake-out, and the song immediately takes a haunting left turn: "Everyone wishes for it / How do you measure its worth? / Just by the pleasure it gives here on earth."

Listening to it now, I find myself asking how much worth I'd assigned Zain before. Why, when we had so much in common, didn't we connect more? Why didn't I really try to inquire about his life? Where was my curiosity about the human behind the account?

How do we measure our worth on social media, and the worth of those we interact with there? Just by the pleasure they give? For years I filled in the gaps in ways that made it easy for me to go about my business online without giving Zain a second thought. All the little red flags I saw that maybe he was going through something—things that gave me pause, suggested there was a human behind the account—I ignored.

Zain and I exist in different worlds, and the internet brought us together. But even as it collapses distance, helping us connect with people on the other side of the world, distance may also be inherent to the connections social media forges. We are, in certain respects, forever at arm's length online; we may never be able to get all the way there. Or, if we can, it might take a little more work.

And yet there is also something about the internet's expansive commons—its anonymity, its distance—that can enable novel kinds of connection and vulnerability if we let it. Surprising ways of being and belonging that can help us close profound distances. In this way, the internet is kind of like Grand Central station. In *How to Disappear*, Busch describes seeing a woman bid farewell to someone who appeared to be her son in the midst of the busy train hub in New York City. "Tears are streaming down her face," Busch writes, "and I am reminded of how this vast public space not only allows for intimate moments but also reinforces them."

Sometimes the best place to find yourself is in a space where you almost cease to exist, like when I moved to Chicago on my own with no savings at twenty-one years old and lost myself in something immense. Or like when, in the fall of 2019, I found myself in Grand Central for the first time since moving back to the Midwest. I was there to catch a train from New York City to New Haven. Like Zain, I had some distances of my own that I still needed to close.

Shortly after arriving, I went to meet up with my ex Alex. Though we'd kept in touch over the years after my move, it was our first time seeing each other since he'd come over on my last night in New Haven to help me finish packing up my car and say goodbye.

In the first months after we broke up, enveloped by a depression so thick I refused to open my bedroom curtains even once, I'd told myself that we had never *actually* connected, not fully. This was more comforting than the truth: that closed distances aren't guaranteed to stay closed. But sitting together again, I could see more clearly than ever what a lie that had been. He still knew me better than just about anyone, even in friendship. In fact, my move had enabled us to make our way back toward a friendship because we were able to work on understanding one another with the safety of distance.

After a few hours together, we walked over to my favorite restaurant in the world—Miya's, a one-of-a-kind, sustainability-driven sushi restaurant that defies categorization, run by the Lais, who became my second family while I lived in New Haven—for dinner with some of my closest East Coast friends. As we all laughed and fumed about the things that had once enraged us,

I found myself wondering what I'd been trying to escape when I fled New Haven a few years before. Why had I thought my life in Minnesota would be so much realer than what was available to me in Connecticut?

But I already knew the answer. As in adolescence, I had run from my circumstances, toward what seemed like better ones. Yet when I got back to Minnesota, things were still a mess. No amount of physical distance or social media scrolling could make my problems disappear; they had to be dealt with. But with distance from that difficult period in my life, I knew I didn't need to run anymore, or to feel split between my past and present lives. Alex and I could pick back up where we'd left off, in friendship; the distance hadn't made our love for each other less real. It had just given us a chance to reestablish our boundaries and return to them in a more appreciative way.

One of the high points of that night's meal was Miya's "chickenots." As their name implies, they are *not* chicken—they are in fact breaded and fried oyster mushrooms—but that almost requires pointing out because they taste very similar. However, maybe it's because I haven't eaten chicken in many years, but I actually don't think that they're "almost like the *real* thing." That isn't what makes them good; they're their own thing, just as real as chicken. That night, we all screamed with delight over how good they were. We ate several baskets and wished for more. There was no bit of us that would have preferred to consume the "real" thing instead. Like our digital lives and the various ways we use online tools to close and establish distance, the chickenots were their own distinct version of something different, something real.

If we expect our digital efforts to close and maintain distance to feel exactly like their offline counterparts, we will perhaps perpetually feel as if something is slightly (or majorly) off.

But if we let them be their own thing—real in their own way, with their own gifts and challenges—we can better navigate their limitations and appreciate what they offer.

After dinner Alex and I hugged goodbye at the New Haven Green, and I turned to walk toward the friend's place I planned to stay at that night. Not until several blocks later did I realize I hadn't turned back to look over my shoulder or wave.

But it wasn't because I was in a hurry to take off, like I always was in high school, or like I'd been when I ran from New Haven several years earlier. It was because I was in a haze in which time seemed not to exist. The night had stretched on far longer than I'd planned; it was late. But I took my time walking through the town I'd been eager to flee only a few years before. I was full of mushrooms that tasted kind of like chicken, nostalgia for a city I'd once called home and that would always be, and memories of a man I'd once loved and now loved in a different but just as real way. I passed through the dark quietly, stopping in moments to look not just forward or back but up, around, and inward. To take it all in. I was in no rush to put distance between myself and this night.

It's rare that I feel that way—that I don't need to be moving toward or away from something. That there isn't somewhere else I should be, somewhere that might be better, or at least different. I walked on, continuing into the night, leaving my phone in my pocket. The phone with pictures I've posted of past selves. The self that fell in love with Alex one Halloween. The self that moved with him to New Haven. The self that ran back to Minnesota as everything in my life came undone. But no matter the distances I establish online and off, these selves will always be with me. I will forever be forged by the places I've been and the people I've known.

Even as digital tools allow us to put distance between ourselves and our circumstances, to run, they also present new ways of anchoring us to who we have been. Sometimes, as it did that night, this feels freeing. But in the age of screenshots and archives, it can also feel suffocating. To better understand this strange new permanence in our digital lives and what it reveals about becoming real, I began by looking down at the ink in my arms.

6

INKED

T he week I turned eighteen, my mom took me to an unassuming tattoo parlor nestled among mechanic shops, secondhand stores, and dive bars in Saint Paul, the same one she'd gone to for her first and only tattoo.

The shop was messy, but also sterile, like a disorganized doctor's office—though instead of freshly laundered lab coats, exam tables covered in sheets of smooth white paper, and inoffensive pop hits from the '80s, there were guys in oil-stained cutoff motorcycle tees, a leather couch worn and cracked with age, and unintelligible screaming lyrics blaring from the speakers of an occasionally skipping CD player. (Same unfortunate fluorescent lighting and overbearing disinfectant aroma, though.) I was ready to cross the threshold and leave my childhood behind.

Getting inked at eighteen couldn't be more of a cliché, especially in the part of the Upper Midwest I call home. There's a reason it's a timeless and compelling rite of passage for those entering adulthood: it's the ultimate act of permanence. *I know myself well enough to get something I'll want on my body forever,* a tattoo says. *I am now a fully formed human being, and I can do things of consequence.*

Just minutes after the tattoo gun began buzzing, my mom drove this home when she got up and walked out of the shop. "You're an adult now," she said over her shoulder without looking back. "Good luck!"

Of course, just a few years after getting that tattoo, I decided I hated it.

The tattoo, a stalk of wheat on my right calf, was accompanied by a Bible verse—John 12:24, in which Jesus explains that a grain of wheat must die and be buried in order to bear fruit. Within a few years of getting it, though, I no longer believed in God. As I tried to establish my identity as a newly nonreligious person, the ink in my right leg—evidence I had not always been the person I was now—complicated my narrative. When I wore shorts, I found myself justifying my journey even to casual acquaintances, trying to explain how I could go from being a believer so earnest that I'd marked myself permanently with a Bible verse to a sincere atheist in a few years. *I wasn't really an adult when I got it,* I'd think resentfully. *Not like I am* now.

Several years later, as I was beginning graduate school, a documentary film about LGBTQ Christians at summer camp in which I'd appeared while in high school was bought by a cable network. They aired it once a week, sometimes more, and made it available to stream for free on their website. One moment from my life, spent on an island in the middle of a northern Minnesota lake with a dozen other queer Christian teens, broadcast across the internet and on display forever.

Before long, strangers were reaching out to me through my out-of-date Myspace page. Their messages were often deeply powerful accounts of their own struggles to find a place for themselves in Christianity—struggles like the ones I'd articulated as a teenager—coupled with expressions of gratitude for my example as someone living as a queer Christian and questions about how my faith journey was going.

Between the lines of their gratitude and questions, I could hear their hope, their expectations, their excitement. And, once again, I had to explain. Like the stalk of wheat meandering up my leg, my digital trail told the story of a past that strangers assumed was my present.

When I stopped believing in God, I felt a sense of loss but also relief. Among the sources of that relief: I stopped worrying about whether or not there was a heaven or hell.

Eternity had always freaked me out. I couldn't understand it, the idea that you could exist forever. The fact that I couldn't understand it scared me. I also sometimes found myself wondering whether or not what I was doing in the present was going onto a permanent record by which my eternal fate would be decided. My fears about eternity weren't consuming (though there's actually a word for when they are—*apeirophobia*), but I was happy, when I let go of my belief in God, to let them go, too.

As an adult living in the time of Twitter, though, some of my old anxieties about forever have returned. The strange permanence of the social media age, when so many of the things we say and do are documented, may be transforming our understanding of forever and introducing new versions of old anxieties. And that's not all it's altering.

There's nothing new about the impulse to keep a record of your life—long before the internet, we had journals, scrapbooks, and tattoos. But rather than being hidden in a drawer or covered by jeans, this documentation is much more visible. It's more public and much quicker and easier to perform. As a result, our relationship to documentation and our sense of how long it lasts are undergoing a massive shift.

Tattooing, once considered a fringe practice, the chosen adornments of sailors, soldiers, scoundrels, and circus performers, has gone mainstream. A 2017 report from the American Academy of Pediatrics reported that 38 percent of Americans between the ages of eighteen and twenty-nine now had at least one, which has shifted a number of cultural norms. The internet is quickly shifting our norms, too. Things that were once abnormal—like tattoos, or constantly cataloguing your life, documenting and publicizing minor events on a daily basis—have become the standard.

After joining Instagram in 2016, I started taking and posting a lot more photos, and I cherish many of them and the memories they evoke. But there are some that, in hindsight, I wish I had just saved for me. There are also so many I didn't need at all, and I suspect that taking them was disruptive to the experience I was having when I took them—getting my phone out to photograph food during dinner with a friend, for instance. This new standard, under which we're always inputting entries into our digital record, can function like the religious anxieties that once pulled my attention more in the direction of maintaining a sterling permanent record than toward the actual present.

We've all felt it at one point or another: that moment when, rather than allowing ourselves to exist in and enjoy a particular experience, we find ourselves reaching for our phone. Thinking of your social media posts as permanent entries can lead to moving through the world with how you'll record it in mind. To prioritizing postability. To doing or not doing something because it might be a good photo opportunity or a sensational story to thread. To sharing or not sharing things based on what has been rewarded with retweets and likes in the past. To even changing *the way* you tell a story, highlighting certain things and deemphasizing others based on what works for the medium. And if a more vulnerable or risky post from the past comes back to bite you enough times, it can be easy to decide you should err on the safe side, just in case future you is uncomfortable with what current you is posting, and keep that kind of stuff to yourself next time—or even avoid vulnerability and risk altogether.

Social media also makes it all too easy to post thoughts that we *should* keep to ourselves, at least in their infancy. Not only do our digital platforms invite us to share whatever we're thinking about the moment it occurs to us, but they also encourage us to share them *on the record*, no matter how embryonic they might be.

A number of years ago I wrote an online column for a news agency several times a week, and I was often urged by a staff member to produce faster, while the things I was writing about were still trending. Unsurprisingly, I regretted some of the pieces I wrote under those conditions, when nudged to issue opinions developing (or undeveloped, as the case may have been) in real time. Yet those opinions are now out there, eternally attached to my name.

On social media, many of us have felt an unspoken pressure to comment on every event lest we give the impression that we don't care about it. It's as though we're constantly being asked to prove we're not only paying attention but also not just watching in silence. These days, however, I've become more interested in staying quiet in certain moments—in listening to the perspectives of the more informed and, instead of inserting my own take into the mix, retweeting *those* perspectives.

And while it's especially difficult to form a thoughtful opinion on an event as it unfolds, my perspective often shifts over time even when it comes to things I've had ample time to consider. And what do you do when that happens?

When emerging ideas are shared in a permanent way they can end up shaping our understanding of ourselves. Feeling like we need to defend those half-formed thoughts instead of leaving them behind can stunt the growth we experience through experimentation. Social media "can play a part in constructive identity play," writes Sherry Turkle, founding director of MIT's Initiative on Technology and Self, in *Alone Together*. But "it is not so easy to experiment when all rehearsals are archived."

When we do remember that our posts are permanent, we often end up playing it safe and playing to the crowd. "There is nothing more deliberate than the painstaking work of constructing a profile or having a conversation on instant messenger in which one composes and recomposes one's thoughts," says Turkle. Digital communication encourages us to edit in real time because what we post is public and permanent, and the stakes are high. And yet this is in tension with how ephemeral it all *feels*. So we continue to share updates from our lives as they unfold, half aware that they're forever, and half convinced they're just for now.

Does writing about things in the moment lock us in to that perspective forever? And can that be, in part, a good thing?

Memory, even short-term memory, is notoriously unreliable. In court cases, more experts now argue that eyewitness accounts shouldn't be called upon unless they can be used in conjunction with other evidence that validates them. "Memory distortions are basic and widespread in humans, and it may be unlikely that anyone is immune," a 2013 study in *Proceedings of the National Academy of Sciences* states. Already unreliable, memory can become even more inconsistent with time. A 2012 study from Northwestern University's Feinberg School of Medicine teases this out. "Every time you remember an event from the past," writes Marla Paul of the findings for Northwestern Now, "your brain networks change in ways that can alter the later recall of the event. Thus, the next time you remember it, you might recall not the original event but what you remembered the previous time." Keeping a real-time memoir, then, can help us sharpen our memories and access how we understood an event closer to the time it happened.

But as we age, we may also look back on experiences with a new, more appreciative and careful understanding. Our memories can change as we change. This was something I didn't anticipate when writing my first book. Recording events from my childhood and the first half of my twenties made growing in my understanding of those significant events more difficult. To some extent, my perspective on those experiences—many of which are foundational to the person I've become, like kissing my first boyfriend for the first time, learning of my parents' divorce, or sitting on a towel in the passenger seat of my mom's car in a soaked swimsuit after lifeguard training and coming out to her as queer—has been frozen forever.

The most significant aspect of digital permanence, it turns out, may in fact be its impact on memory. At first blush this seems unquestionably positive: as we create digital archives of our lives, we are each assembling a database of supporting evidence for our memories. Can't remember that one restaurant you went to a few months ago? Just scroll back through your Instagram feed or Yelp reviews.

But even as it helps us to validate our memories, our social media activity can also potentially distort or taint them, Julia Shaw explains in *The Memory Illusion*. As we livetweet an awards show, text while having an offline conversation with someone else, or read detailed restaurant reviews online while discussing plans with a friend, we might think we are "multitasking," but we are in fact "just over-loading our brains," writes Shaw.

This is called *interference*. Far from a new problem, it's something humans have always struggled with. Interference, psychologist Larry Rosen and neuroscientist Adam Gazzaley explain in *The Distracted Mind*, comes in the form of "both *distractions* from irrelevant information"—like the Twitter notifications that keep pulling your eyes down to your phone during a friend's concert—"and *interruptions* by our attempts to simultaneously pursue multiple goals"—like attempting to both watch and livetweet your friend's concert. And while Rosen and Gazzaley acknowledge that our cell phones and social media platforms have certainly made some tasks easier, "they also threaten to overwhelm our brain's goal-directed function-ing." When you're task switching between digital and analog experiences, something has to give, and it's often the analog that folds.

The reason for this appears to be a hardware issue: our working memory can only store so much information at any given moment. Which is why, inundated by a digital stream of content, our ability to remember what we're experiencing beyond it may be dramatically reduced. "Indeed, while the resources of the internet seem infinite, our attention spans are not," An Xiao Mina writes in *Memes to Movements*. "As we scroll through our feeds on the subway or bus, click on websites in the office, and listen to podcasts on the way home, we are making critical decisions about how and where we want to drive our attention."

But our memories aren't just altered by all of our digital distraction and interference. As we post our memories online in real time, they become "part of a social landscape," writes Shaw. Online, our memories are no longer just our own but rather are a collaborative process in which we invite others to participate. There are of course positives to the increasingly collective nature of our memories; we are now able to document historic events in ways we never could have dreamed of just decades ago, with records produced by many different people, not just powerful gatekeepers.

With this perspective, we can also look back at whose lives weren't adequately documented in the past and correct those mistakes accordingly. As Yale University's Aimee Meredith Cox told Mashable about the #BlackWomensHistoryMonth hashtag, social media can help us tell a new story. "Black women have traditionally been written out of history unless it is in the context of victimization," says Cox, explaining why Women's History Month has often failed to highlight the important contributions and achievements of black women. But today many marginalized people are now seizing the opportunity to correct the mapping of our shared history—and write their own histories in real time. Looking at the impact of digital movements, the power of social media to amplify narratives that have often been overlooked, intentionally distorted, or silenced is clear.

However, even with the good it brings, our mass digital documentation can also quickly lead to memory conformity—when our understanding of events is so deeply influenced by the accounts of others that we can no longer tell what we actually experienced ourselves. Shaw cites Brian Clark of Western Illinois University, who argues that, due to the internet, "the distinction between public memory and private memory . . . has been blurred to the point of erasure."

In the age of Twitter, it seems impossible that our memories of certain experiences aren't being at least partially shaped by what Shaw calls "post-event information." And as Duke University's Dan Ariely has found, our membership in groups makes us irrational when it comes to memory (and in general). We are much more likely to conform our recollection to the accounts shared by people we see as in-group and reject those maintained by people we see as out-group—a dynamic especially potent online.

But social media's impact on memory isn't just limited to how we remember things. It also affects what we do with those memories. We are living in a time of *transactive memory*, where we not only build our memories online but also off-load much of our memory retention to digital platforms, where it continues to be influenced by others. One of the consequences of this is found in a study conducted by Betsy Sparrow, then with Columbia University, which found that the sense that we can always search the web for information later makes us less likely to try to remember things. In light of this, Sparrow suggests that "we are becoming symbiotic with our computer tools, growing into interconnected systems that remember less by knowing information than by knowing where the information can be found." Outsourcing our memories may have benefits, including freeing up space that allows "our cognitive resources to remember other things to which we are less likely to have immediate access elsewhere," writes Shaw. But offloading our memory has consequences—in terms of both post-event misinformation and the risk of not being able to access it when we need it.

The good news, Shaw says, is that "in a very basic sense, remembering life events through social media is going to enhance memories for those particular events." This is because of something known as *retrieval practice*, which is the idea that a memory gets stronger the more we revisit it—like each time we scroll back through our Instagram history. But we can only retrieve certain memories: those we've shared digitally. And this is the thing that worries me more than any of the other issues regarding social media and memory, especially as it relates to realness. "Every time we remember something," Shaw writes, "the network of cells that make up that memory becomes active, and that network has the potential to change and lose the details about which we do not directly reminisce."

She gives the example of Facebook reminding you about a vacation photo post, which prompts you to return (again and again) to the memory of that specific moment when the photo was taken—and how you framed it in your post and caption. Repeatedly reflecting on that specific (post-worthy) moment, and not on other memories from the experience, changes how you think about the trip as a whole. Like the aforementioned Northwestern University study demonstrated, as we revisit a recollection, we often remember the recollection, not the experience itself.

Of course, Shaw adds, this is not a new, social media–only phenomenon. Looking through the family photo albums of my childhood, for example, has the same effect. But she suggests that social media differs in the sense that "the prompts are being selected from your online persona so they already represent a distorted, social-media appropriate, version of your life. This amounts to a double-distortion—distorting the memory in your brain with a previously distorted memory from your online persona." While this was also true of my childhood family photo albums—our trip to Michigan was represented by a smiling group photo of us on a ferry making its way across the great lake, not a picture of the tears after my sister purposefully stoked an argument as revenge for being forced to come on the trip (don't worry, though only she was laughing about it then, we all do now)—those albums were viewed occasionally, whereas most of us are on social media daily. The photo albums weren't integrated into the platforms I now use to make sense of my life, connect with others, and express my identities to the world, whereas my digital memories are.

This is why it's vital to think about these issues in light of how we understand who we are. "By having social media dictate which experiences count as the most meaningful in our lives," says Shaw, we run two risks: one, that we will discard the memories we've deemed as less postable, and two, that whatever memories are rewarded with likes and engagement will come to seem more meaningful than they in fact were. Because of this, Shaw says we should ask ourselves: "How do you know whether you are recalling your experienced reality or your online, crafted, reality?" She suggests that we probably can't tell the difference.

If we can't trust our digital memories, what does this mean for who we are? If our memories are a big part of what makes us who we are—Augustine once wrote that he couldn't "even call myself myself" without his memory—does this mean that social media, which encourages us to document more, is helping us become more real? Or is it making it harder to feel real, as it distorts some of our memories? The fact that it seems to be a bit of both is all the more reason to use it carefully.

In the months after my breakup in the summer of 2016, I was barely keeping it together. A lot of the energy I'd put toward keeping up appearances online and off for most of my twenties—the kindness I'd tried to show to critics, the self-editing I was doing on social media—was suddenly being expended elsewhere, like in service of ensuring I didn't cry in a meeting or break down in the middle of a Target.

This also meant that, after years of carefully engaging on social media, I was finding it more difficult to be patient with online detractors and to filter my cattier thoughts out of each post. As my friend Ony put it, I was running out of fucks to give. But Ony proposed a solution (inspired by the fact that he teased me so often a local radio station ended up giving us a show that was probably at least 50 percent him dragging me on air): embrace my petty side.

So I did. I began replying to annoying, bad-faith comments sarcastically. I posted more of my flippant observations about mundane things. I shared juvenile jokes and memes. I even acknowledged that I, a human being with a body, sometimes had sex. I started worrying less about what I should or shouldn't say—stopped thinking of every tweet as a permanent entry in an ongoing public record—and started speaking a bit more candidly, sharing more of what was on my mind even if it edged sometimes into the rude.

Before long, friends started coming to me privately and saying they'd noticed a difference in how I was posting online. It wasn't exactly an intervention, but more than once someone joked that I was destroying my brand. In one such conversation, an acquaintance said that while they were enjoying my increased openness, they hadn't realized that I'd been putting on airs before, that I'd been a phony. That now I was showing the real me.

But the truth is that I was always both people: the bridge builder and the petty poster. I had simply compartmentalized and made space for one over the other, especially publicly. That meant that my pettiness got expressed elsewhere. In Gchats, Twitter DMs, and even online forums, I blew off steam under anonymous accounts or in private conversations in ways I wouldn't publicly. For years I was a person at odds with myself.

I first recognized this inner conflict not through my online behavior but through my tattoos. For years, my tattoos had marked me as an outsider; in spaces like Harvard and Yale, they signified that I wasn't like many of my colleagues. I rolled my eyes whenever someone would gawk or comment, but secretly, I loved feeling like an outsider. It was a preemptive, defensive move. I was going to show that I didn't belong in these worlds before anyone could tell me I didn't.

A major part of this was related to my profound discomfort with the pressures of being a representative for my communities, especially in environments where I already felt so out of place because of my very different academic background. Hired to support and advocate for the nonreligious, I wanted to help people see that nonreligious identities are acceptable, but I also didn't want to be anyone's representative. I may have been a chaplain at Ivy League schools, but I wasn't going to look the part. I wore bright-colored clothing, got a lot of tattoos, stretched my earlobes, and chain-smoked. The sides of myself that I normally didn't broadcast—my pettiness, my rebelliousness, my discomfort with respectability politics—began pushing themselves through the cracks. So I found other spaces for them outside of the professional spheres in which I moved, including on my body and, when tattoos and pastel-purple pants weren't enough, online. I was different people in different spaces.

We all need to roll down our sleeves to hide our tattoos sometimes. But the need to do so can feel especially acute online, when we remember that anyone can see most of what we post. We often end up exercising caution out of fear of alienating others. On the other hand, because we can't see people's disapproval, or because we think of social media as somehow less real or more fleeting than it really is, we also sometimes feel more free to express ourselves than we do in other spaces. So we waffle between overthinking and oversharing—between carefully choosing what we say and saying too much, depending on the space or the moment. Memes about "me on Twitter vs. me on Facebook," where the former is outrageous and the latter is restrained, are popular (on Twitter).

But this disconnect is complicated by the fact that everyone is encouraged to have a strong—and consistent—"brand." For most of my twenties, I had one. I was the queer atheist who worked with the religious for social justice. I wrote a blog about it, and then a book. For years my social media was laser focused on related issues. But like everyone, I've changed. By the end of my twenties, I no longer felt like that online representation. The truth, of course, is that I was never just that.

As I began to abandon that carefully designed, overthought public image, I found that even though the shift felt big to me, little changed. I lost some followers (the US Department of Education was among the first to go, I believe, after I made a joke about poppers). I also gained some. Mostly, though, the biggest change was that I felt more myself online, and those who knew me offline thought so, too.

This feeling of relief was a long time coming. Years earlier, as my writing began reaching a broader audience and my social media profile grew, I started getting invited to speak at colleges and bookstores—to move the conversation from online to off. Though not explicitly stated, those invitations often felt contingent on the book and social media version of me—the patient bridge builder—showing up. But "book me" was never the full me, and over the years he became increasingly difficult to summon. Though I didn't want to, I began to resent the expectation to be a one-dimensional self.

That tension between my professional, public self and my individual messiness came to a head in early 2015 when I was approached about a possible White House appointment. It wasn't something I had ever wanted or even considered, and I never imagined I'd be asked.

Seeking more information about what I should expect if I decided to pursue it, I got on the phone with a representative from an organization that helps prepare people for the presidential vetting process. They began to run through a list of things that might come up. Were there any compromising or incriminating photos of me? (Uh.) Had I smoked pot? (Well.) Had I gone to any protests? (HA.)

The representative continued, but I lost the ability to focus on what they were saying. It's impossible to adequately express how completely overwhelmed I was by just the initial questions they raised. I hadn't made past decisions thinking I might someday pursue public office or a political appointment.

I consulted with friends and colleagues, and almost all of them couldn't believe I was even debating it. "Of course you say yes to something like this. It's Obama!" they said. "Your speaking fees will quadruple. It's the highest honor you will ever achieve in your career. Don't question, just do it. It's worth dealing with any anxiety you might feel."

But none of their reasons felt compelling enough. I was fully committed to my work as a community builder, and I didn't want to take an opportunity that would pull me away from it, especially if the only reasons to say yes were ego, status, and money. But deep down I knew my commitment to my local community was not the complete answer or even the biggest reason. I declined to pursue the appointment because I didn't want to live in fear that something I might have said or done in the past—or anything I might say or do in the present—could be weaponized against me. How I was seen by others already gave me a lot of anxiety; this would have made it infinitely worse.

I'm not good at saying no under normal circumstances, so saying no surrounded by a chorus of people urging me to say yes was incredibly difficult. But it was also liberating in an unexpected way. After I turned down that opportunity, I got a tattoo. It was, simply, the word NO. Underlined, to make it clear that it wasn't ON—but the underline had an added benefit of making my NO more emphatic. It continues to remind me what I learned, which helps me live it out.

If properly understood, the permanence of social media can be a useful tool like this tattoo—one that helps us deescalate our inner conflicts and become more integrated. Like the underline beneath my NO and how I hadn't considered it would emphasize the tattoo's message, social media's permanence can surprise us by driving home things that help us feel more real, things we might not have otherwise seen clearly in ourselves.

Though not everyone will have to navigate the exact situation I did, the joke is often made that, due to social media, pretty soon only those who have never done anything fun in their lives will be able to run for public office. In *Trick Mirror*, Jia Tolentino writes that "people who maintain a public internet profile"—in other words, almost all of us—"are building a self that can be viewed simultaneously by their mom, their boss, their potential future bosses, their eleven-year-old nephew, their past and future sex partners, their relatives who loathe their politics, as well as anyone who cares to look for any possible reason." No pressure.

The need to be digitally coherent, and at the same time acceptable to everyone, is exhausting. If we want to combat this pressure to always be consistent and coherent, we can learn from queerness, which often seeks liberation from restrictive norms by blowing a hole in the wall of acceptability. In rejecting cultural norms and expectations, it offers an answer to the impossible consistency currently demanded by the internet.

But even in queerness and other marginalized identities, we see the pressures of the expectations of consistency. The editing queer people, women, people of color, and others learn at a young age can metastasize online. Tolentino says that "the self-calibration that [she] learned as a girl" has helped her to "capitalize on 'having' to be online." That rings true for my queerness, too—the compartmentalizing I learned at a young age has helped me navigate the world's demand for digital coherence and consistency.

But perhaps our inelegant attempts to be human online present a chance to reframe these demands and reapproach them as amateurs, like the drag performers who reframe and reapproach the demands of gender. As Zeynep Tufekci notes in *Twitter and Tear Gas*, the feminist movement of the 1960s brought attention to the fact that "the personal is political." Today, Tufekci points out, social media platforms "mix people's personal lives with their political trajectories." As we do more and more of our political and civic work online, and more and more of our socializing online, these things intermingle. In other words, "many personal aspects of one's life and interactions expressed on social media—tastes in music, travel, offhand statements about current cultural events—have become part of political expression."

This linkage is a double-edged sword. In a 2015 paper for the *American Journal of Sociology*, Cornell University's Daniel DellaPosta, Yongren Shi, and Michael Macy observe that social media has made cultural taste an indicator of political identity, and this raises the stakes for appearing inconsistent. They found political-cultural correlations—liberals like Starbucks, conservatives enjoy Cracker Barrel—have gotten stronger over time. While this has often been explained by implying a psychological difference between liberals and conservatives, the authors show that the deepening preferences are actually caused by social networks. Close social ties amplify cultural preferences and make them more bound up in political identities. This causes us not only to conform but also to conceal when our tastes deviate (again, I don't post when thirtysomething atheist me is still listening to Relient K on my Instagram story).

Instead of seeing our deviations as things to be siloed off to the side, there is opportunity here for greater integration of the political with all other aspects of our lives. It is harder to sidestep living one's values when you can't see them as a part of your life that exists apart from the rest of your interests. For example, once upon a time it was easier for a self-identified progressive person to enjoy homophobic and transphobic humor without realizing it conflicted with their value system. In the early 2000s, *The Daily Show with Jon Stewart* was a go-to for progressive viewers, and its host an icon of the political left. But Stewart, like many others at that time, dabbled in anti-LGBTQ humor. One egregious example comes from a segment in 2003, when he mocked Ohio representative Dennis Kucinich for saying he would nominate "any gay to the supreme court, or lesbian, or bisexual, or transgender person." After calling it the "craziest thing" said by any of the Democrats seeking the presidential nomination that year, Stewart pretended to introduce such a Supreme Court appointee. "Yes, yes," he said, "all rise for the Honorable Justice Chick-with-Dick." The audience roared with laughter. Today, if that were to happen, a sea of Twitter users would immediately swell to point out the contradiction. There is accountability in this.

But there are also challenges we won't be able to overcome if we don't allow people to be incoherent. Being able to contradict yourself, to be more than one thing, is essential to being human. Which is why there's so much at stake in considering the digital demand for consistency. In *A Circle of Quiet*, Madeleine L'Engle warns that people who overthink themselves—those who are "always turned inwards" and probing into their actions—"usually become less and less individual, less and less spontaneous." While they are "perhaps more consistent than the rest of us," she concedes, they are "also less real." On the other hand, she explains, "the deeper and richer a personality is, the more full it is of paradox and contradiction."

Not only does the demand for coherence risk making us less human, but online harassment often hinges on weaponizing people's contradictions against them. On the internet as it currently exists, "the multiple social roles that each person plays—a natural part of human society—have become harder to maintain," writes Tufekci. Or as Robert W. McChesney says in *Digital Disconnect*, "Viktor Mayer-Schönberger writes about how people can never escape their pasts in the Internet era, and something very important to being human is being lost." We haven't lost it yet, not fully. But it won't just stick around on its own, either.

■

Many of my tattoos have happened during times of transition and change: moments rife with contradicting emotions, like turning eighteen or turning down a possible White House appointment. Tattoos are both a way of reinventing yourself and a way of cementing that reinvention. Which is why I also got a lot of tattoos in the year following my breakup.

The first postbreakup tattoo came after the Pulse nightclub tragedy, which snapped me out of my own personal melodrama. In the earliest hours of a Sunday morning in June 2016, a gunman descended on the LGBTQ club in Orlando, Florida, and committed a massacre that took the lives of forty-nine people and injured fifty-three others, making it (at that time) America's largest mass shooting in modern history. Though violence is a part of queer reality, I and many other queer people were stunned.

In a world that constantly demands queer people edit and hide to ensure our survival, queer bars have, for many of us, been one of the only spaces where we can truly be ourselves. While the majority of Pulse victims were Latinx, and my understanding of the tragedy as a white queer person is fundamentally limited and different from that of my Latinx friends, the shooting represented a violation of one of the few safe public spaces many of us in the LGBTQ community have ever known.

Given my role as a humanist community organizer, I was asked to represent a nonreligious perspective at an interfaith vigil in New Haven alongside Christian, Muslim, and other religious community builders. I agreed to give remarks that would make space for the fact that people process these kinds of tragedies in many different ways, including without religion, and also acknowledge that, for some, religious words can actually remind them of past and present traumas. But, personally devastated, I felt unequipped. Though as a chaplain I had set aside my own struggles so that I could support others in theirs many times over the years, this time I didn't know how to put on my blazer and play the part.

So, on the morning of the vigil, I drove forty minutes to an unfamiliar tattoo parlor. I was there for two small tattoos I'd wanted for years, but always hesitated to get: the word QUEER in thick, blocky letters and a queer-liberation triangle, both on my right wrist.

I'm six foot four and still don't know how to buy a shirt with sleeves that make it all the way down my comically long arms to meet my wrists. Which means that, if a person is going to see any of the tattoos that cover both of my arms, QUEER is the one they'll notice. I wanted to put it in a visible spot because it's tempting to try to conceal my queerness, especially when I feel unsafe. But if you do it often enough, hiding can become your default. Reflecting on the lives cut devastatingly short at Pulse and the privileges I have as a white, cisgender gay man, I knew had done enough hiding.

"We're here, we're queer, get used to it!" is a rallying cry for many queer people, but in the past it was a hard one for me to embrace. Partly because I've sometimes struggled with confrontation, but also because it took me a long time to "get used to" being queer. I spent years concealing my queerness. This helped me grow accustomed to something else altogether: if you can't hide completely, you need to at least hide the messier parts of your identity, to ease others into understanding.

Being the only openly gay person in my high school or in Christian churches as a teen, I felt the need to be a better, more acceptable version of myself. I couldn't be flawed in the ways others were allowed to be. I had to be a good representative for my community. And the same thing happened years later, when I was a representative for atheists and humanists in interfaith spaces, in media, and as a community builder at institutions like Harvard and Yale.

But as I got those tattoos and reflected with the community on the Pulse nightclub massacre, I was struck by how important it has felt to make a concerted effort to integrate the aspects of myself I used to tuck away—and I think social media has helped.

For many of us, social media can function as an accountability tool. We see it frequently. Someone will share a goal on Twitter and explicitly state that they're putting it out there so that they're more likely to see it through. Photos are uploaded with captions updating friends on a "fitness journey" or a large tattoo in progress. Writers tweet #AmWriting even if it's only technically true in the sense that they wrote that tweet. (No judgment; I speak from experience here.)

Just as my tattoos offer an image-based account of my personal development over the years, social media helps many of us keep a history of our own lives, our own previous selves. By publicly sharing things in a permanent way—on our skin or online—we are forever linked to the person we were in that moment. And because social media is a tool for naming and sharing things about ourselves, we have the opportunity to harness it to learn more about who we are through this ongoing documentation, enabling us to keep track of our patterns and see things about ourselves that we might otherwise miss. For instance, if we begin to notice we're always tweeting (or tempted to tweet) frustrations about a certain thing and excited exclamations about another, it can motivate us to seek out resources and develop strategies for coping with the former and to carve out more space for the latter.

If that sounds like a mindfulness exercise, it's because it basically is. But while mindfulness is about not judging, social media can sometimes feel like the opposite. How can we feel real in a space where we're constantly afraid we will be judged? While our real-time memoirs can be a good thing—I feel more integrated now that I am being more honest about my pettiness on Twitter, more visible in my queerness both on social media and in my skin, and more accountable because of the things I share (this book exists in part because I sometimes posted about working on it to hold myself accountable!)—there are also consequences to the public nature of social media's permanence.

Shortly before getting that tattoo of the stalk of wheat and the accompanying Bible verse, I did something profoundly cruel.

It was my senior year of high school, and I had to take one last math class to meet my graduation requirements. My math teacher was very smart but struggled to command the attention of final-semester seniors. Occasionally she questioned herself aloud, and we pounced on that vulnerability—criticizing her, protesting assignments and pressuring her to change them, and generally ganging up on her—hoping to exacerbate her questioning. We were legitimately frustrated by some of her methods, and by our own inadequacies. But like all people, especially adolescents, we weren't always kind about our grievances, and were prone to flashes of cruelty.

One day, I escalated the situation. During a particularly challenging lesson in which the teacher gave a large assignment and then refused to budge when students protested, I went to the back of the room, emptied out a box of tissues, wrote COMMENT BOX on it, and passed it around the room so that we could each share our "feedback" on how our teacher was doing. While some of my peers had cell phones at that point, there was no such thing as Snapchat or Instagram. So the incident wasn't documented, wasn't posted on Instagram or broadcast live.

For a long time, only those who had been in the room or who had been told about it knew the story. It didn't follow me around; it wasn't attached to my name. Until, in 2012, I published my first book, which contained a passing reference to it near the end:

> I've still got a mean streak. The kid who lived to provoke my siblings, who once made a "suggestion box" out of an empty tissue holder in the middle of a high school math class for a bungling, ineffectual first-year teacher and passed it around the room—that occasionally rude rabble-rouser still lives in me. But I have found more productive uses for that energy, for my desire to challenge and change.

But while I took ownership of it there, I ensured I controlled and contextualized the story. I shared it to show how *I had changed*. It wasn't uploaded to the permanent record of the internet—out of context, out of my control, out there forever. It's only in the world because I decided to share it, to explain it from *my* vantage point (she was "bungling" and "ineffectual"; I'm "occasionally rude" but "have found more productive uses for" that rudeness now).

What I did was cruel, full stop. Indefensible. But that doesn't mean context is totally irrelevant (especially for those with an interest in understanding *why* things happen and how they can be prevented). I was going through a deeply difficult period in my life: I was openly queer in a hostile high school and frequently the target of others' cruelty. Additionally, shortly before I made the comment box, my boyfriend's parents had discovered our relationship and forcibly broken us up on my eighteenth birthday, days before I was going to take him to prom. So much of my world didn't understand me, but he did, and suddenly he was gone.

I was in agony—perhaps more so that week than at any other point in high school—and felt constantly disempowered. I didn't have adequate resources or support at school. Overwhelmed and isolated, with nowhere to turn, I made a comment box and took my pain out on an innocent bystander.

Today, such a moment captured in just the right way can go viral through happenstance and define a person forever, and no amount of context can stop it from happening. And because we all know this, it's easy to feel like we're walking on thin ice on social media. We understand that we're all just a series of retweets away from internet fame or infamy, and the consequences can be significant.

In a piece titled "We Are All Public Figures Now," written in response to an incident in which someone posted a Twitter thread about two strangers interacting on a plane that led to the subjects becoming unwitting social media stars, Ella Dawson writes, "the erosion of the division between public and private has been coming for a while now." We all know it on some level, but we never expect to be subjected to that kind of scrutiny ourselves. We groom our internet presence, Dawson says, but "we don't think about this as a public act when we have only 400 connections on LinkedIn or 3,000 followers on Tumblr. No one imagines the *Daily Mail* write-up or the *Jezebel* headline." This isn't hyperbole. The evolution of average online poster to internet dartboard can happen in minutes.

In some parts of the world, the freedom to not have a moment from your life plastered all over the internet is now considered an essential human right. In 2014, a European court ruled that people have a "right to be forgotten." In the first four years after the ruling, more than half a million Europeans submitted requests to Google to have information about them removed from search results. It's a start, though it's still only in Europe, and Google decides on a case by case basis whether those requests are worth granting. We have a long way to go before we live in a world where social media no longer has the power to define almost anyone forever based on one moment. Even when it seems innocuous, it's worth interrogating. Think about it: is the Walmart yodeling kid *really* going to want to be *that* forever?

I made a joke near the end of my first book about being too young to write a memoir, and while I don't regret writing it and I think anyone of any age can reflect on events in their life, I do look back and see a lot of my fear of being exposed bubbling up between the lines. Even as I shared intimate details about myself, I was hiding, concealing my terror at the idea of being fully and permanently seen.

When I toured with the book, someone asked me during a Q&A why my father wasn't really in it. I was taken aback by the question, but I couldn't argue with him; my dad only appeared on one page. I didn't write much about my father, I said, because it wasn't relevant. Barely concealing my annoyance, I moved on to the next question.

Over the years I've thought more about that person's question, and I know the answer isn't that my relationship with my dad is irrelevant to the way I see the world and the work I do. It's that the story of that relationship was messy and still evolving. I wasn't sure how to talk about it, and I didn't want to be on the record forever. So I cleaved off that piece of my self and my story.

I'm still not entirely sure how to talk about that relationship, but I'm tired of cleaving. I want to be a whole person, as difficult as the internet can make that feel. Compartmentalization is often the norm online. Synthesizing who we once were with how we'd like to be seen and known today can feel impossible. Especially when we watch someone else's past get dredged up—and the instant stream of online vitriol that sometimes follows, reply after reply like slips of torn paper stuffed into a cruel teenager's crudely fashioned comment box. But I'd like to believe that we can integrate our permanent past into our present without having to pretend it isn't there, and without having to be completely consumed by it, either.

———■———

There's real value in challenging people in positions of authority, online and off. Prejudicial social media posts from elected officials, media personalities, and other powerful people—like when a politician tweets a white-supremacist dog whistle or an entertainer says something homophobic—shouldn't be ignored. Pointing out xenophobia, racism, LGBTQ antagonism, and classism wherever they appear, online and off and in ways both overt and subtle, is important: both to demonstrate that we won't tolerate it and to teach others about the various ways in which these things manifest.

But, as someone who has engaged in callout posts and jumped into the fray of public shamings, I don't think we ask ourselves often enough whether we're punching up (calling out those in power) or punching down (calling out the disempowered). Especially because I am a believer in restorative justice, which requires that a person take responsibility for their actions, but also assumes that, once proper steps are taken, the person will not have to endure a lifetime sentence for their transgression—especially something as banal as a stupid tweet. We all have foolish thoughts and do reckless, harmful things. But people can and do change. Without excusing, ignoring, or justifying bad behavior—while also still expecting accountability—we can extend understanding to people posting online as they grow and change.

Without restorative justice in our various spheres I fear that, in a time when we know that a careless moment can define us forever, people will hold back their less formed thoughts, keeping them quiet instead of bringing them out into the light where they can be engaged, challenged, or celebrated. There are, of course, positive things about the impulse to keep some half-baked thoughts to yourself. But I also don't want to live in a world where people only share safe, focus-group-friendly opinions. "Let's not turn [social media] into a world where the smartest way to survive," Jon Ronson writes in *So You've Been Publicly Shamed*, "is to go back to being voiceless."

Of course, it's essential to ask ourselves who benefits the most from calls for digital nuance—and for whom the calls are typically made. Those who rail most virulently against what is sometimes called "cancel culture"—typically political conservatives or those who like to tell themselves that they're not—are often more concerned about preserving power than encouraging compassion for people who make mistakes. In a piece for the *New Republic*, Osita Nwanevu puts it exceptionally well:

> The critics of cancel culture are plainly threatened not by a new and uniquely powerful kind of public criticism but by a new set of critics: young progressives, including many minorities and women who, largely through social media, have obtained a seat at the table where matters of justice and etiquette are debated and are banging it loudly to make up for lost time. The fact that jabs against cancel culture are typically jabs leftward, even as conservatives work diligently to cancel academics, activists, and companies they disfavor in both tweets and legislation, underscores this.

Ultimately, while it's important to think critically about our impulse to "cancel" people online, a power analysis must *always* factor into how we consider these situations—because cisgender white men are almost always given the benefit of the doubt in ways that others rarely are. While this does not make calls for nuance inherently bad or wrong, it's clear that some people are much more likely to be allowed to work through their digital tattoos than others.

But we should also ask ourselves who has the most at stake when it comes to reconsidering redemption in the age of forever. In fact the permanence of our posts favors the already advantaged: they have more of a safety net in place if the internet turns on them. The privileged have less to fear from social media's permanence, not only because their actions are more likely to be interpreted generously but also because their advantages make it less likely they will lose it all—their financial stability, their relationships, their future opportunities—if they lose their reputation. They are more likely to have other ways of getting by if they do lose their career or income, too, more opportunities to start over. The most vulnerable among us—those lacking the safety nets and advantages of the more privileged—might also be those most vulnerable to having their lives undone if a careless tweet gets picked up by the wrong account.

Looking at the white supremacists who harass people of color online, the Twitter accounts who target feminists with the #Gamergate hashtag (an online harassment campaign focused on people who raise concerns about sexism in video games), and websites that dox social-justice activists (cobbling together personal information and past photos and posts in an attempt to blackmail them or harm their reputations and livelihoods), it's striking how casually people use social media to target and harass people they don't agree with, and to use their past or present inconsistencies against them. How easily people's digital tattoos get weaponized against them by digital bullies.

The online means with which people young and old can bully one another have compounded; they can use Facebook, Snapchat, Instagram, Twitter, and, perhaps worst of all, anonymous apps like Whisper. No one needs to make a comment box out of cardboard when digital comment boxes abound.

The consequences of this bullying can be fatal, as they were for fifteen-year-old Audrie Pott in 2012. After sexually assaulting her at a party, a number of her classmates took naked photos of her. The next day, those photos began appearing on social media, and people started saying atrocious things about her. Days later, panicked and ashamed, she took her own life. Horrifyingly, Audrie's isn't the only story like this; more and more young women are being publicly shamed online, and for some, the idea that these photos or stories could circulate for the rest of their lives is an insurmountable horror.

Once something is online, it's eternal, which can make it feel inescapable to victims. There was a time when a parent could reassure their bullied child that they would soon leave behind the whispers and taunts that followed them in the hallway, as my mom once did, but cyberbullying can follow you forever. And many bullies know this. They know the inherent power of the internet, its permanence, and they gleefully wield that permanence as a weapon. Sometimes, perhaps more often than we even realize, it isn't so overt. People don't mean to be bullies or have malicious intentions. They may even perceive the attention they're offering as positive. But the effect can still be completely overwhelming all the same. Threads of people publicly analyzing you and your life, discussions that forever lock you into the person you were at that time.

Other times, the bullies aren't even other people but the platforms themselves using our digital ink against us. Algorithms are constantly mining our posting and browsing habits and targeting us with their compiled data, and sometimes this targeting takes a dark turn. In 2018, Gillian Brockell wrote a piece for the *Washington Post* detailing how, after she had regularly posted about her pregnancy on social media before experiencing a stillbirth, she continued to receive targeted ads for months—each sponsored post for diapers, blankets, and toys reminding her of her personal tragedy. "Please, Tech Companies," she writes, "I implore you: If your algorithms are smart enough to realize that I was pregnant, or that I've given birth, then surely they can be smart enough to realize that my baby died, and advertise to me accordingly—or maybe, just maybe, not at all."

Some say that if you didn't want it out there forever you shouldn't have posted it. And it's true that sometimes the things weaponized against us are things we shared willingly. But the permanence of social media requires us to reflect on the matter of consent. While people opt in to sharing things on social media, they haven't necessarily asked for a single thing they posted to become what defines them. When something you shared is used for a purpose other than what you intended, whether it's going immensely viral or being turned against you by a bully, it can be a denial of agency. "This story you didn't choose becomes the main story of your life," writes Dawson. "It replaces who you really are as the narrative someone else has written is tattooed onto your skin."

Even still, we probably shouldn't share everything about our lives on social media. Not to keep it from bullies, but because the constant glut of personal updates and information may be too much information, too much noise.

Online, we can learn more about others than is helpful. For years my mom and I weren't Facebook friends, and that's how I wanted it. But one day in my early twenties, in a bout of home-sickness a year or two after I'd moved away from Minnesota, I decided I didn't care about all the embarrassing college drink-ing photos I was tagged in or the revealing things my friends posted on my wall. I wanted to be her Facebook friend.

To my surprise, she rejected the request. She didn't need—or want—all of that information, she said. She trusted me to share with her what was relevant and appropriate. Beyond that, she was fine. All that access would give her too much with which to imagine.

With a permanent social media record available for most of the people we meet at our fingertips, it's tempting to "research" new acquaintances and create our own mental picture of who they are based on who they've been, instead of giving them the opportunity to introduce themselves to us as they are now. Perhaps it seems safer—making us feel like we know what we're walking into—but it can also skew our interactions with them, causing us to tailor what we share with them based on who we think they are (itself an image cobbled together from what we could glean about who they've been in the past).

That may sound extreme, but today it's routine; I can't even tell you how many times some guy has said "I Googled you" after a first date. Or, often, before. Each time I feel robbed of the opportunity to decide for myself in what order I want to peel back the layers of who I am. We all do this, search the internet for information about someone we've just met, but whenever it happens to me it feels like a veto of my autonomy. Like the Bible verse on my leg making someone assume I'm still a Christian, my online past can now bear a greater influence on how someone I'm just getting to know understands me than my offline present.

—■—

A couple years ago, a group of friends and I tracked down a used copy of the documentary in which I appeared in high school, and when the DVD arrived in a nondescript envelope we quickly huddled around a laptop for a screening. After it was finished, we discovered that the most hilarious and horrifying thing about it can be found on the DVD menu, among the deleted scenes. It is a short clip mortifyingly entitled "Chris Feels Misunderstood."

In the clip—excerpted from a self-recorded session in the "confessional" cabin, where a camera was set up for campers to record personal commentary akin to the vlogs of today—I talk about my concern that my actions aren't being properly interpreted by the other attendees at the summer camp for LGBTQ Christian teens. It's perhaps the ultimate teen refrain—*no one understands me*—but in this short clip I take it to ridiculous new heights, explaining that though I'd been goofing off a lot that week (perhaps my biggest plot point in the documentary was when, confronted about waking up early and using all the hot water in the showers, I brattily suggested the other campers look at what the Bible says about forgiveness) I could in fact be quite serious.

The confessional clip is objectively amusing, but it's also painful to watch. I can see myself trying *so* hard, worrying so deeply about how I'm being perceived. Wanting desperately to "[come] across right," as I say in the clip. I was so concerned that, because I was letting go and having a good time, people wouldn't see me as smart or thoughtful—the things that I had been told were my strengths, were what gave me value, for so much of my life—that I sat down in front of the camera and gave a monologue defending myself for having fun at summer camp. It's absurd, and funny, and also kind of sad.

Sensing that I wasn't giving the cameras what they needed to portray me in the way I'd hoped, I entered the confessional cabin and clumsily attempted to wrestle back control of my story, because I knew that everything that was being filmed was potentially going to be forever tied to my public self. Even then, in the very nascent years of my social media use, I had a sense that I should be worried about how my life was being documented—and how permanent that documentation would be.

Many of us use social media in part because we want to be understood. But the truth is that we really just want to be *partially* understood. We want to be understood in a way in which we call the shots, in which we're in control of what others understand. The cameras concerned me because I wasn't controlling them and because they were capturing a permanent record. On social media, I have often tried to be in complete control of the story, a story that feels temporary, ephemeral, changeable, even if it isn't—not really. This has made me afraid to be too loose or silly online, and instead I've worked to project a careful, more serious image.

When you feel like you need to monitor what you say and do in order to be understood, it's easy to constantly fret about whether or not it's working, to overthink the story you're writing. Worry about it too much, and it can begin to feel like you're living primarily for the image you're projecting online. The story you're trying to broadcast can become the story of who you are.

These days, I'm trying to tell a different story from the one I've often told online. In an age when the stories we tell about ourselves are eternally etched into the world like tattoos on skin, rewriting your story can feel nearly impossible. But I'm trying anyway. I don't want to live with permanence in mind anymore.

A year after my first book was released, I received a very last-minute invitation to appear on *The O'Reilly Factor* on Fox News. At one point in the segment, when I was talking, the chyron below me read "CHRIS STEDMAN, ATHEIST." A screenshot of that moment has been shared a number of times online and has become a bit of a running joke. (The memes are great.) But the reality is that for years after my book came out, I was invited to speak in venues where I really only got to be one thing: Chris Stedman, atheist. I had a brand, and it felt dependent on me being uncomplicated. A singularity.

But I am more than just an atheist. I am more than Chris Stedman, comma, plus one descriptor. We are all more than any one aspect of our identities. And we shouldn't have to choose between being our full selves and trying to be understood.

To be understood as an atheist, I often felt asked to reduce myself to just that. This is a broad problem: when members of misunderstood communities challenge the stigmas placed upon us, we're often tokenized and flattened out. Our national culture is uncomfortable with people possessing a complex mix of identities, so it reduces us to the most digestible version of those identities.

When you feel like you have to flatten yourself out and reduce yourself in order to be understood, you often end up self-policing. But that is a fruitless project without end, because no full human fully aligns with the brand.

I've come to believe that making more space for people to be messy, complicated, contradictory, imperfect—to feel real—is not just fundamentally important to ensuring that we live in a world of healthy individuals. It's important to society as a whole. Allowing people to be more fully human changes the way we talk about difference and increases our ability to understand one another. It helps us recognize that we all enter into these debates with biases and baggage, and that we're going to fuck up but also, hopefully, grow when we do.

Our aims in flattening out our stories and identities, in presenting a more digestible public self, are often noble. Sometimes we simplify our stories to help others better understand things that are complicated. Sometimes we do it because we don't want to take up too much space. Sometimes we do it because we want to fight bigotry and break down stereotypes, and we believe that being an exemplary, unimpeachable representative will help us do so.

But in the end, it will always bring us to the same place: a place of not really being known, of not really being seen, of peering out from behind a mask. And that makes it harder for us to humanize our differences. We need to be full humans, imperfect permanent records and all, first.

The first tattoo I got after the stalk of wheat was, in a sense, a rejection of it.

A simple outline of a capybara, the tattoo was inspired by a television show I'd watched that said the Catholic Church considers the capybara a fish because a pope once said it was. According to the program, even once it became obvious that it was a mammal, the church couldn't change their position on the matter because of the doctrine of papal infallibility.

Though I was never able to verify the validity of this story, the tattoo served as a kind of symbol to represent my views on religion at the time—that it was backwards, outdated, unthinking. I saw that tattoo as a kind of counterbalance to the stalk of wheat on my right calf, like they were competing symbols in opposition. But over time, as I continued to study religion, I came to understand how complex it can be. Still, the capybara tattoo remained.

In the year following my breakup, I decided to change it. Not to remove or cover it up but to add to it. To update it and make it more detailed, like my now more complex understanding of religion.

Today, this more detailed capybara tattoo is a symbol of a different kind: a representation of how we can evolve. It reminds me that we are shaped by our pasts but not defined by them. That we can and will change, and that things are rarely as simple as my original tattoo—or as our digital ink.

Social media forces us to confront the fact that we are forever *becoming*. That we never completely *arrive*. Our online posts are never the full story of who we are, not even in the moment when we upload them. Like the finger pointing to the moon, they point the way to something deeper, something truer, but they will never capture the full story. The sooner we recognize this, the better we'll be at understanding how their tattoo-like permanence can actually be used as a tool for positive ends. How we can learn from social media about accountability but also about the fact that people are forever works in progress, forever growing, and never the sum of their public parts or their worst moments. We aren't just our scrapbooks, all highlights and smiles—but neither are we only our most selfish impulses or thoughtless cruelties.

Part of being a person, an essential part, is screwing up. Does having every mistake, every half-formed opinion, on our record make us more real—or does it make us less? Perhaps knowing everything is being documented makes people less inclined to take risks, to experiment, to put themselves out there and speak freely. If so, I suspect we'd be better off letting go of the sense that we need to have a coherent online identity and instead embrace that feeling real requires the freedom to reinvent yourself. That parts of you can be contradictory and still equally real.

At its best, the permanence of social media can make us more aware of ourselves. After all, part of being a person is *learning* after you've screwed up. As large numbers of people continue to abandon older ways of holding ourselves accountable—the practices, rituals, and shared space of religious communities and other civic organizations—social media could be rising to take their place in helping us connect, reflect, and hold ourselves and one another accountable.

We are more than our tweets, yes, but we *are* our tweets, too. Just as I am more than my wheat tattoo, it also communicates an important piece of my story. Like tattoos, we use tweets and selfies to remember but also to communicate and build ourselves into being. We are what we post, and if we struggle with the fact that it all feels so permanent, perhaps it is because the permanence of our posts shines a light on their realness.

Even the things that feel temporary and fleeting are building our world. "It's a common misconception that memes are ephemeral," An Xiao Mina writes in Memes to Movements. "A hashtag trends, a selfie meme circulates widely, and then they disappear as quickly as they seem to have emerged. But many of these memes are part of something longer term, which is a political narrative, and these narratives are driven by memes that go viral, garnering responses from people on the street, the media, and the world's most powerful politicians."

If memes seem ephemeral, Mina argues, it's only because they are "like the scattered seeds of a story with deep roots, informed by culture, geography, upbringing, and a wide variety of other factors." She continues:

> Creative media alone cannot change a long-running problem in a matter of years [because] legal and cultural change can take generations, especially in the face of powerful opposition . . . But what art and media do, online and offline, is create an archive of cultural memory, a record of conversations and subtle shifts that have transpired, making forgetting an impossibility and all but ensuring future conversations can ensue.

The accumulation of many fleeting things can make something lasting.

Besides, we can put at least some of our anxiety to rest in knowing that a lot of our digital ephemera is actually *not* as permanent as we think. "Too often people assume that digital content will last forever," writes Astra Taylor in *The People's Platform*. "In reality, we lose an estimated quarter of all working links every seven years and digital files can quickly become incomprehensible due to the swift churn of technological obsolescence." Still, we don't know what we'll lose and what will last.

Digital permanence can function as an equalizer in a world where only a small group of gatekeepers—typically wealthy, white, cisgender heterosexual men—have been allowed to record history. But it can also make us feel like we're living in a world where older versions of who we were are imposed on the person we've become.

At its best, though, social media can hold us more accountable to ourselves, revealing who we are—the good and the bad—and helping us become better. Digital permanence might force us to become more honest about how we all evolve and maybe even learn to be more comfortable with past mistakes, like laughing at a bad first tattoo. But without intention and care, we also risk creating a world where we're policing ourselves in every moment, worrying about things we haven't even said.

The permanence of our digital lives is equal parts revealer and reducer, equalizer and restrictor. It has the power to make us real and to stunt our growth. Which of these roles this strange new permanence will play in our lives depends entirely on how comfortable we can become with the simple fact that it exists and, like the wheat on my calf, isn't going anywhere. But like the capybara on my arm, we still have a chance to redesign, to add some detail.

Redesign takes many forms, but one of the most delightful and generative is through play and experimentation. To better understand how our digital lives give us space to reimagine ourselves, I went to talk to game makers and the people who play their creations.

7

THE ROLES WE PLAY

In the summer of 2018, I went to an LGBTQ variety show to kick off pride weekend. Near the end of the night, after an extraordinary lineup of queer poets, burlesque artists, and punk bands, local illustrator and author Archie Bongiovanni did a live reading of one of their comics. In the strip, two characters are talking when one of them gets a match on the popular dating app Tinder. The person who got the match, Taylor, begins to panic. "How does one translate their personality into the digital world?" Taylor wails, before adding: "Isn't social media just a <u>GAME</u>?"

In the age of catfishes and clout chasers—people, typically online, whose approach is to "strategically [associate] themselves with the success of a popular person or a current contemporary trend to gain fame and attention," as rapper Snoop Dogg defined it in a video posted to YouTube in 2018—many of us share Taylor's fear that the internet is just a game. One in which everyone is trying to score points and level up. But while there's some truth to this concern, it may also be a bit cynical to say social media is *just* a game. Or, rather, to say that the games we play online are about being fake.

Yes, people can pretend to be characters online as one does in a game. But our digital games can also teach us something about what it means to be real, if we're willing to look at them more closely. Like a good game, the internet is essentially a laboratory for identity—one that presents unprecedented opportunities to learn more about what it means to be human, to cooperate, and to belong.

On a sunny spring afternoon a few months before that variety show, I pulled into the parking lot of the Saint Paul headquarters for Atlas Games, maker of board, card, and role-playing games (or RPGs).

I walked in and took a seat across the table from Jeff Tidball, Atlas's chief operating officer and an award-winning game creator. Shortly after, we were joined by Atlas's warehouse manager, Travis Winter, and RPG director, Cam Banks. Between the three of them, they have over seventy-five years of experience playing and creating games. It was clear—not just because of all the gaming paraphernalia crowding their offices—that they lived and breathed gaming. I was eager to find out why games appealed to them and hoped our conversation might help me better understand how the imaginative impulses we engage in gameplay are (and aren't) mirrored in our online behaviors.

Playing games, Winter began, is about "taking a break from being in charge." He has a lot of responsibilities in his day-to-day life, and games give him space to play.

In some ways, the parallels between this and our online lives are obvious. But to explore both spheres, it's important to be clear about what constitutes a game. In *A Theory of Fun for Game Design*, game designer Raph Koster explains that most people who study games agree that a game is a voluntary, rule-based "free activity" outside of "'ordinary' life." Within this context, "different outcomes are assigned different values, the player exerts effort in order to influence the outcome, the player feels attached to the outcome, and the consequences of the activity are optional and negotiable," says game designer and video-game theorist Jesper Juul. Sid Meier, creator of the Civilization games, describes a game as "a series of meaningful choices," and authors Ernest Adams and Andrew Rollings add to the definition, describing a game as "one or more causally linked series of challenges in a simulated environment."

Sound familiar? For many of us, social media can feel like a "simulated environment"—a "free activity" set apart from "'ordinary' life" where different outcomes, like getting engagement or increasing your reach, have different values. As in a game, there are rules, and we feel attached to what happens when we use it; yet, in both cases, while we are attached to the outcome, consequences can feel optional and negotiable. As with a game, there is sometimes a sense that the stakes are lower online—that what happens there is perhaps less real and has less of an impact on the rest of our lives. That if a conflict happens online, for example, it is somehow artificial, or at least less real than an argument that occurs in person.

In light of these definitions it's easy to see why, as Winter said, games are often a place we go to unwind if we have a lot of responsibility in our lives. They feel like a place where we can play out high-stakes stuff in a low-stakes environment. Whether it's an escape game, in which you're trying to get out of a room in a limited amount of time all the while knowing you're not in any real danger, or a game of Dungeons & Dragons (D&D), in which you're battling imaginary monsters instead of the real difficulties we all encounter in life, gameplay can be an opportunity to conquer challenges with fewer far-reaching consequences. (By the time I was doing final edits on this book, I'd become so convinced of this that, to my own surprise, I'd purchased my first ever video game console.)

Our online behaviors often function similarly. When I look back on my digital habits in the year leading up to my breakup, it's obvious to me how much I was using it as a space to meet some essential needs. There was so much going on at work during that time; I was on the job seven days a week, working from morning until late into the night, and Alex was building a small business. We both rarely took breaks. In the brief moments I could find between all the work—as Alex was often busy during them—I would turn to the internet for relief. I began goofing off online, separate from the social media accounts associated with my name, writing, and activism—jumping anonymously into the comments sections of pop-culture pieces, mouthing off on things that felt inconsequential and disconnected from the rest of my life.

I wasn't able to articulate it then, but joking around anonymously online was a way of blowing off steam at a time when I felt overwhelmed by responsibility. In online venues, I wasn't the executive director of a nonprofit, the partner of someone starting their own small business, or even just someone who had to go on long walks in subzero weather trying to tire out a young dog who never encountered her limit—I was a faceless avatar making jokes and commentary about pop culture. It may have felt small and inconsequential, but there were days when posting playfully online was the one thing that kept me from being overcome by stress.

We do things like this because play is a necessity. It's not something extra, some luxury to indulge in if we can spare the time, but rather something that fulfills important needs. Research has shown that play contributes to our well-being in numerous ways, perhaps most importantly in how it reduces the impact of stress. When we don't actively seek out opportunities for play, we sometimes go about meeting our need for it in less intentional ways—as I did behind faceless avatars, and as many of us do online.

Our digital play can either be an unguided way of blowing off steam and forgetting our problems or a game with goals and achievements; it all depends on how we play. So if we're going to use social media playfully, it would benefit us to do so more intentionally.

—■—

After Winter finished explaining what draws him to games, Banks jumped in.

"For some, gameplay is less about taking an active role and more about being a spectator or chronicler of the story," he said. "They like to keep records and create a write-up after. But at the table, they're not doing a lot."

The watching or narrating aspect of play made immediate sense to me—after all, there are now entire online platforms dedicated to giving people the opportunity to watch others play video games. Less literally, I'm willing to bet we've all watched a digital drama unfold and, even if we don't want to admit it, enjoyed the experience of being a silent observer. The kinds of digital games we act out on social media—the dragging and exposing, the calling out and putting on blast, the actually high-stakes dramas that unfold on our timelines—show the power of our platforms to impact offline life, from someone getting fired when an employer is alerted to Facebook posts made on company time to a social media manager losing their job after accidentally liking the wrong tweet from their employer's account. And yet our online dramas are so often regarded as harmless entertainment, even when they're not—a reflection of our broader sense that our digital lives aren't real.

Because we often consider the digital pieces of our lives as not (or less) real, the playful things we create to express ourselves online, like memes, are generally considered silly trifles. But, like the fallout people experience over a bad tweet, they can in fact be a real—and immensely powerful—tool. The collaborative nature of internet memes, in which we take someone else's SpongeBob meme and remix it to create our own, may just feel like goofing off. But this process can actually help us reimagine the world together—one way digital play can cause us to feel more real.

"Memes help us envision another world, a practice known as *prefigurative politics*," writes An Xiao Mina in *Memes to Movements*. In other words, playfulness lets us experiment with and build narratives that we can then use to reshape the world around us. "In creating space for the imagination," she argues, our digital play "can help motivate action." Like memes or tabletop RPGs, our digital games are often about collaboratively reimagining the world. By enabling us to enter into prefigurative politics together, play can help us become who we want to be.

On the one hand, it's true for some that games are a space set apart from the rest of their activities, to play out something seemingly unrelated to the rest of their lives. Live-action role-playing, or LARPing, is one such kind of play, which runs a wide range from model United Nations to sci-fi scenarios. I'm also reminded of escape rooms, horror movies, and haunted houses—all of which can be ways to play out high-stakes drama in a safe environment, letting participants carefully experience catharsis. If you have a lot of responsibility in your life, these practices can provide a useful outlet. Yet we can also take the things we learn about ourselves in these spaces and integrate them into other parts of our lives.

But for some this identity play runs even deeper. In *Life on the Screen*, Sherry Turkle writes about MUDs, or multiuser domains—early digital spaces where people came together to create imaginary worlds, usually through the written word—which actually grew out of D&D, the most famous RPG of all time. Turkle suggests that participants weren't just building new worlds through text on MUDs. They were also "constructing new selves," she says—and some MUD players would come to see themselves as refracted between selves as a result, because on MUDs one could "play a role as close to or as far away from one's 'real self' as one chooses."

The apparent anonymity of online forums for play, like that experienced in MUDs, gives people an opportunity to "express multiple and often unexplored aspects of the self, to play with their identity and try out new ones," says Turkle. But she seems skeptical about how real this identity exploration is. "MUDs make possible the creation of an identity so fluid and multiple that it strains the limits of the notion," she writes. "Identity, after all, refers to the sameness between two qualities, in this case between a person and his or her persona. But in MUDs, one can be many."

One has always been many, Turkle acknowledges, but she suggests that the internet changes *how* we are many. "The self is no longer simply playing different roles in different settings at different times, something that a person experiences when, for example, she wakes up as a lover, makes breakfast as a mother, and drives to work as a lawyer," she writes. Online, she says, we become "a decentered self that exists in many worlds and plays many roles at the same time."

I'm not sure the segmented self represents a fundamental change, though. That person woke up a lover, but she never *stopped* being a mother or a lawyer. Those pieces of herself may be more in the forefront at certain times and more in the background at others, but they are always there, informing how she sees herself and the world around her, and how she moves through it. I suspect it's always been true that we've existed as a self partitioned, like the tabs we shift between on our internet browsers. It's just that perhaps we are more able to see their distinctions now. Online and off, we shift between selves. Sometimes we want to play an active role, and other times we just want to observe.

When I was a kid, my siblings and I played a lot of imagination games with complex rules and ongoing story lines (as well as more lowbrow fare like "Hide-a-Bed," which consisted of folding someone into the retractable mattress of our sleeper sofa and seeing how long they could tolerate being pinned between layers of foam and fiber before panic set in). Among them was our favorite and most frequently played game, which we called "Zoo."

It wasn't terribly complicated. My sister's character, a monkey named Banana Bug, ran the show. Her accomplice was my younger brother, a mountain lion who loved to lounge and whom I named Mahi-Mahi. My youngest brother was added to the game as a wild squirrel who lived in the zoo uncaged. His name was Blar Blar, but he took "wild" to mean "rabid" and bit each of us whenever he got the chance.

And me? I was the zookeeper. I resolved conflicts between the different animals; I addressed the issues and cleaned up the messes. The animal characters had idiosyncrasies and unique characteristics, but the zookeeper was just that—a zookeeper. It's not that it wasn't a glamorous role, or that it didn't have a creative name like Banana Bug or Mahi-Mahi or Blar Blar. It's that it wasn't even really a character at all. The zookeeper didn't have a personality. He was just a title. Unlike the animal characters, playing zookeeper wasn't a chance to step outside of myself and be something new and different. I was still a human. My siblings' characters were about creating fun chaos; mine was about keeping order. Their characters drove the story; mine reacted and resolved. For my siblings, "Zoo" was a hugely imaginative game. But for me, it sometimes felt more like a job. When I was the zookeeper, I was still me, but I was a more responsible, more *together* version of me.

This isn't an uncommon kind of game among children. Kids often inhabit adult roles that carry a degree of responsibility, like a doctor. But what stands out to me about the zookeeper role is that I was the only one in the game playing this kind of character. In hindsight, I also notice how frequently I found myself drawn to this sort of role as a child—how eager I was to play a more responsible, more adult version of myself.

So often this kind of *playing up* has been true of my digital play as an adult, too. For years my Twitter felt so sanitized that it was almost as if I were just a title, just my professional roles. Like I didn't have a personality beyond them. Social media has frequently been a vehicle for trying to control how other people see me—something the game makers at Atlas identified as one thing that sometimes draws people to games, especially those who want to guide the narrative of the game like a Dungeon Master in D&D.

But I wasn't always trying to exert control when playing games as a kid. Sometimes my youthful gameplay was actually about *letting go* of control and having a space for experimentation. Though the world around me often felt defined by constraints, I grew up in a household that encouraged us to break some of society's rules. For example, my mother stocked a basket full of dress-up clothing, and my siblings and I constantly utilized its contents for imagination games. Frequently this resulted in us wearing items of clothing that were intended for people of a gender other than the ones we were assigned at birth; our family photo albums are full of pictures of my brothers and me wearing dresses and skirts from that basket. Not for laughs, but to play fully developed and sincere characters.

Though I'm cisgender, meaning I identify with the gender I was assigned at birth, I often felt restricted by the expectations of my assigned gender as a child—and sensed that any deviation from gendered norms could have grave consequences. But play was a place to start breaking some of those rules. To experiment, try things out, and explore aspects of my personality that felt unsafe or risky to express elsewhere, much like the queens I saw on amateur drag night as an adult.

In this sense, our digital games are more than a vehicle to control how others see us. They also enable us to experiment with identity and express ourselves in radical and often vital ways—giving us the power to shape not only how others see us but the number of ways in which we can see *ourselves*.

The September after my summer breakup—shortly after my boyfriend moved out of our apartment—I went to Washington, DC, to speak at a White House event on interfaith cooperation. It was hosted by a university where Lia, one of my close friends from childhood, worked.

After the event Lia and I caught up, drifting to stories from childhood, like the birthday party she had at a paint-your-own-pottery studio where it came to light that two of our mutual friends, also at the party, had outed me as gay to peers without my permission. The story climaxed with me literally chasing them outside with paint-covered hands while everyone else wondered what the hell was going on. It's a funny memory now, but I remember the panic that set in once it hit me that word of my sexuality was spreading; how I imagined it expanding exponentially like a wildfire I once witnessed by the side of a Minnesota highway. I still feel it, that bone-deep fear that can take over when you lose ownership of your own story.

But my favorite of the stories she shared that day was about how, early on in our friendship in elementary school, I invited her over to my house. We went into my room, and I opened my closet doors to extract a doll I kept hidden under a blanket. My mom had given me this doll when I was three; she gave one each to both of my brothers, my sister, and me, because she wanted us to learn how to be nurturing. I showed the doll to Lia and asked if she thought it was okay for a boy to have a doll. She said yes, boys could have dolls, but she didn't really like them that much herself. She preferred "rocks and dirt." (A verbatim—and truly iconic—quote.)

Listening to her, I understood how powerful it can be to let go of the desire to control how you're seen—a desire that makes losing control feel so terrifying. In Lia's example, I saw the power of play as a vehicle for sharing yourself, and how that can invite someone else to do the same.

It's hard to be a kid who doesn't fulfill society's gendered expectations. From a very young age, it was clear to me that I wasn't what a boy was *supposed* to be. But a number of my childhood games—from dolls to dress-up and the games I played with Lia—gave me space to step outside those boundaries. In play, I could pretend to be things I didn't think that I was. And I could express things that I *knew* I was but didn't feel safe expressing in my "real life."

Playing by the rules ("boys play with rocks, girls play with dolls") boxes us in, but play can also be expansive—a way of going beyond the images of ourselves we've adopted or constructed in order to access something more real. "In real play, which is real concentration," Madeleine L'Engle writes in A *Circle of Quiet*, "the child is not only outside time, he is outside *himself*."

"A child playing a game," she continues, "is completely *in* what he is doing. His *self*-consciousness is gone." In other words, play can be a way of losing yourself in order to find yourself; of transcending the norms you've inherited so that you can go deeper into who you really are. Because, L'Engle says, "when we are *self*-conscious, we cannot be wholly aware; we must throw ourselves out first." In play we can dispatch of the old and start anew.

This reconstructive aspect of play became clearer to me in conversation with the game makers at Atlas, who talked at length about games as a place to try new things and experiment with how you understand yourself. But it revealed itself all the more in several interviews and conversations I had with people who have used digital spaces to explore their sense of self—none more illuminating than my conversations with a woman named Merisa.

—■—

A few years ago I met Merisa on Twitter, and we started messaging regularly. After she mentioned that she was an avid online gamer, I asked if she would be willing to tell me a little more about why games are so important to her.

She loved video games, she told me, from the very first moment she held a controller in her hands. It was the 1980s, and video games had suddenly become much more affordable and accessible to a broader range of Americans. At the beginning of their heyday, with blocky graphics that were more agender than anything, it often felt like they were for everyone; it wasn't until the 1990s that a broad number of people started thinking of them as "more of a guy thing."

It was in this specific window that Merisa, a transgender woman who was assigned male at birth, found herself entranced by video games and their blocky 8-bit graphics—in large part because they were one of the few things that seemed acceptable for both boys and girls to be interested in, especially in the early days. Little did she know that her love of gaming would lead her to the space where she would first come out.

In the mid-'90s, when Merisa was around fifteen years old, she started participating in an online chat room for people interested in *ZZT*, a computer program with simple graphics in which you could build your own games and share them with others. It was there, in those chat rooms, where everyone was just a display name, that she first came out as trans.

It was actually quite simple: she just changed her display name to something more feminine and said that if anyone had any questions, they could ask her. But no one did. The non-chalance of their acceptance—their unquestioning willingness to simply start calling her by a different name—was almost shocking. And in fact, as it turned out, there were many other trans people in the chat, too. Online spaces—especially those that orient around creative endeavors, whether it's a chat room for users of a cooperative game like *ZZT* or the pop-music stan forums of today—often allow for a degree of anonymity that appeals to queer and trans people in need of a safe space to express their identities.

While her experience of coming out in a chat room was surprisingly simple, Merisa's journey to coming out offline was anything but. She initially came out as trans to her family and many of her friends in the late '90s, during her senior year of high school. Some of her friends were supportive, but her parents refused to accept her identity. So after graduating from high school, Merisa moved to live with her sister in San Diego, California, where she could put on a dress and go to the gay bar for ladies night on Saturdays without her parents' judgment. But after her sister graduated from school and moved back in with their parents, Merisa was laid off from her job and had to move back in with them, too. Living with parents who didn't understand her, with no health insurance and only a part-time job, she felt her only choice was to go back in the closet. *I'm going to try being a dude*, she thought. *I'll do my best to make it work.*

But after almost ten years in the closet, it definitely wasn't working. With each passing year, she felt more and more hopeless. Naturally creative, Merisa loved to express herself; it was a huge part of what appealed to her about gameplay. Her one outlet for self-expression was online RPGs. She got very involved in *EverQuest*, a massively multiplayer fantasy game in which users create custom characters that work in teams to explore dungeons and slay beasts. And even though she generally played with a group of coworkers to whom she wasn't out, she was able to play as a female character. Because she was gaming with people who saw her as a man outside of the game, it felt subversive to pick a female character. *EverQuest* is what's commonly referred to as a "persistent" game, meaning you stick with the character you create—unlike, say, selecting Princess Peach for a single round of *Mario Kart*—resuming play as that character every time you return to the game. As a result, there was an assumption among many *EverQuest* players that men wouldn't play a female character.

But this choice represented more than just subversion; it was also a way for Merisa to express aspects of herself that she couldn't in just about any other area of her life. To feel closer to being understood for who she really was than she could at work or home. To be seen as a woman and have people engage with her as one.

Yet even though she had online games, the stress of living at home was eating away at Merisa. Sleep became increasingly evasive, and she would often get panic attacks. But one day, someone she knew from the chat rooms she'd frequented as a teen tweeted about a YouTube series in which people played *Minecraft*. Merisa found the videos soothing and discovered that watching them helped her fall asleep.

Eventually she started talking with one of the women in the videos. After five years of chatting they became good friends, and eventually Merisa told her she was trans and planned to transition someday. After that, she became a confidante and resource, helping Merisa navigate and improve her relationship with her parents and even helping her get in voice practice over Skype. A few years ago, after Merisa had saved enough money from her full-time job at a school district to move out of her parents' house, she came out again and began to transition, and the two started dating. Today, Merisa and her girlfriend run an online game community together—an explicitly queer- and trans-inclusive space for people to play, because they want to create the kinds of welcoming gaming spaces that Merisa benefited from when she was younger.

But the benefits of gaming have extended far beyond Merisa's youth. A few years ago, when she was trying to figure out how she wanted to present herself as a woman, gameplay gave her an opportunity to explore different things and discover what she liked. She knew she was a woman, but she didn't fully know what that meant to her. Merisa didn't have the experimental teenage or young-adult years to try out different styles of dress and figure out what works best, a period of self-definition and exploration cisgender people so often take for granted. Gameplay was more than just trying on different styles of clothing; it was a means of experimenting with an overall aesthetic and with different ways of being in the world. Even today, Merisa finds games helpful for learning new things about herself and bringing different elements of her personality to the forefront.

Whether we're regular video game users or not, I think play in a variety of settings helps us function and teaches us new ways to see ourselves. When I was in high school, a good friend from church hosted a murder-mystery party. I was assigned the role of an undertaker, and we agreed that I should dress in a manner consistent with what we thought "goth" meant. As I was trying to figure out what to wear, I asked her if she would paint my nails black. I was already out as queer at that point, but I still had a great deal of internalized homophobia, and I was constantly trying to prove to the world that being queer didn't mean that I was different from everyone else. But here, in this game, was an opportunity to experiment. To try something I was curious about, something that felt subversive, under the guise of "play" and see how it felt. Sure enough, I liked it, and I've gone on to paint my nails outside of gameplay since.

This may be what draws many queer and trans people like Merisa to gameplay. Considering the number of queer people who love video games or role-playing and tabletop games like D&D, she's far from alone in her interest. Games let us experiment. We're often not as bound by the conventions and norms of our hetero- and cisnormative society. Games aren't necessarily escapism but rather vehicles for self-expression: creative, cooperative, world-building exercises where we can define ourselves and the world around us on our own terms. And with enough practice, these invented versions of ourselves can become more real than any game.

One important aspect of this conversation—particularly in light of Merisa's story—is that the question of what it means to be "real" is sometimes used to police the self-expression of people who deviate from norms.

This is something Thomas Page McBee explores in detail in *Amateur*, his account of navigating the sport of boxing as a transgender man. Diving into the world of boxing—one dominated by cisgender, heterosexual men, and hypermasculine norms more broadly—McBee explores the anxieties that come along with the questions of whether his fellow boxers know he is trans and whether they'd still see him as a "real" man if they did.

While it is acutely and distinctly challenging for trans people, McBee ultimately discovers that this pressure to be *real* in a way the world dictates acceptable—for men to be *real* men, or women to be *real* women—is something we all experience in one respect or another. And these pressures often manifest in ugly ways, particularly among men. "It quickly became clear that all men proving their 'realness' did so through fighting the policing and shaming of other men," he writes, "sadly often by shaming and policing them back." In trying to fight the gender regulation inflicted upon them, men often discover that the quickest route is to police other men themselves.

This impulse to regulate the way others play with and perform their identities—in the context of gender, to be sure, but also in race, sexuality, socioeconomic status, and other axes of identity—goes all the way back to the time in our lives when we learn our first games. It's as early and intrinsic as patty-cake and hide-and-seek. "Most of us experience gender conditioning so young—research shows it begins in infancy—that we misunderstand the relationship between nature and nurture, culture and biology, fitting in and *being oneself*," says McBee.

A big part of how we come to feel as if we're real is by proving it to others within our in-group and earning their validation—or trying to elevate ourselves above them. "Boys become 'real' by proving their masculinity to other men," McBee continues, "mostly through taking risks and dominating others who haven't fallen in line." Under the rules of masculinity, the game of being a man is one in which the only way to win is by ensuring there are losers.

I've learned a great deal from friends of mine who are trans or nonbinary about how we're ultimately all performing gender—it's just that some of us are rewarded for our performance, whereas others, those who deviate in ways that are deemed unacceptable, are punished.

Just as we all perform our gender identities, we broadcast other pieces of ourselves, receiving reward or punishment (or enforcing reward and punishment) depending on the part we play. We are always performing in our interactions with others and sometimes even when we're alone. At times the performance is intentional, but it is often unconscious or automatic. And these performances become more complicated in the digital age.

"Offline," Jia Tolentino argues in *Trick Mirror*, "there are forms of relief built into this process." The audiences change, for example; the self you perform in a professional setting differs from the self you perform with your significant other's family, which differs from the self you perform with close friends. We don't have to feel like we're always "on" with any one of them. But online, the lines between our performances become distorted, blurred, blended. "Worst of all," she continues, "there's essentially no backstage on the internet." While you can go home and leave your work audience at the office, our digital audience is always present, just as our digital histories are tattooed on our skin.

The impulse many people have to police our identities makes it feel impossible to be at all complicated. Especially because we sometimes bring pieces of ourselves into our digital identities that we normally wouldn't share with everyone in our lives. As Turkle notes, it all *feels* private, even though online all of our "rehearsals are archived."

The tension between the parts of ourselves we are comfortable sharing and the pieces we wouldn't want to broadcast raises important questions about which parts of our digital selves are real—or rather in what *sense* they are real. Sometimes people use digital platforms to explore things about themselves that they have no desire to integrate into their offline lives. This is perhaps most obvious in the arena of sexuality, but people do it all kinds of ways, including those who adopt an online persona with characteristics they have no interest in embodying offline. Sometimes, fantasy is just that—not something someone wants to actually act on but a means of working something out in the realm of imagination. In play, people can explore and subvert norms they've internalized in a space safe and set apart from other parts of their lives.

I once mentioned in a therapy session—a safe, set-apart space where I work through things, not entirely dissimilar from what we sometimes experience in gameplay—that I occasionally find myself attracted to a type of guy I'd be surprised to find myself dating "in real life." In fact, this type, what we might call a "dumb jock" or "gym bro," stereotypically embodies characteristics I generally find off-putting. In my experience, this has typically not been the type of guy I would want to share an extended conversation with, let alone my life. Yet I've sometimes found myself thinking about such a guy, and I couldn't figure out why (beyond the fact that society conditions us to do so, but that's a bigger conversation). Was I just in denial about the fact that I was attracted to this type because it contradicted my own image of myself and what I should or shouldn't be drawn to? Should I try dating someone in this category, no matter how annoying I might find many of them? I was sincerely open to that possibility. But my therapist suggested that sometimes we use fantasy to sort out things that exist apart from what we want in our actual experiences—to experiment, as we do in other kinds of play. In play, we can sift through the cultural baggage we inherit and try to make sense of our relationship to it.

Some play is real-world practice—work on the self that gets brought in to other areas of someone's life—but other stuff is just play, just fantasy. Is it real? Or do we need to develop a better understanding that there are degrees of realness within us— things we need to wrestle with and explore without broadcasting them to the world? (If so, I don't recommend being a writer.) The fact that so much of our digital play and experimentation is monitored doesn't seem particularly helpful in this respect.

Anthropologist David Lancy argues that children need unsupervised playtime away from adults in order to learn and grow. The work of developing the self is never done, so adults need unsupervised play, too. But when so much of our digital play is archived, supervised by platforms that track and sell our data—and when we are given overly prescriptive and boundaried ways of playing through our digital platforms and are thus limited in our ability to try new things—perhaps we lose that opportunity. And as we become more aware of how our platforms surveil and manipulate us, we learn to adapt the ways in which we explore ourselves online to the things our platforms and peers would deem acceptable. This creates problems when it comes to feeling real because we end up making decisions about how to express ourselves and connect with others based not on what feels truest to us but, at least in part, on what we think others might find acceptable.

We also train ourselves to perform our values for an audience under these conditions. It is "because of the hashtag, the retweet, and the profile" that expressing one's values online "gets inextricably tangled up with visibility, identity, and self-promotion," argues Tolentino. We're told we need to have a brand, a strong online identity that everything we post gets filtered through. Which means that when we try to express our values online, our actions get filtered through a hypermonitored self, a self with a forever audience, a self that has been shaped by platforms that make us think first and foremost about, well, ourselves. And because we've gamified our digital content—we get a rush of dopamine from engagement; likes and retweets mean we're *winning*—it's easy to perform a digital moral identity that brings your own self into everything. A self that ultimately exists to perform a moral identity that gets you attention. I've watched friends and acquaintances get sucked in by it, transforming their digital identities into constant outrage machines, jumping on whatever the latest viral incident is and connecting it to their own experience. I've done it, too.

This doesn't mean it's always wrong to tie issues to your own experiences, and not just because I'm doing it all over the place in this book. Making associations and connecting dots is one of the best ways we learn. It can be a vital means of closing the distance between our own experiences and issues that feel far away. But in the digital age, it's easier than ever to confuse the experiences of others with our own. "A virtual experience may be so compelling that we believe that within it we've achieved more than we have," Turkle writes in *Life on the Screen*. She explains that she has interviewed many people who play digital games as a character of another gender. They often claim that, for example, playing a woman allows a man to fully understand what it's like to be a woman. But Turkle cautions that there are limitations on how much we can actually understand through this medium.

In *The Future of Feeling*, Kaitlin Ugolik Phillips writes of how some people are trying to take advantage of advances in virtual reality (VR) technology to develop empathy-expanding experiences. One VR experience allows someone to step into the life of a person living with homelessness; another shows the sometimes traumatic journey undertaken by someone making their way through a group of protestors into a Planned Parenthood clinic. Others still give a window into the experiences of refugees and immigrants. But, of course, the VR goggles come off after the program is done. And while there is research demonstrating that VR can in fact help people become more empathetic, Phillips also interviews people who voice concern that it can morally confuse us. There is a risk of thinking we understand more than we do, creating a kind of moral laziness. If we assume we already understand someone else's experience, we might not feel the need to make a consistent effort to understand and empathize with those who are different from us.

Ultimately, so much of what we get out of digital play depends on the goals we each bring to our games. Are we using digital play to process and experiment or just to broadcast a palatable self? The truth is that many, probably most, of us do both. Which means we need to better understand how and why we play in these ways, especially in a world where others stand ready to say we've broken rules we never agreed to.

—■—

Few communities better exemplify the value we can find in breaking rules we never agreed to than the furry community. Yes, you read that right. We're going to talk about furries now.

I turned the corner, pulling onto the road for the hotel by the airport, and suddenly I saw them: the furries I was there to meet. First there was one, a fox with an enormous tail of unnaturally red fur, and then another, a grinning blue wolf with a jaunty tongue slipping from his jowl. Soon there were swarms of them, packs of humans wearing tails and ears, and some even wearing bright, full-body animal suits, all migrating toward the Chicago O'Hare Hyatt. To the uninitiated, like me, there was something almost unnerving about seeing giant fuzzy creatures out in the open, walking down the sidewalk unashamed instead of holed up in one of the hotel's conference rooms. And there was also something thrilling about it.

The costumes looked hot and clammy, but I was the one who was sweating. I was about to meet real-life furries—a community of people who create and sometimes play out animal alter egos—in the flesh.

A few weeks earlier, I had interacted with my first furry, Steve, on Twitter. After he drew an illustration of my friend Tarik as an animal, he said that he could draw me, too. We DMed for a bit, and I asked if he'd give my fursona (or "furry persona") a family resemblance to my dog, Tuna. I sent him a link to my Instagram so he could see pictures of Tuna and me, and he got to work. A few hours later, he sent over his illustration: a human-dog hybrid with giant ears, teal-streaked hair, and a playfully protruding tongue. It was a cartoon of an animal, but somehow, it felt like me: the smirk, the glint in his eyes, and the human hands making a posed selfie peace sign. He even had my nose rings and my QUEER tattoo on his wrist.

But the resemblance was more than surface level, and taking it in felt revelatory. The drawing hinted at an unseriousness, even a friskiness, that I sometimes have a hard time seeing in myself. Grinning, I leaned forward on my bed to show Tuna, and she looked back and forth between my phone and me. I may have been imagining it, but it looked like she approved.

Steve and I kept chatting after that, and while I didn't want to be a cultural tourist, I had never knowingly interacted with a furry before. He gracefully and patiently answered my dumb inquiries, then mentioned that he and his boyfriend would soon be heading to Midwest FurFest, an annual gathering of thousands of furries. I was already going to be in Chicago that same weekend, so he suggested he could get me into the closing party of the convention, which he was scheduled to DJ.

I immediately wanted to say yes—but I suddenly became anxious. There would be cameras, he said. What if someone saw a picture or video of me there? Steve understood my anxiety. When he was fourteen, his dad found some furry art he had drawn and sat him down for a talk. "I'm not saying you're a freak," his dad said, "but this isn't stuff that normal people look at." Shamed, Steve repressed his interest for years.

Eventually, he began to dip his toes back in the water online, following furry artists and posting some of his own work. Surrounded by people who understood him, Steve knew immediately that this was his community. Today he is a leading voice among furries—creating furry art, DJing furry events, spurring conversations about social justice online, and taking on "alt-right" and Nazi furries.

Because of my exchanges with Steve, I've now interacted with large swaths of Furry Twitter and even went on a furry podcast. Taking in the illustrated avatars and animal names popular among furries online, it's easy to think about furry identity as a means of hiding. But I've discovered from Steve and others that donning an animal identity can actually be about revealing, not concealing.

As I learned at the furry convention, creating a fursona or wearing a furry suit (or "fursuit") can encourage vulnerability. For many furries, like Steve, a fursona is an extension of who they are as a person, something I got a glimpse of when I saw elements of my own personality captured in an illustration of me as a dog created by a stranger, based entirely on pictures I'd posted online. Putting on a fursuit or adopting an animal identity can help some furries get past social anxiety, bringing out aspects of their personality that they may have a harder time expressing on their own. For others, it can even be aspirational—a way of creating a version of themselves that they can live into, something that conveys who they are working toward becoming.

Furries are a hugely misunderstood community; they exist at the margins of our culture. If they're mentioned at all, it may be as the butt of a joke or something regarded with suspicion and fear. But "normies" (as many furries call nonfurries) can learn from the ways in which furries push back against that shame and embrace the complexity of being real. Because the community can provide a path to all kinds of self-discovery—Steve was starting to figure out that he was gay when he first became involved with furries, and it was among furries that he learned to become comfortable with his sexuality.

Steve's story is not uncommon, and it's not incidental that he and others might find queer acceptance among furries. In fact, according to research conducted by the International Anthropomorphic Research Project (a multidisciplinary team of scientists studying the furry fandom, which is both real and incredible), while just over 80 percent of nonfurries report being exclusively heterosexual, fewer than 25 percent of furries do. Similarly, 2 to 2.5 percent of furries identify as transgender, and 10 percent identify as genderqueer—both significantly higher percentages than among the general public.

I may not be a furry, but I understand the fear of being made to feel vulnerable and judged. But I am learning to let some of that go, which is why I not only went to the convention but, once there, accepted Steve's invitation to join him on stage. Dancing in front of hundreds of people during his DJ set as cameras filmed the scene, I looked out over a pulsing sea of conference attendees—some in oversized suits of neon fur, some wearing just ears or tails, and others largely unadorned beyond badges stating their characters. They jumped and laughed, lifting their hands, paws, and hooves into the sky, giddy to be in a space where everyone could express themselves without scrutiny. And when I posted pictures and videos from the convention, I didn't worry about what people thought, either.

Shame can kill, but it doesn't always. More often the fear of being our fullest self just eats away at us like acid, gradually hollowing us out until the version of ourselves that we share with others feels like a costume. This fear can consume our inner complexity, reducing us to a shell of the person we really are, leaving us peering out from behind a mask we think will protect us. But playfully letting that fear go, even just for a night of dancing, can help us get closer to embracing the things about ourselves that the world says we should hide.

As Steve's bass-heavy music flooded the crowded hotel ballroom, I felt my shame and fear ebb. I was in a place where I was safe from judgment, a warm and welcoming den from which I could reenter the world with the confidence of the dog in Steve's illustration. I never would have guessed it, but going to a furry convention made me feel more human.

Despite its benefits, play can absolutely be a means of running away from yourself. To understand this element of play better, I asked the game makers at Atlas if they thought that games could be a kind of escapism, as is frequently charged. They acknowledged that there is, in some cases, truth to this.

"I've seen it," concedes Banks, "though more often it seems to be the case with online games—you're alone in your place, safe from the rest of the world, with welcoming groups of people who are only associated with you because of the game, and that's where you're happiest." Playing with people who are otherwise total strangers can allow you to remain isolated while still meeting your basic need for interaction, he says. D&D, on the other hand, requires you to be more social.

Tidball echoed his comments, saying that while you can sit alone online, "the actual activity of tabletop games actually fights against escapism." Banks chimed back in, saying, "These experiences help break down walls instead of setting them up and hiding behind them."

Are they right about the games we play online—are we often just hiding behind walls? And if that's true of online games, is it true of our identity play and experimentation, too?

In *Life on the Screen*, Turkle suggests that offline RPGs can help people engage important questions about who they are because RPGs "stand betwixt and between the unreal and the real; they are a game and something more." But unlike offline RPGs, she argues that digital play is different. Online, identity play "has no endpoint" and has "fuzzier" boundaries. Rather than being set apart from our lives, a separate space for working through issues, which she suggests RPGs are, online play becomes integrated into our lives.

Though Turkle is writing about literal online games, I have felt this way about Twitter sometimes—like it's a game that never ends. But maybe there's another way to play. Our digital identity play *can* be integrated into every moment of our lives, but that doesn't mean it *has* to be. We can be more purposeful about how we use it, stepping in and out of it instead of fully integrating it into our lives. Because as helpful as social media can be when it comes to experimentation and self-discovery, we also need time to understand ourselves outside of our public performance of who we are—not so much a break *from* our digital lives as much as a break *for* the kind of living we can only when we're not on display.

Beyond their blurry boundaries in terms of having a clear start and end point, Turkle argues that online games run into issues because they also "blur the boundaries between self and game, self and role, self and simulation." Sometimes players describe "their real selves as a composite of their characters," she says, while other times describing "their screen personae as means for working on their [real-life] selves." Still, on some level that's kind of how it works offline, too. We are always alternating between seeing the different pieces of our lives as making up a composite that is *who we are* and seeing assorted parts of our lives as spaces to work out things and bring them back to the rest of our lives. The digital is ultimately one more layer in the composite that is your life—as much a space for discerning what makes you real as any other.

Further, for some people, digital play provides a *different* but *equally important* kind of community. In an interview for *Esquire*, musician and actor Donald Glover tells Bijan Stephen that online he can "talk to people as a regular person," not a celebrity. For someone like Glover, online anonymity is a way to experience something he can't elsewhere, something that makes him feel more real.

On the other hand, Glover has said that the social media accounts associated with his "real," offline identity have made him feel *less* human. In the *New Yorker*, Tad Friend quotes Glover as saying, "I felt like social media was making me less human, and I already didn't feel that human." Our digital tools have immense power, and we can wield them in many different ways, including ways that make us feel less human. Yet there are also times we need digital space to express or experiment with various pieces of ourselves. Before the internet, writes Turkle, this kind of "rapid cycling through different identities" was more difficult. While there is something valuable about continuity, for many people in the past, Turkle acknowledges, the inability to move between identities "chafed."

When I moved away from my home state in my early twenties, feeling chafed and ready to start over, I would sometimes look at the people who stayed—my family, high school and college friends—and think it was a shame that they were having such a limited experience. I, on the other hand, was moving from city to city, challenging myself by stepping outside of my comfort zone and finding my footing in new spaces. What I didn't understand is that the people who didn't leave were experiencing different positives: the kind of sustained friendships they could develop that moving around made more difficult for me, or getting to know their cities in a deeper, more intimate way than I have mine. Each approach is probably better suited to different people, depending on their personalities and the ways they need to grow and stretch. But just as cycling had benefits for me, their approach had gifts I didn't see.

When we cycle and experiment, though, Turkle says, we ought to ask ourselves a question: "What relation do these [different identities] have to what we have traditionally thought of as the 'whole' person? Are they experienced as an expanded self or as separate from the self?" The way we answer this question will inform how we understand what it means to be real. We can become more able to cycle, to be multiple, in a way that makes us feel whole. But if we're not careful, we can also split and try to escape ourselves.

Play and the identities we form through it don't have to be about escapism, though. Sometimes they're about empowerment. Sometimes, like in Merisa's video games, play is a kind of resistance to the limitations of our world as it is. In fact, some people find set-apart spaces like conventions—such as the furry convention I attended—*more* real than other parts of their lives. And this can be true of digital gatherings, too.

This isn't new, either; church retreats often felt this way when I was younger. Even though leaving them was hard—and even though they were an escape from the challenges of my life, like the overt homophobia expressed by some of my high school peers—they were also immensely valuable spaces where I could practice becoming more comfortable with myself and then take that back with me to my high school. This is what the imaginative impulse we explore in play can do: help us envision and practice a better world.

These kinds of playful spaces can be a retreat that gives us the opportunity to go back into the rest of our lives feeling like a person again. This was absolutely true of the drop-in LGBTQ center I attended in high school, for example. Every Friday evening, I left my town and traveled to Saint Paul to get away from the rest of my life. For several hours I was just among other LGBTQ people—playing games, sitting on a couch talking shit, learning how to help someone get into drag, listening to CDs burned for me by a friend, or sneaking outside and making out with a football player behind the building. At this drop-in center, I could walk around fully at ease, which I couldn't do just about anywhere else in my life. It was respite and resistance all at once. In a time when I found myself constantly monitoring how I was being perceived by others and whether or not I was safe, the drop-in center was an essential space where I could just goof off, relax, and play.

These playful spaces, online and off—the parts of our lives where we can just *be*—are incredibly real. Escapism? Yes—they help us escape the constraints of a world that doesn't always let us be ourselves.

Sometimes we escape the confines of our current reality in ways that make us happier and healthier. But some of the ways that we play—overt ways, like gambling, but also the ways we play with identity online and off—are more about self-medicating than about experimenting. And they can become addictive.

New York University's Adam Alter compares social media to cigarettes by laying out information about how much—how frequently—we use our technology. "Each month almost one hundred hours was lost to checking email, texting, playing games, surfing the web, reading articles, checking bank balances, and so on," Alter writes in *Irresistible*, using information collected by Moment, an app that tracks the amount of time users spend on their screen. "Over the average lifetime, that amounts to a staggering eleven years."

Sometimes our digital games—literal and figurative—can make us feel as if we're losing valuable time. The Center for Humane Technology, a nonprofit dedicated to fostering healthier and more human-centered technology practices, partnered with Moment to ask people to report how much screen time left them feeling happy or unhappy. On the unhappiness list—the ranking of apps that left users feeling the most dissatisfied after use—Grindr (the queer dating and hookup app) sits at number one, which did not surprise me. Seventy-seven percent of Grindr users said it left them feeling unhappy, perhaps because it can feel like a bad game: one in which you have to keep repeating levels, one that feels impossible to win. (The second-most misery-inducing app is in fact a literal game, *Candy Crush Saga*, while fifth on the list is *Candy Crush*. Apparently these are different things.)

Another entry on the list is Reddit, which lands at number six. Reddit has some really nasty sections, but it also has entire areas devoted to feel-good content. So why does it make users feel bad, too? Is it the arguments and flame wars? Trolls? Dispiriting content always rising to the top? "For me," a friend who frequently uses Reddit said, "the negative comes when I'm like, 'Oh, I just wasted ninety minutes.'"

It's rare that I feel I've wasted time when I've just finished an enjoyable board game, but I've definitely felt it after goofing off on my phone for hours. Indeed, it seems that the longer people spend on an app or website, the more likely they are to report feeling unhappy after using it. Which suggests the problem isn't fundamental to the apps themselves but lies in how they currently tap in to vulnerable human instincts.

This, I think, is the mistake some people make when talking about social media and addiction. The issue they're really identifying is the difference between *deep* play and the kind of *passive* play that just keeps you clicking. The latter occurs when platforms gamify the good feelings they offer. Compulsive social media use arises when we get "forms of social approval—likes on Facebook and Instagram, retweets on Twitter—that are intermittent and unpredictable," writes Jia Tolentino in a 2019 essay for the *New Yorker*, "as though you're playing a slot machine that tells you whether or not people love you." The randomness and evasiveness of digital social approval—the fact that some tweets go viral but others don't, that the moment you think you figure out the rules they change—can keep you hooked, chasing the initial feeling it gave you.

But there are *also* real digital communities engaging in deep play, like Merisa's online games or the deep bonds I've forged by cracking jokes and creating memes in that group Twitter DM—the kind of play that leaves you feeling satisfied, as opposed to the passive play of digital gamification that keeps you mindlessly feeding in quarters and wasting your time.

In *The Ethics of Authenticity*, Charles Taylor suggests that "views that portray us as totally locked in and unable to change our behavior short of smashing the whole 'system' . . . [are] wildly exaggerated." We may not need to smash it, but the system does need transforming.

Without transformation, the system as it exists can play to some of our worst instincts—including our aversion to boredom. The strange imagination games my siblings and I invented in childhood often emerged out of a feeling of insufferable boredom. Seeking relief, we developed elaborate games, which became spaces for self-expression and exploration. In the age of social media, smartphones, and streaming, that effort is no longer necessary, because there's always a cure for boredom just at our fingertips. But I worry we've lost touch with something valuable by being able to evade it so easily—by our compulsive aversion to it and our reflexive actions to kill it with digital play.

In my preinternet life, whenever I felt bored, I was forced to brainstorm solutions: to try things I might not have otherwise tried, read things I might not have otherwise read, explore places I might not have otherwise checked out, and discover things I might not have otherwise noticed. This wasn't just when I was a child; I didn't have a smartphone until I was twenty-three, so up until then there was a significant part of my early adulthood spent waiting—at the bus stop or at an airport, in the lobby of a doctor's office or the parking lot outside work before a shift started, between classes or meetings. Life's idle moments were exactly that: idle. In many of these instances, especially if I forgot to bring a book or some other distraction, I remember feeling profoundly, deeply, maddeningly bored. And it was in those moments that my mind wandered. Sometimes, inspiration would strike. I'd write a poem or a bit of a song, or remember that I wanted to reach out to someone I hadn't spoken with for a while, or start wondering about a question that I felt I needed to find the answer to later.

Boredom was fertile ground for new ideas and insights. But these days I just pull out my phone and check email or Twitter. I've gained many things with social media, but I've lost the ability to be bored.

Our society values achievement and activity above just about anything else, pressing into us the notion that we ought to derive our sense of identity and purpose from productivity and labor, leaving little time for leisure or aimlessness—but that's not the only reason boredom often *feels* deeply wrong. Boredom opens "the shutters on some very uncomfortable thoughts and feelings, which we normally block out with a flurry of activity or with the opposite thoughts or feelings," writes psychiatrist Neel Burton in a piece for *Psychology Today*. So often, the cultural pressures of productivity and our desire to avoid the discomfort of boredom converge to keep us clicking.

Filling up our time with activity has consequences. The last four years of my twenties, when I threw myself into building that program at Yale, were probably the busiest time of my life. On the whole it was a transformative and deeply rewarding experience. I got to do amazing things with incredible people. But it was also really hard on me. I was constantly exhausted and not doing a good job of modeling balance for those around me. Three years into this work, Alex and I broke up. As we separated, and even more so in the year following, I spent a lot of time reflecting on why it happened. One of the biggest reasons that emerged is that we were both bad at making time to do nothing. By the time we stopped and realized that we weren't in a good place, we weren't able to salvage it. We had avoided uncomfortable truths with our busyness for too long.

But as our relationship came to an end, I also spent a lot of time reflecting on its beginning, and its gifts. In particular

I began to remember how, especially early on, he helped me get better at making time for play, and fun, and boredom. He showed me that fun isn't frivolous, like when he got me tickets to see Britney Spears in Las Vegas, something I'd wanted to do but considered trivial. I'll always remember that concert, and not just because an extremely dramatic gay to my left began sobbing and spraying a branded Britney Spears fragrance toward the stage upon hearing the first notes of her song "Perfume." Alex also taught me that it was okay to just do nothing sometimes. We would spend Saturdays lounging around the empty warehouse in Boston's Southie neighborhood where he lived and designed footwear, and in those lazy, formless days we learned a lot about ourselves and each other. But old habits die hard—eventually we both slipped back into currents of busyness that pulled us away from one another.

Talking about the end of our relationship is hard for me. It feels vulnerable. And true vulnerability—not the things that seem vulnerable yet are easy for me to share, but the things I don't want to confront in myself, let alone share with others—is one of the hardest things in the world. I avoid it, which is also a big part of why I avoid boredom. Because boredom is a vulnerable space. When your mind wanders, it can wander to the harder things in life, the existential and personal questions or concerns that you might be avoiding. But avoiding boredom and the information it can reveal doesn't keep you safe.

Besides, in order to *feel*, sometimes we just need to be useless. In the *New Yorker*, Tolentino writes of taking steps to "declutter" her digital life. During the first few days of a social media break, she writes, she compulsively checked her email inbox, reread text messages, and went back to news headlines she'd already skimmed in search of new information—all things I've done on social media breaks. Then, she began taking her dog for longer walks (again, same). And eventually she "acquiesced to a dull, pleasant blankness." On one boring afternoon, she lay on her couch "and felt an influx of mental silence that was both disturbing and hallucinatorily pleasurable." In this silence, she "didn't want to learn how to fix or build anything, or start a book club." Instead, she writes, "I wanted to experience myself as soft and loose and purposeless, three qualities that, in my adulthood, have always seemed economically risky." I have felt all of this, too, and it has shown me that I don't want to think of myself as needing to be "useful" at all times. Sometimes, I want to feel soft and loose and purposeless, like I did back in Southie with Alex, when we were momentarily good at letting ourselves be bored.

There is value in questioning the very idea of productivity. Our ability to just *be*, to exist outside of a framework that assigns value or worth to our actions, is an essential piece of what it means to be human. Sometimes boredom is its own answer. Like deep play, it can be an imaginative, self-building space.

In *Finite and Infinite Games*, New York University's James P. Carse proposes that there are two kinds of play: finite, in which the point is to win and finish, and infinite, in which the point is to keep playing. Carse argues that what makes life meaningful is finding ways to set up or join infinite games—in relationships, art, literal games, anywhere. Finite games are fun, of course, but not fulfilling in the big ways. What makes the play of childhood imagination games, D&D, furry fandom, Merisa's ongoing play, and, at its best, life on the internet so fulfilling is that they are all infinite games. The point is to keep playing with other people. Finite play, on the other hand, is sometimes unfulfilling—the gambling, the feeling of wasted time, the addictive qualities of mindless gaming where you're not really engaged and just try to win over and over. We tend to look at social media as empty play, for likes and clicks and shares and views. It can be. But our digital lives also have immense potential to hold space for infinite play. It's not just a roll of the dice; we can decide which kind of game we want to play.

I'm not proud to admit it, but sometimes I have used the internet to feel *cool*.

As a kid, I was often picked last, or at least near the end, when we had to play a team sport in gym class. I was lanky and uncoordinated, and my face radiated fear as I stood in the queue to be chosen. No one needed to say it, but everyone knew: picking me wasn't a good call if you wanted to win.

But games were a different story. When playing a board, card, or other tabletop game that required people to be strategic or cunning or to know things—like charades or Trivial Pursuit—I noticed that people often wanted to team up with me. It wasn't that they liked me, though of course some did. It was that they wanted to win, and they knew that I got good grades.

In school the things that were most often valued—both tangible, like cool clothes or expensive video games, and less so, like social graces or knowledge about sports—were things I didn't have. So I learned that the trick to getting people to like you was to emphasize the things you excelled at, and conceal your weaknesses—something we all learn but that feels particularly necessary for queer kids. Like the games at which I excelled, I discerned that being strategic got you further.

When I began blogging and using social media as an adult, I started hearing from a growing number of people around the world who weren't interested just in my words but also in me as a *person*. In the happenings of my life, even the mundane stuff like what music I was listening to or where my dog and I walked that day. It became especially true on Twitter, where even people who hadn't read a single word of my writing started following and regularly interacting with me. In a space where a certain kind of self-expression is valued—where people who can comment on a broad range of events seem to do well—I found myself gaining popularity. Twitter felt almost tailor-made for some of my strengths and also made it easier to mask my shortcomings.

In this sense it eventually started to feel a bit like the games I excelled at in my youth. On Twitter, I could emphasize certain skills—skills I already possessed, like being able to come up with a quick retort or clever caption to a meme, or to make connections between disparate topics in a short amount of time—while deemphasizing my weaknesses. As my followers grew, Twitter allowed me to become, or at least to feel, popular, even if it was on a small scale. (Like, seriously small.) On Twitter, I was no longer picked last. It was a game I knew how to win.

We might look at people who inhabit characters in video games or at furries, at D&D players, or even at the perpetually online (like I've sometimes been) and say: well yeah, sure, they're playing with identity, but ultimately they're *playing*. Long before Twitter, though, I learned to play by the rules—to succeed, to get by, to get people to like me. Which is why the desire to dismiss the kinds of identity sorting and performing that people do through the internet as somehow less real than what happens offline is ultimately just a comforting fiction. "To align oneself with the real while intimating that others are at play, approximate, or in imitation can feel good," writer Maggie Nelson says in *The Argonauts*. "But any fixed claim on realness, especially when it is tied to an identity, also has a finger on psychosis." To drive this home, Nelson quotes Jacques Lacan: "If a man who thinks he is a king is mad, a king who thinks he is a king is no less so."

I take this to mean that we're fooling ourselves if we think there is a hierarchy of identities, in which some—the offline— are more real, and others—the digital—less. By sealing off the digital as somehow *less real*, we forgo a space to experiment and play with identity as amateurs. Everyone's needs and interests are going to be different. For some, the internet is less important when it comes to understanding themselves and connecting with others. But no matter how online we are, there's rich information about what it means to be human to be found in the digital pieces of our lives.

Drawing on psychologist D. W. Winnicott's notion of "feeling real," Nelson says that we can aspire to feel real, we can help others feel real, and we can feel real ourselves. It is "a feeling Winnicott describes as the collected, primary sensation of aliveness, 'the aliveness of the body tissues and working of body-functions, including the heart's action and breathing,' which makes spontaneous gesture possible," she writes. (This is what happens when we play!) "For Winnicott, feeling real is not reactive to external stimuli, nor it is an identity. It is a sensation—a sensation that spreads. Among other things, it makes one want to live."

Being human isn't easy. But play can enliven us enough to keep going in the moments when that feels most impossible. The games that make us want to live are worth playing.

How do we know which games are good, which ones make life worth living? As our meeting came to end, I asked the game makers at Atlas.

What makes for a good game, said Tidball, "is not so different from what makes any kind of social interaction positive." At its core, a game "is a shared desire to have a certain kind of experience." But as simple as that might sound, this is actually where things get most complicated of all. While some players assume everyone present is trying to have the same kind of experience, that's rarely the case.

In order to avoid this problem, a successful game needs to be accessible, Tidball continued, as there will be people with varying levels of investment and understanding. Some people are there to play the game, but others are there first and foremost because they want to connect with others. Any good game host will understand that different things bring different people to the table and accommodate the approach to playing accordingly.

I experienced this intimately when, after my meeting with Atlas, I attended my first-ever D&D meetup at a local comic shop. The immediate camaraderie I felt with this group of strangers—their nonjudgmental welcoming, as well as the carefree abandon and surprising degree of investment I felt simultaneously—reminded me so much of the most positive experiences I've had online, like in the aforementioned DM chat. Online spaces are often regarded as zones of intense disagreement, trolling, and flame wars, but they can also be wildly supportive—a "yes and" space. In improv theater, participants generally agree to "yes and" one another, meaning that when they work together to develop a scenario, they don't cancel out someone else's actions but instead build on them. This is how RPGs are, too—one person I interviewed who loves D&D told me that, at their best, RPGs are about saying "yes and" as much as possible. What makes the difference is welcoming in people with varying goals, working to understand them, and not projecting our own agendas onto others' play.

It's easy to think that we're all trying to have the same experience online as well, and that the struggles and desires of the perpetually online represent the interests and challenges of everyone. But some people go online to post pictures of their kids or find a recipe for buttermilk pie. Others see it as their primary space for making meaning, forging connections, and experimenting with their sense of identity.

Banks added that a game is ultimately about players "creating an experience they can remember later on." At its best, our online play can give us the tools we need to become fuller, more complex versions of ourselves. To discover who we are and remember it.

Our digital games can be about cruelty and voyeurism, escape, or control. But they can also be about experimentation with the self, imagining new possibilities, world-building, and community-finding. Problems emerge from these very different goals because we often don't know how to be in relationship with one another or how to understand one another. We're playing different games.

"When people become intimate, they are particularly vulnerable; it is easy to get hurt in online relationships," writes Turkle. "But since the rules of conduct are unclear, it is also easy to believe that one does not have the right to feel wounded. For what can we hold ourselves and others accountable?"

That becomes all the more difficult because even when we *do* sense others' rules, they often don't align with our own— and yet we sometimes still feel weirdly beholden to these rules we didn't create, holding ourselves to standards we don't like or even respect. "I sensed I was being judged through a collective lens made up by idiots," one person told me of their digital experience, "but there was no other way to look at myself."

It doesn't have to be this way. We can work together to create new rules, to draw up a new board on which to play. But we have to begin by ceasing to tell ourselves the story that our digital lives are "just a game." Or, rather, if they are a game, we need to expand our understanding of what games are—how they function and what they make possible. We need to decide which kinds of digital games we want to play. We can use our digital play for escape, or we can use it in the ways games can open people up and help them imagine a fuller self and a better world. The next move is ours.

8

UNCERTAINTWEETS

On any given day, a sizable chunk of the people I follow on Twitter are joking about their anxiety. All of a sudden everyone has it.

While I first attributed this to An Xiao Mina's Internet Cat Fallacy—suspecting more people have had anxiety than many of us realized, and the internet now provides a safe venue to discuss it—it turns out anxiety actually *is* on the rise. In 2019, the American Psychiatric Association reported a statistically significant increase in national anxiety since 2017.

It's not surprising; we live in anxious times. As a 2019 piece by Talia Lavin for the *Atlantic* puts it, "America seems to be in the midst of a full-blown panic attack." It's not just America, either. Many nations are experiencing immense economic and political instability. The seas are rising. Systemic racism persists and adapts. The chasm between the wealthy and the rest of us grows larger every day. Climate change and pandemics (as was starkly apparent to me while working on final edits to this book in the early days of the COVID-19 crisis) increasingly force us to reimagine how we live, travel, and interact, sometimes making digital connection the best or only option. Each year, immense new challenges emerge on an unprecedentedly global scale, and as we move more important pieces of our lives to digital spaces (at times by necessity), we find ourselves not only more aware of the world's problems but also left feeling powerless to do anything (or, at least, enough) about them. And as if being inundated with bad news we're largely helpless to change weren't bad enough, we also often feel unsure how to even understand ourselves and one another on a basic level in this new digital land of likes.

Is this anxiety at the heart of our digital efforts to find belonging and realness? It was, after all, in the summer of my own immense anxiety—the summer my life came undone— that my search for a better grasp of digital realness really began. To better understand that, to go past the rising numbers on my own anxiety, I knew that I would have to go back to that summer. To the anxiety that drove me to start this search in earnest. I would have to go back to scabies.

I pulled into the parking lot of an unassuming health clinic a half hour outside the city. Sitting in my car, the windshield coated in rain, I took the deepest breath in the history of human civilization before walking inside. Ronda Farah, a dermatologist and professor at the University of Minnesota Medical School, welcomed me into her spotless office. "So," she began with a bright smile, "you want to talk about scabies?"

Despite my incessant Googling in the months leading up to and following my scabies diagnosis, I still didn't really understand why it had exacted such a profound psychological effect on me. While it's one of humanity's oldest documented afflictions, many people still don't understand scabies—or the human response to it—that well. So it was time to consult an expert.

Part of why scabies is so maddening, Farah began, is because itch is one of the most difficult things to treat and for people to tolerate. It can be harder to endure than extreme pain. And it's cyclical: the itch-scratch cycle just intensifies your misery because once you scratch, your body releases a neuropeptide that makes you itch even more. As she described this, I thought back to pacing outside my apartment just days after my diagnosis, refreshing my Twitter and Instagram feeds, desperate for something to distract me from my itchy misery. And I thought about every time I've posted something online and watched the notifications roll in, only to feel an even stronger hunger for more engagement. It can seem impossible to satiate our digital itch sometimes, like each scratch just fuels it.

I asked Farah if she thought shame was another reason scabies isn't well understood or researched. She agreed but added that while scabies is particularly stigmatized, other skin diseases, disorders, and infections that *aren't* contagious share similar stigmas. "The skin is our visual to the external world," said Farah.

She emphasized that dermatological issues have a strong psychiatric and mood overlap for this reason. Skin conditions like psoriasis or acne scarring can have a significant bearing on psychological well-being, causing us to see ourselves in a distorted way. As she talked, I thought of something as small and as visible as a typo in a tweet—how it shifts to the surface, becoming the object of stressful fixation even though few may notice, and even fewer will care. We often worry about what our digital skin communicates to the world, and perhaps what it betrays about us—holding ourselves to a standard we typically don't impose on others.

But while the itch and visibility of scabies were both factors, I knew I was dancing around the primary reason I'd come to seek Farah's insights. I wanted to understand the thing I'd struggled with most: that ongoing treatments didn't guarantee the scabies would be gone. Since it's difficult to find evidence of their presence, and your skin often continues to react for a long time after they're gone in ways similar to how it reacts while they're present, you can't be sure in the short term that the treatments have worked. You have to sit in the unknown for a long time.

Farah agreed that the challenge of diagnosing and treating scabies—like, as she put it, finding a tiny bit of jelly in the middle of a gigantic donut (not sure I'll ever look at jelly donuts the same way after *that*)—is probably the hardest thing about it. She's seen scabies wreak major psychological havoc on patients, especially those who already struggle with uncertainty.

After she said the word, I repeated it with a growing recognition. The reason scabies had exacted an *extreme* degree of havoc on me is because I'm really bad with uncertainty. OCD bad. Not in that flippant "I'm *so* OCD—I arrange my books by color!" way. As in I literally have obsessive-compulsive disorder.

In adolescence, struggling with my sexual orientation and my parents' disruptive divorce—things that felt out of control, and more specifically out of *my* control—I started developing compulsive rituals. I would rub one eyebrow and then I'd have to rub the other; I'd flip one eyelid inside out, then the other.

Weird shit. Though I didn't know it, these strange little rituals were attempts to infuse my life with a semblance of balance and order, even on the micro level. These tics made me feel in control of my life, if only for a moment.

Eventually I went to therapy to deal with them, and as the behaviors faded away, I told myself I was rid of OCD. But during the summer of my scabies diagnosis, it became undeniable that it had just gone dormant. Almost two decades later, I had developed a new set of irrational rituals.

Though it was apparent that my OCD had returned in these rituals, I'd actually never been rid of it. I had just gotten better at addressing the obvious rituals while missing the smaller ways my OCD had expressed itself in the years between—including in my online habits, where I was *especially* less aware, given how infrequently we're prompted to reflect on our digital behaviors.

For years much of my social media use was about order. I tried to build meaning out of events that felt out of my control or meaningless through strange digital rituals. But many of these attempts to create order hadn't worked because, just like my OCD rituals, I wasn't addressing the root problem.

While OCD is a less common form of anxiety disorder than others—the lifetime prevalence rate for OCD is about one in every forty people—I think many of us, with or without OCD, use social media for the purpose of trying to keep uncertainty at bay. After all, those who study it suggest that OCD is actually just a maladaptive expression of the discomfort we *all* have with uncertainty. "We'll do anything that we can to get away from uncertainty," clinical psychologist Jonathan Fader tells journalist Rebecca Jarvis in the ABC podcast *The Dropout*, "and this is evolutionary." We're wired to ward off uncertainty and seek a sense of security, and many of us now use digital tools to do so.

This doesn't mean the impulse to give order to our lives is itself wrong. But when we're not aware of the hidden structures of our digital lives and the directions they move us in, we can easily maladapt to meet this need. For some it's the obsessive refreshing or the reflexive ways we log on without even thinking about it. Like how, on that lonely summer day when I felt so isolated and alone, I posted a selfie without knowing why. Just as I thought I had left my OCD behind in my adolescence—only to miss the ways it had continued to manifest for years, until it again became impossible to ignore—when we're not aware of how and why we use digital tools to try to set aside the discomfort of uncertainty, we lose the ability to harness the impulse in a healthy way.

The greatest fears we have about social media are the what-ifs. What if my identity gets stolen? What if Facebook is providing my private data to people trying to hack our elections? What if I said something terrible a long time ago and it resurfaces? These questions point to a bigger one: how much of social media—where we can shape the ways others see us perhaps more easily than ever before—is about feeling like we're in control? And what happens when that facade crumbles?

OCD symptoms are repetitive behaviors used to neutralize or suppress unwanted anxious thoughts, which may sound familiar to anyone active on social media. The regular checking to see if someone we haven't heard back from has posted on Instagram; the repeated refreshing to see if anyone's liked the selfie we just posted. The little habits a person with OCD develops to try to eradicate life's what-ifs can begin innocuously and logically enough—washing your clothing in hot water to kill any scabies you might have, or refreshing your Twitter notifications to make sure no one is mad at you—but the trouble arises when you *keep* doing them in an effort to keep doubt at bay even when they're not necessary. While only people with a biological vulnerability to it develop full-blown OCD, any of us can ritualize to try to keep uncertainty away.

In order to become more comfortable with uncertainty, we have to learn to overcome what is called *operant conditioning*, or the idea that if something works in the short term we will pursue it, even if it's not logical or causes us harm. For example, if I frequently wash my hands and then I don't see any signs that I've reinfested myself with scabies, I will probably continue to wash my hands a lot, just to be safe, even if there's no evidence excessive hand washing keeps scabies away and really it just dries my skin out. Likewise, if social media offers me an immediate feeling of connection, a disruption to loneliness, then I may start making sure I'm always logged on, just to be safe, even if there's no need or if it causes other parts of my life to suffer. We go online even when we're not lonely, just to make sure we don't ever have to be.

For me, Twitter has often been reinforcing in the short run, as a way of going after something positive and pleasurable—interaction, connection, affirmation—even at the expense of investing in things that will give me connection and affirmation in a more long-term sense. And it has also been helpful in avoiding anxiety, like when I used it to distract me from my scabies, even as it sometimes causes more anxiety. Because it's reinforcing, I've gotten in the habit of using it for those things even when I didn't need them.

But the problem with operant conditioning is that it keeps escalating. We find ways to justify our behaviors. "Why not? It isn't a big deal, it doesn't take much time, and this way, [we] won't have to worry," as Jonathan Grayson, founder of the Grayson LA Treatment Center for Anxiety and OCD, puts it in *Freedom from Obsessive-Compulsive Disorder*. But the problem is that, "without realizing it, [our] problem is getting worse. *Over time [we are conditioning ourselves] to feel more anxiety and to find more ways to avoid* [it]."

Many people blame our era of anxiety on social media, especially when it comes to anxiety among young people, and it's understandable why they might assume it's the cause. But an eight-year longitudinal study led by Brigham Young University's Sarah Coyne suggests that more time on social media doesn't actually make teens more anxious or depressed. In a press release, Coyne pointed out that "two teenagers could use social media for exactly the same amount of time but may have vastly different outcomes as a result of the way they are using it." Because of this, she suggests we move beyond the screen-time debate and look at *why* and *how* we're using social media to understand why it makes us feel the ways it does.

This puts the study from Moment and the Center for Humane Technology in a new light. Whereas that study suggested that more time online led to feeling worse, a different study deepened the measurements. Internet-induced anxiety may not be related to the amount of time someone is online itself but rather how that time is spent. For the person actively engaged—in deep play instead of passive, reflecting on their use and asking themselves honestly what needs they are trying to meet—it's unlikely they'll feel like they're wasting time.

Like scabies, our habits and rituals can be difficult to locate and properly identify. But social media can bring them to the surface. Where, if we're willing to be honest with ourselves, we can see the underlying motivations that drive them.

Not everyone has an anxiety disorder like OCD, but we all experience anxiety. And uncertainty—life's what-ifs—is at the heart of all anxiety. When most of us signed up for our first social media platform, we had no idea how much of our lives would become digital, and how much many of us would come to rely on the internet to give us a sense of security, connection, and control. Today, our digital practices have become ways of ritualizing our lives to rid ourselves of anxiety. But like the rituals I developed after my scabies diagnosis without knowing what needs I was trying to meet, we can only get better if we understand what purpose our digital rituals—the games we play, the tattoos we ink into our skin, the distances we close and establish, the maps we make—are serving, and if we address the anxieties about *who we are* that sit at their root.

The greatest crises we face today—those inspiring immense anxiety, like climate change, violent racism, or terrifying and difficult-to-contain new diseases—are national or global in scope. But because the internet connects us across geographic expanses, it gives us an opportunity to address them together.

It's like the books I read as an adolescent—the ones that expanded my horizons and opened me up to experiences and perspectives so far beyond what I knew as a white kid growing up in the Upper Midwest. They helped me see that, whatever my story was and the particular privileges and disadvantages that story afforded me, I was part of an interconnected web of other people's stories. Their stories were different, unique to them and replete with challenges I would never know experientially. But I could understand them, at least in part, if I made the effort, and that understanding could translate into action, into changing the way I moved through the world. The internet can help us do this, too. It can make us more visible to one another and help us chart a new path forward—a path toward a better, kinder, more connected world.

But part of what makes this difficult is that this visibility depends on the electricity we require to run our devices and our internet. In light of climate change, the connected world is also a troubled one. As we move bigger pieces of our lives online—more and more of what makes us human—it will become harder to disentangle our need to be real from our need for fuel. Especially because, in an increasingly digital world, we get the message that everything should be immediate: same-day delivery, streaming video, instant downloads. This desire for immediacy—this itch—will make it harder to fight climate change and harder to handle global challenges, which in fact will need us to move in the direction of giving up immediate gratification for the long-term viability of the planet and the well-being of the most vulnerable among us.

When considering the dilemma of climate change, it's striking how our virtual worlds manifest in a tangible way on the earth. Some say our increasingly digital lives drive a wedge between us and the physical world, suggesting that the time we spend in digital space makes us feel more distant and disconnected from the natural world and thus less invested in preserving it. Conversely, others argue we're now more able to become aware of how climate change impacts people in faraway parts of the world and thus more inspired to work for change.

Wanting a better perspective on how the increasingly digital pieces of our lives may be helping or harming efforts to raise awareness about and take action on climate change, I reached out to Jon Ozaksut, digital director of the Yale Program on Climate Change Communication (or YPCCC). We'd never connected during my years at Yale, but I asked if we could meet when I visited New Haven in fall 2019. As the member of YPCCC—which does in-depth research about what kinds of messaging most effectively impact people's understanding of the reality of climate change—who focuses on digital communication, Ozaksut seemed like the perfect person to speak with.

We sat down in his office, and, beneath a sloped ceiling, Ozaksut began explaining that climate change was a testing ground for the battle over what "real" is. The war over fake news is much older than climate change, he said, but that's where the modern debate over the real took shape. What early battles over climate change laid bare was that factual truth is not enough, said Ozaksut. We need to look at the emotional truths our beliefs communicate.

So the first question I brought to him—Does digital distance make us less invested in the physical world?—is only answerable if you look at the emotional truths behind it. It's debatable whether our increasingly digital lives cause us to care less about the planet, Ozaksut said, but one thing that is very clear to him is that many of the lines that used to define our communities have degraded. We see it in the development of an alternate news reality, the filter bubbles we enter online, and the dissolution of certain forms of offline community. Ozaksut traced much of this to the "mass systemic collapse in the perceived integrity of institutions, from Major League Baseball to the Catholic Church."

At the same time as this collapse, algorithm-based online communities came up, and these end up atomizing us along lines we don't always recognize. Ozaksut said this is because our social platforms are "sentiment agnostic but engagement driven." What this means is that if your post gets more reactions it will show up in more feeds, regardless of its content. And, he said, you can get these reactions as easily by driving negative emotion as positive—in fact, it's easier to tear things down than build things up. So sentiment agnosticism "rigs the game a little bit" in the direction of content that divides us. The polemicists online are turning us away from the information and action steps that could help us make meaningful change on climate.

In response to my second question, the divisions that emerge online again came up as his answer. Yes, he acknowledged, more people are now *able* to become more aware of climate change; the *New York Times* climate desk, for example, is doing incredible work bringing the climate crisis into people's social media feeds, he said. But if you're getting the *NYT* climate newsletter or seeing their content on social media, it's probably because you've already signed up for it, or you're in Facebook groups where people are already alarmed about climate change. So, once again, the issue is our online filter bubbles and the inflammatory content that drives them.

Ozaksut's observation that our social media platforms boost divisive content—and how that's a more urgent issue than the distance social media puts between us and the physical world—confirmed my sense that we face a monumental issue when trying to use the internet to become more real. One that towers above most of the others: the internet we have today is shaped first and foremost by the priorities of profit.

At a time when we should be working to ensure that social media is bringing us together instead of driving us apart, we are instead having to fight against the fact that our platforms prioritize what makes them money even at the expense of our well-being. What keeps people scrolling is fear, anxiety, and anger, and constant use is how these platforms currently make money. When money is the most important thing, platforms will drive whatever keeps people plugged in. Mindless, anxious scrolling is a win; mindful use is not. It doesn't matter to Facebook if we're enjoying our time online—it just matters that we're online.

"This situation results not necessarily from conspiracy, but rather from the quite visible, unabashed logic of capitalism itself," writes Robert W. McChesney in *Digital Disconnect*. He continues:

> Capitalism is a system based on people trying to make endless profits by any means necessary. You can *never* have too much. Endless greed—behavior that is derided as insanity in all noncapitalist societies—is the value system of those atop the economy. The ethos explicitly rejects any worries about social complications, or "externalities."

This makes it almost impossible to have conversations about how to ensure social media helps us open up rather than wall ourselves off. Ultimately, under a model that values profit above all else, conversations about ethics will be deprioritized or dismissed outright as complications or externalities.

These externalities include the fact that an internet driven by profit will inevitably encourage us to simplify ourselves down to obvious identifiers: what we do for work and what we consume and spend our money on. Undergirded by capitalist notions of what makes for happiness—the accumulation of material goods, work and achievement, status and stuff— platforms that prioritize profit urge us to reduce ourselves to posting about those kinds of things. They limit us to, or at least emphasize, sharing updates concerning status, achievement, and success, the constant posting of which merely serves to strengthen capitalist notions about what makes us real, whole, and worthy. We thus compare our full lives—all our failures and mundanity—to other people's accomplishments and status symbols, which then makes us want to pursue and prioritize those things ourselves. As a result, we end up competing with one another for prestige. "Our practical identities are inseparable from the society to which we belong," writes Martin Hägglund in *This Life*. If our society is one in which "the dominant way of relating to one another is to compete for resources"—be they financial resources or digital attention— "we will understand ourselves primarily as creatures who are competing for resources."

Of course, the fusing of the self with stuff isn't just an internet problem. But this stuff-infused self is reinforced by the very platforms themselves. The image that you project via social media becomes commodified in the age of big data. The self you put out into the digital public square is sent back to you via targeted ads shaped by data about you harvested by the platforms (which is how they make money).

This self-simplification is made easier by the fact that the platforms started with our trust. Like the privacy statements and terms of use we never read, we took on faith that they had our best interests in mind. And because of our trust and optimism, digital platforms were largely able to avoid scrutiny during the formative years when we began migrating our search for meaning, belonging, and realness online. They thus fused these pieces of our self-exploration and discovery with their efforts to sell us things. While the self under capitalism has always been influenced by its norms, the internet has taken it to new heights. Largely operating covertly already, the fingerprints of capitalism completely disappeared in the early digital years.

However, even in all of this, it's debatable how much surveillance capitalism *actually* understands us. The tools that track us base their understanding of us on what we share online, which we've been told time and time again is less real or not real. So without the full picture, they continue to nudge us in the direction of the simplified versions of ourselves we sometimes share online. These digital platforms are now, for many of us, *the* space where we reflect on our lives, process major events, forge connections. Even if they're not the primary space for some, for most people they're a piece of the puzzle, an increasingly large one. So the fact that they're designed to encourage certain kinds of use—more shallow kinds—and discourage others; that they're designed to keep us scrolling, clicking; and that they muddy the waters of what makes us real is all cause for concern.

Ultimately, when our digital platforms turn our online activities—the connections we forge, the ways we experiment and express ourselves—into monetizable activity, they transform it into a kind of labor. If the things we do with our free time become a form of labor, that time is not *really* free. Which is why we need to disentangle these digital forums—which more and more of us use to understand ourselves and become who we are—from profit.

How we organize our society says something about who we are and shapes who we become. If the internet is supposed to be a public space—for and by us all, where we seek meaning, belonging, and a sense of who we are—that's now complicated by the fact that, as Astra Taylor writes in *The People's Platform*, "the public good is increasingly financed by private money." And this money bends our public space in the direction of corporate interests, not all of ours.

Ultimately, as with climate change, when it comes to addressing the problem of a profit-driven internet, individual behavior change isn't enough. We need systemic changes within the platforms themselves. "To reduce the issue to individual choice and character is to disregard how exploitation is *systemic* under capitalism," writes Hägglund. "As an individual consumer, I can choose not to buy certain products, but without a collective transformation of the system of exchange I will continue to participate in capitalist exploitation."

Part of why we tend to think about our digital challenges in terms of individual behavior changes is because of the obsession with the individual that results from these conditions. Only in a world of hypercapitalism can we focus so much on an individualized conception of ourselves instead of one rooted in an understanding that we are part of a collective.

We see this emphasis on defining yourself singularly in the way these platforms emphasize individuality and self-expression above all else. Facebook asks you "What's on your mind?" and rewards you if you always have an answer. As a generation leaves institutions that are, at their core, about helping us see ourselves as a part of a greater whole—moving instead to platforms that often push us to think about ourselves as unique individuals—I worry that these platforms are training us to locate our value in whatever increases theirs, regardless of how it affects the common good.

In short, if the self we're constructing online is being built in venues inherently designed to make money, that informs who we become. And because these platforms also encourage us to see ourselves as individuals rather than part of a greater whole, we begin to think more and more through the lens of our own needs and interests. Thinking in terms of ourselves makes the collective issues we face feel too large to address, which makes us really anxious. As bigger pieces of our self-construction happen online, we could become all the more anxious as a result.

Like a mapmaker restricted by the conventions of cartography, there's only so much we can do online within the boundaries created by the architects of our platforms. Which means that our approach to using these platforms isn't the only thing that will have to change. The platforms through which we connect, reflect, and share our lives will themselves need to change the ways in which they operate, shifting away from models that prioritize profit above all else.

In the meantime, by opting out of traditional institutions, we have just transferred the work they were doing to new ones. Our digital platforms now give us spaces to connect and share our lives with one another—but are these platforms committed to our ability to better understand ourselves, explore what gives our lives meaning, and forge meaningful connections?

While many of us leaving long-standing institutions for the internet believe that we are rejecting the scripts of institutions and forging our own, most of us are *really* just embracing different institutions with different scripts. In a digital world guided by the priorities of capitalism, many of us have replaced religious scripts with ones shaped by the ways brands can monetize our lives, which is why so many corporations have embraced buzzwords like *self-care* and *authenticity*. While we might think we are leaving institutions and making our own way in the world, Craig Martin points out in *Capitalizing Religion* that this new freedom is heavily scripted, confirmed, and controlled by market forces—which means it's not really freedom at all.

Independence is valued in my family because we've needed it to survive, and as I became an adult it was easy to tell myself that I was as independent as they come. While my family stayed in Minnesota, I moved out of state to Chicago, where I knew no one, then went even farther, to New England. I've been financially independent since I moved out of my family's house as a teenager and have experienced periods of financial insecurity when I had no one and nothing to fall back on. I've scraped my way from one self-created job to another. So, despite all of the help I've received from others, I was able to tell myself a story that I was fine on my own. That I didn't need anyone.

But that story unraveled during my scabies summer. I was back in my home state, where I'd begun. The phase of the career I had worked toward for most of my life, and the job that was supposed to be its culmination, were over. I was suddenly unemployed with almost no savings and quickly burned through what little I had due to medical bills and moving costs. I was physically miserable, in intense pain and discomfort most waking moments (which, since scabies is worse at night, was most moments). The things I'd used to prop up the story that I was self-reliant—my career, my geographic distance from family, my able body—were undone.

However, though I felt profoundly alone in moments, I was far from it. I wouldn't have gotten through that summer without the people who checked in on me and helped me. The friends old and new, the family members who had busy and full lives of their own (my sister came over on the night of my diagnosis with rubber gloves and boots to help me do laundry), and in particular the people online who were my lifeline, who held space for me to vent and weep. As I withdrew from the world and put physical distance between me and just about everyone

I knew—afraid I might spread my scabies and ashamed of what a mess I'd become—it was often people online, like the semi-strangers in my Twitter DM chat or long-distance friends I hadn't seen in years, who, through my phone, kept me going. That summer it became clear to me that this idea that I could get through life on my own had always been a myth, a self-protective story intended to keep me safe.

The myth could have persisted if I hadn't looked a little closer at my digital habits. The irony is that evidence of its untruth has been all around me, and not just in all the people who have helped me along the way. It's right there in the panic I've felt when my phone is low on battery and how I so often keep it on low power mode to avoid eating through too much battery, even when it's mostly charged. In my incessant tweeting, especially in more difficult moments. But until that summer, when I realized my phone was, in moments, the *only* thing getting me through that period of self-isolation and withdrawal—that it was often my sole lifeline to the world of other people, and I shudder to think about how I might have dealt otherwise—I wasn't able to see how I was using it.

What happens when the periods of time where we find ourselves able to be out of communication grow shorter and shorter, yet we come to think of ourselves as ever more autonomous, ever less in need of community or institutions? When even sitting through a movie without looking at our phone feels challenging? When losing our phone makes the world almost impossible to navigate? When the first moment of restlessness, the first uncomfortable thought, prompts us to reach for a device? I have friends, dear friends I adore, who spend more time looking at their phones than at me when we are together. I know I've been that friend, too.

Yet I also don't buy the doom and gloom, either. Not entirely. Before my phone, I would daydream about being with others even when I was with someone I loved. Some other grass always appeared greener. Enough was never enough, with or without a phone.

Still, if we're not careful, the myth of independence that tethers us to our devices could become our shared defining story at the precise moment when we need the opposite story: the one that recognizes that we are bound up in one another. As more of us leave institutions designed to help us understand that we are part of a larger story and instead attempt to meet those needs online, where we can customize an experience around our individual wants and segment our connections to avoid accountability, the risk is that we could ironically come to see ourselves as less connected.

But social media is a tool with the power to show us how connected we are: used differently, intentionally, it can help us identify with more people than was ever possible before. In a moment when our challenges are more and more connected—when problems global in scale force us to confront how our actions impact others—this tool can help us find a path forward.

We will never rid ourselves of uncertainty; we can only learn to abide it together. The irony of turning to profit-motivated platforms for meaning and belonging, seeking it out as individuals instead of through other kinds of institutions, is that these platforms currently turn us back toward ourselves. The apps and tools that promise structure and order, that claim they will streamline our lives and give us security, can never do what they seem to promise—do away with uncertainty—because uncertainty adapts. If we try to resist this fact of life, our responses to life's uncertainty will take on maladaptive forms as they do in OCD. But we can choose another path than that of siloing and reflexive certainty: we can harness the internet to prioritize connecting and demand our platforms change to meet us there.

—■—

With so many people leaving the institutions that have connected us for ages and moving to platforms with a financial interest in driving us apart, it's hard to imagine that individualized story changing. Which is why, while my fellow nonreligious people have cheered on the headlines about the rise of the "nones," I've found myself worrying instead.

While I celebrate that we live in a time when more people are able to change, abandon, or live their entire lives without a religious category without as much fear of social reprisal as they would have faced in the past, I'm deeply concerned about where we religiously unaffiliated turn in times of need. Where are the nonreligious (or even the religious but nonparticipating) getting their narratives about who they are and what it means to belong, and do these narratives help them see the ways in which their well-being is bound up in that of others?

Both from my own work with young nonreligious people over the last decade and from the research I've done with sociologists to study the religiously unaffiliated, it's clear many of them are seeking it out online. As people leave churches and bridge clubs in favor of new ways to feel real, they will seek stories elsewhere. And since the internet is where more and more of our lives happen, it is quickly becoming home to the defining narratives people use to shape their lives. If we don't work to shift the story of social media and how we use it, we cede the internet to people telling a different story. People who wish to capitalize on these new technologies to divide, to exploit fears, to take us backward—among them a growing number of religiously unaffiliated white men making their way into white supremacist movements online, a deeply troubling phenomenon.

In March 2016, writer and critic Baratunde Thurston was inducted into the South by Southwest Interactive Hall of Fame, and in his acceptance speech he laid out the problem:

> The algorithms are coming, and we know they aren't pure or objective. Like journalists, they're embedded with the values of their makers. They reflect the society around them. But if innovation is all about making the world a better place, and the algorithms and code that claim to do so derive from this very imperfect world—sick with racism and sexism and crippling poverty—then isn't it possible that they might make the world a worse place?

We see the impact of this all around us online. As Thurston says, that includes "loss of user information, propaganda, mental health harm from social platforms, and Nazis everywhere." We need to course correct, and quickly.

If we don't, things will move into the empty space created by the institutions people are leaving behind; those spaces won't just sit vacant. They could be immensely positive things, new ways of being and belonging, but there is no guarantee. When digital platforms motivated by profit push whatever drives engagement—which is easier to get by sharing inflammatory content—then it seems likely that the things moving into those spaces will be increasingly extreme.

In a newsletter a few days after mass shootings in Texas and Ohio in the summer of 2019, Kaitlin Ugolik Phillips grappled with the online homes for hate: "If we think about these shoot-ers as people who have been radicalized, it makes sense to ask why and how." According to research, the *why* often has to do with a sense that one's values are threatened as well as the need to feel important and part of a community. These are human needs, and if we want to prevent the radicalization that increas-ingly occurs online, we have to understand them. "A lot of people who end up in places like 8chan—the forum where the El Paso shooter and others have posted about their murderous plans—are looking for community, empathy, and validation," writes Phillips. "They often find those things, but the places they look are rooted in hatred and violence."

That people can find belonging in such twisted ways is nothing new, but today it is certainly related to the fact that, even as we seek out connection online, levels of loneliness are increasing. Some refer to this as the internet paradox: we crave connection to satiate loneliness, and so we find it online, where it can feel less messy. But we aren't always satisfied by what we find, perhaps because we expect it to feel exactly like what we experience offline, and thus feel even lonelier when it doesn't. Increasingly desperate for belonging—and for online versions of it to precisely replicate the ways we've experienced it offline—we can become ever more willing to compromise our values in order to feel it.

Charles Taylor suggests in *The Ethics of Authenticity* that today we should worry not about "despotic control" but rather "fragmentation—that is, a people increasingly less capable of forming a common purpose and carrying it out." What causes fragmentation? Taylor says it "arises when people come to see themselves more and more atomistically, otherwise put, as less and less bound to their fellow citizens in common projects and allegiances." Which is why we should be concerned about the mass exodus from institutions that have historically helped people engage, and their move to online platforms motivated by profit to push people in individualistic directions.

Social media is often about meeting short-term needs, like the immediacy of loneliness, and it actively encourages us to think about our needs in those terms. But the big questions in life aren't short-term questions. They're things we need to spend our entire lives exploring, sometimes in slow ways set apart from the rhythms of our everyday lives.

Besides, strange as it may seem, loneliness is probably essential to being human. What happens when we never allow ourselves to feel that loneliness, with digital institutions connecting us twenty-four hours a day? Today we can engineer our lives so that we never have to feel alone at all. While solitude can be relieving and generative, loneliness is often immensely painful, especially if it is never relieved. But we may lose something essential to our humanity if we *never* feel it—if for no other reason than because loneliness can help us appreciate the times we are not alone, rather than taking the people in our lives for granted and feeling as if we could connect to someone at any time if we really wanted to.

In a now-deleted 2019 Twitter thread on the future of climate politics, David Roberts wrote that "as climate gets more and more chaotic, and the ambient sense of threat and uncertainty rises around the world" reactionary politics will probably gain *more* public appeal, not less. "Threat and uncertainty make everyone more conservative," he tweeted. Which is why, as more people leave institutions of old and seek connection and understanding in a digital swirl of distraction and filter bubbles, we need to develop digital systems that point us in the direction of cooperation. I believe it is possible. As I've tried to understand how we might come to feel more fully human online, I've encountered people doing it all over the internet: the communities that develop and flourish, the times people find solace and meaning, and all the ways the internet *doesn't* fragment us.

To be the people we wish to be, it won't just happen. We need habits that break us out of our self-constructed bubbles, ones that help us recognize our interdependence—especially because we can't escape institutions no matter how much we try. Just as we have swapped out religion for "self-care" capitalism, we have replaced brick-and-mortar institutions for digital ones. "We never start from the beginning—we always inherit a tradition that tells us what we ought to do," writes Hägglund. "The important task is to build institutional practices that acknowledge and enable us to cultivate" lives of meaning and purpose. Online, we tell ourselves we are free of institutions. But this is a lie, and it leaves us vulnerable to those who would prey upon our loneliness and divide us.

The first step toward changing the story, toward changing our habits, is embracing the uncertainty of our digital lives— the challenges, but also the opportunities, that emerge as we build new institutions.

One foggy day in March, I drove to a chain coffee shop in a small town an hour northwest of Minneapolis to meet Erica Stonestreet, a philosophy professor at the College of St. Benedict and St. John's University. I wanted to better understand what it means to "be real" and figured a philosopher could help me get a little closer.

"Our lives are simultaneously a process of creation and discovery," Stonestreet began as a coffee grinder whirred behind the counter a few feet away. When it comes to getting a sense of who one *really* is, there's discovery—recognizing how the factors outside of us have shaped us—and creation—building ourselves into being. Both of these are things many of us now do online.

Still, she said, even as we build ourselves and are built by others, we find ourselves wondering if there is something at the center—something *essential* and *unchanging*. But Stonestreet pointed out the idea that there is a fixed self, a thing that's *really* you, is a very European construct. There are many other ways of looking at this idea. For example, there's a Buddhist notion of no-self that suggests there's no fixed thing that's you, and that everything is impermanent. Looking at my own habits and behaviors, and how many people I can be depending on the circumstances around me, I recognize the unfixed self.

Ultimately, if everything is impermanent and changing, then who we are is "the stories we tell ourselves and others in any given moment," said Stonestreet. "But we are limited by what stories are available to us." To better understand this, she directed me to Hilde Lindemann's work. In *Damaged Identities, Narrative Repair*, Lindemann talks about how "master narratives"—the larger stories in which we place ourselves—aren't always positive. In fact, these master narratives can harm us, as they have in the case of the frequently negative narratives about LGBTQ people.

Looking at our digital lives, it's easy to wonder if the master narratives we absorb digitally are harmful, too. If what makes us real is the stories we tell ourselves about who we are—how we constellate our lives into meaning based on our experiences, roles and identities, relationships, and master narratives, as

Lindemann and others suggest—it is worth asking if our digital tools help us weave these stories well.

One way they seem to is how they've shown us that a wider range of narrative options are available to us. Being real means different things to different people, but for much of human history it has been hard to be real in ways that deviate from the majority. Talking with transgender friends and reading trans writers like Thomas Page McBee, for example, casts the conversation about realness in a different and important light. For trans people, notions of realness are often wielded as a weapon. We've seen this as trans people have navigated the culturally enforced conventions of realness—and, with incredible perseverance and power, shattered many of them. While these individuals have been fighting for their own dignity—a fight they should never have had to undertake—we all benefit from it. Because as McBee writes in *Amateur*, all of us are "proving [our] 'realness'" in different ways—ways that either align with these master narratives about who we're supposed to be and how we signal that to the world or, more often, deviate from them. Even the most privileged among us don't fit the narrative in every way, and all of us benefit from having more paths available.

My own fixation on realness goes back to my early life, times when I saw fewer paths available to me—especially adolescence, as I navigated the questions my sexuality and conservative faith put before me. How they taught me not to trust my instincts about myself, how they warped and distorted the lens through which I viewed myself, and how they convinced me that *I* wasn't real, in the sense that how I understood myself didn't align with the world's expectations and demands of me. But the question of what it means to be real returned in the wake of my breakup, during the tumultuous couple of years that followed, and it nearly consumed me. I wanted to understand what it meant to be authentic, to *truly* know myself.

Why did I care so much about figuring out how to be real? I can see now that it was because, as my world and so much of what I thought was true of me began to disintegrate, I once again wanted the kind of certainty I'd sought in my adolescence.

Why do we buy self-help books? Why do we throw ourselves into a new exercise routine or wardrobe or political campaign, a hobby or diet, or a new social media platform? Why do we find solace in the certainties of fundamentalist religion or self-important atheism? Why do we post status updates or Instagram stories about the minute details of our lives? We want to be understood—by others, but also by ourselves. To document our lives in the hope we might get to a point of self-actualization where we *truly* understand ourselves and the world around us.

In part this may be our attempt to reach a state in which neither the world nor our own selves can take us by surprise. Whether we frame it as such or not, it's chasing enlightenment. Because if we figure out who we are and where we belong, then we'll always know what to do: how to be in the world, and who. If you sincerely understood yourself—knew exactly who you are and why you want the things you want—you'd know what to do in difficult situations and how to avoid them in the first place.

The desire to find this kind of understanding can feel especially acute in times of transition, like during adolescence or after a big breakup. The longing for security, for a deeper understanding of what was happening to me in that difficult year of breaking up, leaving my job, moving, and battling parasites, was what drove me to that tarot reading and what made me ask a search engine what it means to be real. I was confused—about why I wanted the things I did, why the vision I'd once had for my life wasn't matching reality, why I was struggling—and I wanted answers.

I wanted a solution to the problem of being a person, *this* person. A shortcut. My breakup had caught me off guard; I hadn't seen it coming, and I didn't ever want to be caught off guard like that again. I wanted to understand myself so that I could protect myself from myself. To become real so that I could be safe from uncertainty.

Curiously, the things that are supposed to make "being real" easier—these digital pieces of our lives that are supposed to simplify and streamline our existence—often make it feel harder. I felt it on that hot summer day, when I uploaded that selfie and thought, *I'm still here, I'm still here, I'm alive.* It reflected how deeply I'd come to need the feeling of certainty and security that I derived from my existence being affirmed by an audience of others online. In that moment I was grasping because everything felt so uncertain.

I was suddenly so removed from my securities: my relationship, my career path, my independent life away from home, all of these things that propped up my self-image. So I turned to the one thing that had so often offered me that sense of security, the internet. Only it, too, failed to make me feel safe. And now I understand why. For years I used it to seek certainty. To deny my vulnerability and project an image of confidence and independence back to myself and out to the world, hoping it would convince me that I had everything under control. Even in that moment, when I was at my lowest, the instinct to post a polished self that I could try to live into kicked in. But in my face I could see the lie.

"We try to understand ourselves not out of some narcissistic impulse, but because we know that self-knowledge and self-awareness, a sure sense of identity, are what allow us to create a path toward a full and generous life," writes Akiko Busch in *How to Disappear*. "To be ourselves to the fullest degree is what makes it possible not just to experience life at its fullest but to give ourselves most completely to the causes to which we are committed, to our children, to the people we love." Indeed, while the search for the real self can absolutely be about seeking certainty to counteract insecurity, or simply about navel-gazing narcissism, it doesn't have to be. At my best, I want to understand myself, my desires and needs, so that I can learn to more efficiently address them and leave more space to expand toward the needs of others. To do as Busch calls for: "Decide who you are. Then let it go."

Because the question of realness remains and always will, the vital lessons we learn are in uncertainty—lessons we might lose in the age of optimizing our lives digitally. Life is change, uncertainty, incongruity, contradiction. The problem arises in resistance. After years of trying to create a sense of (imagined) security online and off, everything exploded. No longer able to resist change, I was offered an opportunity to approach uncertainty in a new way.

Writing for the *American Sociological Review*, Jacqui Frost explains how she discovered that while some nonreligious people do experience anxiety and social isolation—which is in line with the expectations of concerned social scientists who argue that the decline in religious participation will only lead to harm—many more nonreligious people experience uncertainty "as a *freedom from* former anxieties and isolation."

Some of us run from uncertainty, but others embrace it and see in it opportunities to learn. While I have been among the former, I am trying to be among the latter. And this matters because, as Frost explains, uncertainty is often named as one of the defining challenges of this moment in time. But if we approach this challenge with the assumption that we always desire certainty—and that uncertainty has nothing positive to offer—"we might overlook new and emerging ways that modern individuals are making sense of their lives," says Frost, "through finding meaning in uncertainty."

Uncertainty may thus be the greatest gift of the digital age. Online, we are constantly offered opportunities to see that existence is fundamentally uncertain and that who we are is uncertain, too. In our digital play, our online ink, our maps, and our distance, we see that we are inherently contradictory creatures—hypocritical and confusing, cruel and compassionate all at once. That we can be trolls and angels at the same time, and that doesn't make one "fake" and the other "real."

Being human means containing multitudes. It means constantly working at being kinder, at holding ourselves and one another accountable, because it won't just happen by default. But it also means that falling short is not a failure of humanity. It is not a bug but a feature, a piece of what it means to be human. It is through recognizing and understanding this that we can take steps to address our shortcomings, to change our behaviors, to get better at getting closer to the values we aspire to live out. To learn and change, and to help others not repeat our mistakes, is fundamental to being human.

The complex truth—that social media can make us both less human and more human, depending on how we use it—is uncomfortable. It means we can't just follow ten steps to a better life, can't optimize our happiness if we just use enough apps, can't brand our way to success. It also means that most of us can't just pull the plug, log off forever, and solve the problem that way, either. Instead, if we want to be engaged in an increasingly digital world and also have balance, we will need to make a regular effort to use social media well, to wield its power carefully and mindfully. That feels riskier and harder, and so it is less appealing than the certainty of polemicists. But it's a way forward.

The answer isn't to double down on certainty but to embrace uncertainty instead—something the institutions of the past so often haven't offered us, and what the internet can provide if we learn to use it well. It is through uncertainty, the acceptance of impermanence and change, that we become more real. From my breakup to my job ending to bedbugs and scabies, these hugely disruptive events made it harder for me to curate a certain image online. And, in the end, this proved freeing.

During the most difficult periods of my life, I have climbed into bed, pulled the covers over my head, and yearned to hide my pain from the world. But with bedbugs and scabies, even my bed felt dangerous. I wasn't able to pretend I was someone else—an edited, more polished version of myself. I couldn't curate myself, couldn't hide, so I had to show up exactly how I was: hurting, wounded, and messy.

It was horrible. And liberating.

One of the greatest lessons of the digital age is that even our safest spaces aren't guaranteed to stay that way. If we want to be resilient and real, we need to face the fact that being real means taking risks. Hiding and editing won't save us because we are always at risk of being exposed. The answer, then, is to embrace openness, letting other people see our messier sides more often, not just when we're in crisis.

The second chapter of this book is called "anxietweets," and that's not a flippant play on words. I have often used social media to try to manage my anxiety, knowingly and not. But we need some anxiety for our lives to matter, which is why it is at the core of some of the philosophical classics, like the writing of Sartre and Camus. "If we had no anxiety about what to do with our time," says Hägglund, "we would not be able to discriminate between which activities are worthy and unworthy of who we take ourselves to be." This is why spending too much time on some apps makes us feel unhappy; wasting our time feels like such a fundamental violation because, on some level, we feel anxious about how little we have, and that's what helps us determine what matters and what makes us feel real.

Online, we have to put our faith in something we don't always know will work. But faith doesn't have to mean certainty; in fact, I'd argue it shouldn't. That faith equals certainty is a common misconception, and though most atheists don't consider themselves people of faith, it's often applied to atheists as well. The association between atheism and certainty is based in large part on who has spoken for atheism—the "New Atheists," who represent a very particular kind of atheism, born of very specific life circumstances and experiences. But that's not the only atheism. While the kind of atheism promoted by antireligious polemicist Richard Dawkins is the most visible, it also doesn't reflect the views of many atheists. Prominent white atheists like Dawkins "could do with a dose of humility made possible by a recognition that life is uncertain," Lehigh University's Monica Miller said when I interviewed her for a Religion News Service column in 2014. "White privilege has a lot to do with feeling certain, secure, safe. If atheists want to really tackle such long-standing problems and challenges, then they'd start off well by adopting a brand of atheism or humanism rooted in uncertainty." Like the trust we put in our digital lives without knowing whether or not we should believe what we're seeing—Is this a real person or a catfish?—we frequently have to find ways to operate under uncertain conditions. Faith is a leap.

For some, *faith* is simply another word for *trust*, but theologian Paul Tillich defines faith as having "an ultimate concern." In *This Life*, Hägglund, an atheist, proposes a secular faith that locates its ultimate concern in the sense that life ends. Everything you know, everything you love, will eventually cease to be. Because everything ends, a secular faith is about "being concerned." What does this mean? "Even if my desire were absolutely fulfilled—even if I lived in the midst of an achieved social justice, blissfully happy with my beloved, and with my work flourishing—I would still be concerned," Hägglund writes, "since everything I care about must be sustained over time and will be lost. Moreover, the risk is part of why I care, why it matters to me what happens, and why I am compelled to remain faithful." In other words, even if we get everything we want, we could still lose it. Even if we think we fully understand our digital lives, we can lose that understanding. There will always be unknowns and uncertainties, which is why we must cherish and attend to the things we care about. Uncertainty is the only reason anything is at stake in our lives, Hägglund suggests. In order for things to matter, he says, they must be losable.

The first step of managing OCD is learning to accept that things are losable and see that as part of what gives life meaning instead of just a source of stress. Learning to live with uncertainty and the anxiety it elicits is the goal of OCD treatment, not finding a way to somehow come to avoid it altogether (as I have sometimes tried to do with my digital distractions). It is a process of accepting reality—of deciding you can find happiness in the world as it is rather than the ideal you wish were reality. Otherwise, consumed by life's what-ifs, people with OCD can lose "the only thing any of us can count on having: the present," writes Jonathan Grayson. The same is true for those of us online: we should seek happiness in it as it is, even as we try to make it better, and understand the things we do online as being real, tangible, losable.

When my life started falling apart at the end of my twenties, a dear friend said—empathetically, but also emphatically—"Ah, yes. You're in your Saturn return."

Soon after, another friend said it. Then another. It kept coming. And they all sounded so certain.

I'd never heard of Saturn return, so when my friend first said it to me, I opened my laptop and started searching. The first few links revealed that it is commonly understood as a time in a person's life—usually spanning the end of one's twenties and beginning of one's thirties—that is, supposedly because of events in the stars, primarily defined by major personal changes, transitions, and endings. During your return, life strips away some of the things you've used to define yourself. These changes challenge you to reassess your life and choices and, if you're open to it, make different choices instead. From what I could tell, you're supposed to come out on the other side with a better understanding of who you are. You lose it all in order to gain; you lose your false self to find your *real* self.

The last time I'd felt anything akin to that had been years earlier, when I quit drinking. Some people refer to it as being "in recovery." The meaning of the word *recover* is to find or regain something that's been lost, or to return to a state of health and well-being. It reminds me of one root of the word *religion*, which is to remind and reconnect—to recommit yourself to who you are and what you value. In recognizing the things we don't like in our social media habits, we can attempt to recover some of what feels lost. But we can also let some of it go and reimagine instead. When I stopped drinking, I learned how to better address some of the underlying causes of my drinking, like social anxiety, and came to better understand myself as I reimagined new ways of attending to them.

As we become ever more digital, now is not a time to mourn but to question, recommit, and reimagine. As Elizabeth Rush writes near the end of *Rising*, we need to ask ourselves how we can tell the story of climate change "so that it becomes more than elegy alone, both a record of these uncanny times and a rallying cry." The same is true of our digital lives; but in both cases the challenge is that we have to do so without knowing what lies ahead. Rush describes the efforts to restore coastal wetlands while also knowing the seas are rising as attempts to "bring back what has been lost while readying it for a future we don't really understand." We know what we've gained with the internet—the ability to connect and organize, to experiment, to find options and information. But we also need to understand what's been lost and maybe try to bring some of it back. How do we do so without knowing exactly where we're headed?

Here's the thing about most kinds of change: they happen so gradually that they become the new normal before you've even realized anything's shifted. This is true whether it's climate change—temperatures get a little warmer, weather patterns start to fluctuate, but initially it's all within the range of acceptable variance until all of a sudden islands off Louisiana's coast are gone—or our digital lives—we gradually add platform after platform, Facebook then YouTube then Twitter then Instagram, before suddenly it's everywhere, fully integrated into our lives. If this is our world now, the question becomes what we do about it. If we're in a Saturn return, will we embrace the opportunity to transform and change, and also to recover what we find ourselves missing, or will we dig in and resist?

In *Antisocial Media*, Greg Goldberg writes on the concerns scholars raise about the fact that our downtime is moving to digital platforms and blurring the boundaries of work and play ("playbor," as it's sometimes called). But he argues that these concerns are often actually an expression of a deeper anxiety "about the erosion of particular forms of relationality valued by critics—collective, communal, responsible, accountable, sacrificial, and so on—in a word, social." In short, he suggests that what people are most worried about is the fact that old ways of belonging, ways that they're personally attached to, are disappearing.

Instead of despairing, we ought to embrace our new opportunities to address age-old questions of realness. Even as norms shift, so much about who we are—how we're shaped, how we understand one another—will continue to be relational, even if we become relational in radically different ways than we were before. Charles Taylor argues that throughout our lives we define ourselves "always in dialogue with, sometimes in struggle against, the identities our significant others want to recognize in us." In other words, while people sometimes assume that we develop our own opinions and beliefs mostly through private reflection, this is rarely true, especially in terms of identity.

Even the work we do to understand ourselves on our own impacts everyone around us. The people we are making ourselves into online—including in ways that feel fleeting and irresponsible—shape society. "My *own* existence *is* social activity," said Karl Marx, "and therefore that which I make of myself,

I make of myself for society and with the awareness of myself as a social being." Whatever form our relationships take, we grow and stretch ourselves by being connected to one another. Whether fleeting or forever, I believe that our ways of connecting must always take into consideration the needs of others. We are, in the words of poet Gwendolyn Brooks, each other's business.

"Personhood in European philosophy has long been about reason, rationality, autonomy, self-direction, individualism," Erica Stonestreet explained in our conversation as fog rolled by the coffee shop window to my left. "But we can distinguish individualism from individuality—we all have our individuality, but individualism is this overarching, very American way of thinking about ourselves that suggests we're these little atoms that bounce off each other when it's convenient."

"This idea that who I am is independent of everyone else," I added.

"Right," said Stonestreet. "But then feminist philosophers come along in the '80s and '90s and say, 'Well, actually, you start out dependent—*super* dependent, in fact, if you think about how helpless human babies are compared to pretty much every other animal on the planet." She continued:

> If you're lucky and live to a ripe old age, you end up dependent again. And in the meantime, if you decide to have a family in the middle, people are depending on you. We have these periods of relative autonomy where we're more in charge of ourselves and independence, but we're never fully out of it. So if you start from the idea that humans are not just these atoms that are bouncing around, but that we're actually enmeshed in these webs—my colleague Jean Keller uses the phrase "the encumbered self"—then it's clear that you're always connected to other people.

The encumbered self feels like a particularly apt way to describe our modern condition, but not for the reasons some might think. *Encumbered* has negative connotations—looking up definitions suggests something that's encumbered is weighed down, restricted, burdened, ensnared, held back. But I think of it as a recognition that we are bound up in one another, and that our sense of self is ever more dependent on others. After all, the very reason we post online is because there's an audience. "The only possible reason we can matter to ourselves," writes Madeleine L'Engle in *A Circle of Quiet*, is "not because we are sufficient unto ourselves" but rather because the people in our lives give us meaning and make us real.

An individual conception of self makes it harder to know yourself in some pretty profound ways because it involves a kind of denial. I had a complicated, fraught relationship with my father for years, and in my early twenties I actively distanced myself from him, telling myself and anyone who would listen that he and I were nothing alike. In some ways that denial of alikeness made me unable to see things in myself that in fact are like him, the struggles that are also his struggles and the strengths that are also his strengths, and to deal with those things. It was only once I was honest with myself about our similarities—our shared strengths and struggles—that I could not only work on addressing them but also on my relationship with my father, through which I've been better able to understand him and also myself. It's not just fully positive relationships that make us real. It's the fraught, complicated, messy act of trying to love and be loved. My relationship with my father, mess and all, is part of what has made me real.

It's worth examining our sometimes narrow understanding of what being in relationship with one another entails, like responsibility and accountability. In cracking open our thinking, we can imagine new ways to be human. This is one opportunity our increasingly digital world offers: a chance to look at these things through new, amateur eyes.

At one of the lower points of my supposed Saturn return, I pictured myself as being like a frozen laptop. Sometimes, when your computer isn't responding, you have to hold the power button until the whole thing reboots, hoping it comes out on the other side working. Sitting there watching the rainbow wheel spin and spiral, waiting to see if it just sorts itself out, isn't going to do anything. Sometimes you need to be willing to go back to the drawing board, to hit reset on your thinking and radically reimagine things, as I did when I stopped drinking. It was only once I completely stepped outside of the framework I'd been in and imagined an entirely different way of moving forward that I was able to get in touch with things I'd been struggling with for much of my life. This is what our digital lives can provide. An opportunity to step outside of old ways of being and belonging— the institutions that provided helpful structure, but also so often a certainty that stifled—and go back to the drawing board.

If there is a defining anxiety of this age, it's not that our lives are forever archived. Nor is it the anxiety of not being able to be alone, of always needing to be plugged in and able to connect. It isn't the anxiety of intimacy and distance, either. Though all of these anxieties are very real, I think there's one that towers above them all: our anxiety about uncertainty.

While some people can embrace the digital unknown, many of us seek certainty in our social media use. We turn on read receipts for our text messages. We panic if we don't hear back from someone within minutes. We delete a post if it doesn't immediately start getting likes. We text the hard thing instead of saying it in person so that we don't have to see our fears of how they might react come to life before us. But anxiety is also a sign we care. If our digital lives make us anxious (mine does!) it's because the things that happen online *are* real. And whether we acknowledge it or not, we care about them.

In *This Life*, Hägglund says uncertainty marks "our experience of the present itself, which is already becoming past and becoming related to the future." Which is why—because "neither the past nor the future can be known," not with certainty—Hägglund argues that we have to live on faith.

"Given that your relation to the past and the future depends on faith," he says, "you may be deceived by what you think is certain, mistaken about what you take for granted, and shattered by what you never expected." This necessary faith is what makes us vulnerable. When you put faith in something, yes, you can be let down. But in order to live, we must find a way to live with uncertainty. That is, perhaps, the only certainty.

I can still remember how it felt when, in the middle or even at the end of an AOL Instant Messenger (AIM) conversation in high school, someone just signed off without saying goodbye. (Or when I did the same, usually because my mom unplugged the internet after I'd ignored her request to get off the computer so she could use the phone.)

Any time it happened I'd freeze in panic. Was it something I'd said? Or, if the sudden sign-off was mine, would they think it was something *they'd* said? When someone signed off without warning and didn't come back, there was no closure and lots of space to imagine absurd explanations for their sudden departure.

Even when my AIM chats didn't cut out unexpectedly, I've always been bad at wrapping up conversations. I want to drag the discussion on and on, hesitating before signing off, looking for indications that it was a positive experience for the other person. Just one more text or DM and I'll be good, I tell myself.

I used to think it was just an indication of insecurity on my part (and let's be honest, that's a piece of the puzzle), but a big part of it is because of how jarring text-only conversations can feel in contrast to a lifetime of face-to-face ones. The conversation is, in some ways, flatter. And while text exchanges have complementary strengths that compensate for their weaknesses, like the ability to think through what you're saying a little more carefully, it's challenging to adapt to a different style of engagement. So, confronted with the uncertainty of missing information, my brain attempts to fill in the gaps.

In the age of being constantly connected, it's not hard to feel secure and certain if you want to. You never have to drop out, never have to be alone. You can keep adding new tweets to the thread, editing and adding caveats and adjusting what you're saying based on how people are reacting to it in real time. But this isn't a Twitter feed or a blog, it's a book, and I wrote it as such specifically so that it would have to come to an end. Some things—conversations, relationships, jobs, periods in your life—need to end. Sometimes we have to log off. Saturn returns are, at their core, about endings. Endings that offer opportunities for new beginnings.

To me, letting go of the need for certain kinds of certainty feels like the first step in the direction of the real. Which means that *real* isn't something to conclusively define; it's a thing that happens to you. It's something I will keep working toward, a habit I have to develop and practice. In the words of L'Engle, "a self is not something static . . . a self is always becoming." To become, we must constantly strive to move "from the selfish self—the self-image—and towards the real."

But just because realness defies a static definition, and is instead a kind of dynamic unfolding, doesn't mean we can't put some words to how we might approach practicing it. In the third chapter of this book, I laid out something I noticed early on in my exploration of our digital lives: that the internet has champions and critics. Back in the mid-'90s, in the earlier days of internet commentary, Sherry Turkle noted not only those camps (which she called utopian and apocalyptic) but also a third category, utilitarian, or people who "emphasize the practical side to the new way of life." Those who recognize that while the digital doesn't offer easy answers, it does "provide new lenses through which to examine current complexities."

For a time, I saw myself in this category and hoped to offer some suggestions for simple fixes. But the fixes are anything but simple—and not just because of the platforms themselves, though I do think disentangling them from profit would be a huge step in the right direction. Rather, I think the biggest challenge is how decidedly unsimple *we* are. So, in addition to the utopians, apocalyptics, and utilitarians, I'd like to cautiously suggest we introduce a fourth category: uncertaintweeters.

This category shares some of the hopes of the optimists, the critical eye of the apocalyptics, and the practical willingness to accept our new reality and find workable solutions of the utilitarians. But it differs not only in its ridiculous name but also in its relationship to uncertainty. Like utilitarians, uncertaintweeters also want to reform, interrogate, and experiment. Most of all, though, they acknowledge not only how much we can't actually know about the best way forward but also the value of that uncertainty. Rather than being cause for despair, the uncertainty of our increasingly digital lives might be an *asset* to our search for realness.

People in this category have a strong sense of what poet John Keats called "negative capability." In an 1817 letter to his brothers, Keats wrote that a great thinker is "capable of being in uncertainties, mysteries, doubts, without any irritable reaching after fact and reason." Someone who can practice negative capability is able to follow a thread even when it leads to uncertainty and confusion instead of firm answers. Negative capability is a refusal to choose either/or, to reject or embrace. Applied to our digital lives, it suggests that we are capable of more than just going with the flow or opting out—that we can see both its harms and opportunities and recognize that some aspects of our digital lives offer both simultaneously. Someone operating out of negative capability knows that we can hold views about finding realness and connection online that contradict and oppose one another. That we are as complex and changing as the digital tools we use to map our lives today.

Part of why I think we should be uncertaintweeters—why we should take an approach to our digital lives rooted in negative capability—is that while we know what it means to be false, what it is to be real is more evasive. A fundamental part of being real is the quest to be real itself. Realness is a willingness to let go of the desire for certainty and instead embrace curiosity. It is leaning in to change and the unknown, rather than entrenchment in a fixed understanding of a fixed self.

At one point in *Rising*, Rush describes kayaking with a guide in Maine. When they collapse on the beach after their outing, her guide, Laura, suggests that modern conveniences lead to a sense of security that might not always be good for us:

"Maybe it dulls the senses, makes us less aware of what's happening right in front of us, right now." And I wonder if the sureness we sometimes seek through our digital platforms—always connected, plugged in, distracted—dulls us, makes us less aware of the world around us, less attentive and thus less appreciative. If it is a way to feel a false certainty, instead of embracing life's uncomfortable unknowns.

A 2019 paper from the University of Melbourne's Sean Christopher Murphy and Brock Bastian suggests that rather than positive or negative experiences being more likely to engender a sense of meaning, as has often been thought, it is "peak" experiences—those that are more intense, whether they are positive or negative—that we find particularly meaningful. When we try to optimize our lives or seek constant digital distraction, we leave little room for anything disruptive, good or bad, and life can come to feel less meaningful as a result. We shouldn't lose ourselves in digital comforts to avoid uncertainty and suffering, because as my own Saturn return revealed to me, meaning is found in the peaks, not the undisturbed middles.

A lot of coming-of-age stories are about getting lost and finding yourself. But coming of age in the early days of the internet has felt, to me, like a kind of getting lost and not finding myself. Maybe this a different kind of story, though. A story of getting lost and finding others in unexpected places—in DM threads with semianonymous Twitter accounts, at a furry convention with someone I met online, in a map library and with game makers, on message boards and FaceTime, in between ones and zeroes. A story about getting lost and finding not a single self but rather a number of different selves within me, and learning how to live uncertainly with each one.

Perhaps my Saturn return was a splintering that didn't lead to an eventual rebuilding of a coherent single self on the other side but instead to a recognition of the ways in which I've *always* been splintered, always been more than one self. When I couldn't ignore what felt like a split between my online and offline selves anymore, I was forced to both confront and also accept it. To allow myself to be a different person in different spaces, or even in the same space. To see these splits not as failings but as opportunities to figure out how to be more comfortable with the contradictions and complexities within me and others. To see them not as problems to be resolved on the way to being real but rather as central components of what makes all of us real to begin with.

Social media has helped me recognize these uncertainties and contradictions within myself. But you don't have to use social media to practice negative capability—nor do you have to abandon it. And you definitely don't have to be in your Saturn return, which, to be clear, isn't something I believe in literally. But you do need to give it some thought. It's not going to just happen on its own. It's not going to be triggered by a cosmic event, something in the stars or in the algorithms. It's within you, somewhere, and you can find it if you go digging, if you make an effort to look at your habits and behaviors and try to understand what they're telling you.

Soon after we met, Stonestreet sent me an email. "I had a thought as I was driving away," she wrote. "If someone is asking for my advice on how to figure out who they are, I might start by asking what makes them think they don't know. Getting a sense of the problem can help think about where to look for answers. Why are you asking? What's motivating the project? Is there something that makes 'being real' hard or elusive?"

During my adolescence—years before we got internet access at home, before I could bike to the library on my own to log on, before I could bring myself to type the words "I'm gay" into a computer—I spent a lot of time alone, in my room, in my head, trying to figure out who I was and why I was the way I was. From a very young age, I found music to be a helpful companion for reflection. This was long before streaming, so I would go to my mom's stack of CDs, pick something out, and take it back to my room to listen. One day, I picked out an Indigo Girls CD. She had quite a few. This one had "Closer to Fine" on it.

In the song's chorus, they describe going to the doctor, to the mountains, to the Bible, to exercise—looking everywhere for meaning before ultimately realizing "there's more than one answer to these questions pointing me in a crooked line." In the end, what gets them closer to fine is letting go of the desire for "something definitive."

I definitely didn't get it back then—in fact, I was actively flipping through my teen study Bible with fundamentalist commentary printed in the margins while listening to it, looking for a concrete answer to the questions that plagued me—but I think I'm starting to get it now.

The questions I set out to answer when I started writing this book don't necessarily have answers. Or my answers will be different than yours. I know that's not a great way to end a book. I'm sorry; I wish I could give you something certain. Something definitive. There are other books that claim to be able to do so, if that's what you're looking for.

I set out at the beginning of my search for realness in the digital age looking for answers. I'm ending this process realizing that's missing the point. There aren't answers; there are habits, ways of living, that move us in the direction of realness. A habit of asking questions honestly will always lead you to more. In the words of priest and philosopher Bernard Lonergan:

> We do not know ourselves very well; we cannot chart the future; we cannot control our environment completely or the influences that work on us; we cannot explore our unconscious and preconscious mechanisms. Our course is in the night; our control is only rough and approximate; we have to believe and trust, to risk and dare . . . What has been achieved is always precarious: it can slip, fall, shatter. What is to be achieved can be ever expanding, deepening. To meet one challenge is to effect a development that reveals a further and graver challenge.

Not having the answers isn't just about accepting reality or settling for not knowing—it's actually a "spiritual practice," if you will, one that drives us in the direction of digging deeper. Understanding that there are limitations to what we know or can know doesn't mean that we stop trying to figure it out. Mystery doesn't mean that we just accept not having an answer. But it also doesn't mean that we pretend to have an answer when we don't. It does mean finding joy in trying to figure things out, in celebrating that there are areas where we still don't understand. That the challenges we face are opportunities to learn and grow. That there is realness in uncertainty, in being an amateur. It isn't just something to be tolerated, to learn to live with, but rather a rich source of information. A place where we can learn. Online, there is so much we still don't understand. We can fool ourselves into feeling secure and certain when we use the internet, but it is anything but. Which makes the internet one of the best spaces we have to learn and grow.

If we look at it honestly and fearlessly, the internet shows us what was always there: that life is uncertain, that people are complicated, that existing is messy. In the face of that truth, we got utopians and pessimists—because that's a *hard* truth to deal with. But it is the truth all the same. When I let go of my anxious desire for certainty—when I am an uncertaintweeter, when I practice negative capability—I can use the internet for the purposes of seeking meaning, connection, and realness, rather than just trying to rid myself of anxiousness. Because like the escalating nature of OCD rituals, trying to use social media to self-soothe doesn't address the underlying issue. It just exacerbates the anxiety. But when we lean in to uncertainty, we can use the internet to become more ourselves.

On a cold day in the middle of nowhere, near the end of a three-month social media sabbatical, I read Christine Smallwood's article "Astrology in the Age of Uncertainty," which explains that interest in astrology is on the rise because of the internet and because people are losing trust in institutions like organized religion—but also because, in times of crisis, "people search for something to believe in." At the end, a familiar voice appeared, articulating a familiar phrase.

"It's about negative capability," *Astro Poets* coauthor Alex Dimitrov, whom I referenced earlier, tells Smallwood about the appeal of astrology. "To endure doubt is ultimately the only thing you can do in life—to not strive for meaning or answers, and to endure the state you're in."

Reading this, I was surprised not only to meet my own journey in someone else's words but to meet my own journey specifically in *this person's* words. Because Alex and I have actually known each other for many years now and have developed an unexpected friendship, though our work in life has been very different. (He always teases me for not believing in astrology by saying it's because I'm an Aries.) That a poet astrologer and a professional atheist could come to the same conclusion about how to move through our ever-more-digital world is an example of what we can gain when we let go of our anxious desire for certainty and lean in to the unknown.

Perhaps you can guess where Alex and I met. I'll give you a hint: it is a space as wondrously uncertain, as ripe with possibility, as fundamentally real as we let it be.

OUTRO

THE VELVETEEN HABIT

A couple years ago, someone I love dearly—the person who taught me to drive, who made me dinner in middle school when my mom had to work late, and who drove across the country to sleep on an air mattress on the floor of my Boston apartment, bringing my childhood dog along so I could see her before she died—was diagnosed with Alzheimer's.

My stepdad's diagnosis wasn't a surprise; for years we suspected it was coming, and it was a factor in my decision to move back to Minnesota when I did. But when the diagnosis finally came, when he couldn't hide it anymore, a lot of things had to happen quickly. He retired, he and my mom downsized to a small townhouse, and she got all of his affairs settled while he could still be an active part of the process.

It's a good thing she did, because before long our conversations stopped making as much sense, and soon after that, he couldn't be left alone anymore for his own safety. That's when I started spending a few days a week with him: making him lunch, keeping him company, helping him find things, coloring and doing puzzles with him, taking him to the grocery store or McDonald's, and visiting lots of museums. (He constantly wanted to go to the American Swedish Institute, which, as much as I love it, is a bit less exciting on the seventh visit in two months for someone without memory loss.)

We've spent a lot of time together since his diagnosis, and this time has put many of the questions this book explores into a new light for me. For so much of his life (especially before he came into mine when I was twelve) his work, his independence, riding his motorcycle—these were the things that made my stepdad who he was, in his eyes and in those of others. They were what made him *him*, what made him a full person. But after his diagnosis, he couldn't do these things anymore. Not only that, but his stories, his memories, his understanding of what was going on around him and who he was all began changing, fading, and blurring, too. And the thing that perhaps made him most real in the eyes of some—his relationships with those who love him most—changed, too. He became less able to support others and more in need of support himself.

Even as some things faded away, though, there were openings. New pieces of who he is emerged: new hobbies, new ways of spending time, new questions and interests. He started doing things he would never have done before—we began taking walks together, sandwiching ourselves onto stools between truckers at a crowded diner counter in the city, and coughing up popcorn from laughing too hard at movies like *Homeward Bound* and *Paddington 2*. He came with me to run errands and get my hair cut at a heavily queer salon housed in an old warehouse, and he joined me on walks with Tuna (we always stopped by my neighborhood coffee shop so he could see her put her paws on the counter like she was placing an order, a trick he's obsessed with). Our days were full of activities we never would have done together before. In many ways, for us, a brand-new relationship emerged alongside the new pieces of him.

Spending time with him while writing a book so centrally about realness, I asked myself if these changes make him less *real*. I can't speak for him and his experience, of course, but it doesn't feel like it to me.

For the entire time I knew him before his diagnosis he was, at least with me, somewhat reserved. He would usually hold himself at a bit of a distance. As close as we were, I wouldn't say he opened up much to me. Not because he was against the idea, I'm sure, but because that's just how he was with me. He was a product of generations of quiet men before him, men from a part of the world—the northern American plains—where people, especially men, didn't discuss certain kinds of things.

Because of this, particularly when I was younger, it was easy to focus on the ways in which we were very obviously different. He lived on a farm, attended the giant motorcycle festival in Sturgis, South Dakota, every year, and had a conceal-and-carry gun permit. I was a queer vegetarian, Britney Spears stan, and democratic socialist. We were an unlikely duo, to say the least.

But after his ability to be alone diminished and we started spending a lot of time together one on one, our relationship began to change. Perhaps it was Alzheimer's lowering his inhibitions and removing his filter, or us growing closer. I suspect it was both. Whatever the reason, he started telling me stories I'd never heard before. Stories about his past exploits, his experiences of loss, and his love for his gay brother and his brother's partner (the first gay people I ever met offline). Some of the details would change on the second and third tellings of these stories, and they wouldn't always make much sense—but they were personal stories from his life, the kinds of things he'd never shared with me before. And they didn't stop. He began talking to me all the time, an avalanche of stories. Like the posts in my social media feed, I couldn't always tell how much of what he was telling me was literally *true*, but almost all of it felt *real*.

Alzheimer's isn't well understood. There's no cure, and it largely happens to older people. I suspect many people see someone with Alzheimer's as already halfway or even fully "gone," and some of them—even if they don't come right out and say it—act like people with Alzheimer's have lost their worth, their worthwhileness, their contribution to society. Or they simply ignore them, figuring it's something that happens to people near the end of their lives, so we probably don't need to worry too much about it.

But I think there's another reason many don't want to think too much about Alzheimer's: it reveals just how fragile our selves are and that what is real about us changes, often dramatically. That so much of what makes us real is tenuous and circumstantial.

One afternoon, as we colored together at the kitchen table and watched snowflakes land on the windowsill to our right, my stepdad showed me a sheet he was filling in with brown and purple crayons. It was an illustration of a rabbit and her babies. Below it was some text, a caption about what was depicted in the image. He pointed a crayon at the caption and slowly read to me from it: "Baby rabbits are born hairless and blind."

I'm sure I knew this fact at one point; it seems like the kind of thing I would have learned in school as a child. But in that moment it felt like new information. (He would go on to read it to me dozens of times that day, so I'm sure it will never feel new again.)

As he taught me about baby rabbits, I was struck by how vulnerable they are when they're born; how much rabbits need one another, and how baby rabbits are literally incapable of being alone. I looked over at the man who taught me how to drive, who introduced me to my first gay people—this man now incapable of being alone, who also seems more real to me than he ever did before—and thought about the last time I was that vulnerable, in childhood, and about my favorite childhood story.

As a kid, I was obsessed with *The Velveteen Rabbit*. We had a VHS tape of the television adaptation narrated by Christopher Plummer, which aired in 1985, two years before I was born. From the first time I watched it I thought it was the most glorious thing in the world.

Though we weren't a big television family, I constantly begged my mom to put it on. When she did I'd sit on the floor in front of the television enthralled, unblinking, entirely captured by the story of a rabbit who wanted, more than anything else, to become real.

The Velveteen Rabbit is a dark story to have for a childhood favorite. After the boy whose love makes the toy rabbit feel real falls ill, all of his possessions—including the rabbit—must be destroyed. The rabbit is thus abandoned, discarded like a piece of garbage to be incinerated. But this process—all of it, the love and the loss—shapes who the rabbit becomes. At its core, *The*

Velveteen Rabbit is about how experiences of discovering we're not alone, only to return to solitude again—the comfort we get from being loved and understood and the immense pain we experience when that's taken from us—forge us into something more frayed but also more real.

Now in my thirties, I still love *The Velveteen Rabbit*. But I love it today because I understand its darkness in a way I didn't as a child. I see it less as dark and more as honest. I now know, as the rabbit learns, that it is in both connection *and* disconnection that we become who we are.

Our relationships are a huge part of what make us real, even for those of us who love to spend time alone. It's impossible to know yourself on your own. Since I started taking care of my stepdad, I've learned that Alzheimer's research suggests that maintaining strong social ties can help slow the disease and that one of the absolute worst things that can happen to most people with Alzheimer's is to be socially isolated. In connection, we become more ourselves.

But connection is only half of the process of knowing who we are. Disconnection is also essential to being real. We need opportunities to step back and take time alone in order to understand what we've gained from loving and being loved.

After one of my first breakups, I remember my mom saying that you're born alone, and you die alone. You'll fill the time in between with meaningful relationships that will shape who you become, but nothing is guaranteed. People can leave at any time for any number of reasons. That doesn't mean you don't get attached, that you don't love. But it does mean you need to find within yourself the ability to exist independent of those relationships, no matter how much they shape you. To be okay with yourself.

It's a refrain she's repeated again and again since, including as we've navigated my stepdad's Alzheimer's. And it's what the rabbit experiences—he comes to feel real because he is loved, but then he has to find a way to live without that love. He discovers that he can because even though he was forged into being real through that relationship, he doesn't go back to not being real just because it's over. Once it is done, it can't be undone. And the perspective that he gets from loss enables him to see the ways that connection helped make him real.

But even though I still adore it, *The Velveteen Rabbit* feels like a dissonant voice to me now in a time of constant connection—a time when the digital pieces of our lives are less actions with boundaries, things we step in and out of, but rather things that are almost seamlessly integrated into all hours of the day. If the process of becoming real requires periods of both connection *and* disconnection, does being constantly logged on short-circuit it?

Some of the most painful moments in life are those we have to face alone. My deepest, most anguished wails have almost all forced their way out in solitude. When, alone at my kitchen counter one December evening, I received a personal email from one of the realest people I've ever known, my dear friend Alex (a different Alex than the two I previously mentioned, a dear friend who was central to my getting through that scabies summer by frequently checking in via phone call, text, and video message)—informing me that he had taken his own life, explaining why, and saying goodbye. When I was up all night vomiting with the flu as a child, and my mom had to go to bed after comforting me because she had work in the morning. When my parents told me they were getting a divorce and, after trying and failing to reach friends on the phone, I had to sit alone with my thoughts and feelings. When my ex Alex moved out after our breakup, and I suddenly lived alone again and had to confront the reality of dealing with life's challenges by myself. When I was diagnosed with scabies and found myself completely overwhelmed and utterly on my own. In each of these moments, the devastation I felt was compounded by the sense that I had to endure it by myself. But these were important moments because I had to find a way to draw on the things I've learned from my relationships with others and put them into practice on my own.

Turning inward and finding that resolve feels harder to do now, though, because at the very first hint of loneliness I can just pull up Twitter or send someone a text. Which means it becomes more difficult to know who I am when I'm alone because it so rarely happens now.

I've spent a lot of my life running away from my thoughts, afraid to spend too much time with them. For most of my twenties I filled spare moments with work, parties, relationships, and friends—and, perhaps most of all, with time online. The invention of the smartphone was the best and worst thing that could happen to me because it meant I never had to be alone, that I could always distract myself.

Until that summer when I finally hit a point where I couldn't hold it all together anymore. Overly paranoid of reinfesting myself with scabies, I didn't touch my laptop for at least a month. Itch-walking around the city, I couldn't be glued to my phone because it would run out of battery. I was also told not to drive because my doctor prescribed an anti-itch medication with side effects, so if I couldn't walk somewhere, I wasn't going. But more than anything, embarrassed by what a wreck I'd become, I didn't want to see anyone or even post much online.

Which meant that I spent a lot of time by myself. It was immensely painful in moments, and it was also revealing. Like the rabbit, I had to let go of what had made me feel real—my longest relationship, my career, my independent life far from family. But in that erosion, I was able to ask myself questions about what mattered most to me and recognize what I'd lost. I could hold on to what was useful and discard the rest. Without that forced time to reflect, I'm not sure I would have.

I suspect that if we want to feel real in the digital age, we need to make a habit of disconnecting, despite platforms that actively discourage us from logging off. We need to intentionally carve out time for perspective taking. Otherwise it will only happen when circumstance forces it on us, when things come undone.

This matters because who we are is found in what we do. "It's easy to imagine that the big decisions, things like changing a job or ending a relationship, make the biggest difference in my life, but this is not so," Alan Downs writes in *The Velvet Rage*. "Most often when I make big changes, I quickly discover that I re-create the same mess I was trying to escape before I made the change. Big moves create upheaval and a distraction from whatever may be causing me distress, but inevitably the same old stuff comes back around with a different costume." The real significance, he suggests, is found in small, everyday changes.

Months before my move, unaware that I was doing exactly what he warned against, I read Downs's book. I couldn't see it then, but I now understand that instead of big, landmark moments like moves or job changes, it's the small things—our everyday actions, like how we use social media—that make the biggest difference in how we understand who we are. We are less where we live or what our titles are and more what we do day in and day out. Those big changes can be exciting (or daunting, as the case may be) and can motivate us to take valuable steps to improve our circumstances, but they're not necessarily the places we become most real. Those places are the everyday activities of our lives, digital and otherwise, which is why those activities are a good place to begin making a habit of paying attention.

With that in mind, to honor the writing of this book and the "end" of my search for digital realness, I decided to undertake a three-month social media sabbatical as I finished working on it. Some of my friends didn't think I would make it even three days, and I wasn't so sure I would, either. The first few days were legitimately terrible; I couldn't focus, I experienced dopamine withdrawal, and my friends noted that I kept texting them in tweet and meme format. But then I adjusted.

There were shifts, to be sure. Big ones, even. I suddenly had a lot more time on my hands—the app on my phone that tracks my screen time told me that in the first week my phone use dropped nearly fifty percent, which is especially wild because I was doing a lot more note-taking and writing on my phone that week than I usually do. I also felt calmer; so much of the digital anxiety that I'd become accustomed to faded away. I was less concerned about the online back-and-forths between various people I didn't really know that had for some reason been so entrancing. Now they seemed strange. Of course, I also felt out of the loop, knowing there were events I was missing, commentary. But in many other ways, life largely felt the same as before, except that I wasn't connecting or making meaning online at all.

The calm and ease I felt while being offline—the sense of relief I experienced and the extra time I had—was akin to what I imagine people feel when they go on a meditation retreat.

It was a momentary respite, and helpful, but it was not something I could maintain if I want to live in the world. Especially because the things that felt most difficult about my break—for example, while I started strong, by the final stretch of my break I was doing a fair amount of lurking—actually had a lot to do with the fact that I was no longer present in spaces that have come to feel valuable for me. I had stepped out of the world, but not into a condition in which I thrive.

Whether we stay online, use the internet less or differently, or mostly opt out, the challenges of being human remain. Being a person is hard work; it is anxiety inducing and stressful. But the anxiety is there because things matter to us. It's easier to not feel stressed when you're less engaged with the world. So though I've toyed with the idea of opting out, of extending my social media sabbatical indefinitely, part of what it means to be me is to be engaged with this part of the world. I can change my relationship to the digital pieces of my life, learning to use it more mindfully and developing healthier boundaries—I've considered trying to not use social media on my phone going forward, for example, and instead only sit down to use it purposefully on my computer. But while I have no idea what the future will bring, I don't see myself leaving the internet behind completely.

Especially in the digital age, attention takes work. When everything feels ephemeral, replaceable, deletable—when it's no big deal if a tweet flops because it'll be pushed down the timeline in moments; when it doesn't matter if something breaks because you can just Amazon Prime a new thing for less than what it would cost to fix it; when everything is expendable— then nothing matters. We can become detached from our lives and the world around us. But that comforting detachment is a lie, a self-protective story.

I've always been good at the self-protective story, but it reached untenable new heights after I was exposed to bedbugs and scabies within six months of each other. Both are awful, especially for someone with my particular anxieties. But one of the biggest problems stemmed from the fact that getting scabies so soon after bedbugs—in spite of my OCD-induced over-cautiousness!—confirmed my suspicion that whatever *could* go wrong *would*. For the next few years after that, any time I felt an itch, saw dots on my skin, or spotted even a tiny mark on a hotel bedsheet, I thought, *Well, you were right to worry before, so you must be right to do so now*. The worst-case scenario had come true not once but twice. In an attempt to protect myself, I told myself that it always would.

I've had to work hard to change that story, to remind myself that my worst-case-scenario thinking doesn't necessarily mean the worst-case scenario is inevitable. Likewise, just because social media sometimes pushes us toward feeling less real—more commodified, more defined by surface-level things, less attentive to the world around us—doesn't mean that's how it *has* to be.

Sometimes the doom and gloom we see about it being fake makes us look for the worst-case scenarios. It's easy to do. We have a couple bad experiences—we're fooled by a catfish, one of our tweets makes us the subject of harassment—and we begin to catastrophize. Withdrawal isn't the answer, though, just as it wasn't after my pest experiences, especially for those who want to participate in the meaning-making and connection that now occur online. Nor is the alternative approach some pursue in which, instead of taking distance from the internet, they consider everything online from a distance—seeing it all as less real, as expendable. We should care about what happens online the way we care about what happens elsewhere.

Because when we care about what happens around us, when we are attentive to our lives instead of "safe" in withdrawal, life comes to have more meaning. Rather than stepping back or following Facebook founder Mark Zuckerberg's edict to "move fast and break things," we should care about the things and people in our lives and treat them with care. Understand them not as expendable and replaceable but rather as things that could break—and that could break *us* if we lose them, like when the rabbit loses his boy, or when I lost my friend Alex. This is how we begin to feel real. The risk of loss is a big part of what enables our relationships to go deep enough to mean anything at all.

—■—

Cultivating a velveteen habit in our digital lives—a practice of paying attention, taking perspective, and treating our relationships and behaviors as real and consequential—requires a level of honesty with ourselves about our actions, motivations, and memories.

Once you realize this, it's easy to doubt yourself. I feel it in moments when I reflect back on the terrible summer that played a big role in motivating my search for realness and wonder if I am remembering it as worse than it was. Knowing how unreliable memory is, and how common it is to exaggerate, it's easy to begin second-guessing my experiences. But then I look at that picture I posted to Instagram, and I remember. It's all over my face. Seeing it, I'm transported back to how I felt.

It's painful to remember, but I'm able to see in myself how much that experience affected me. When I start to doubt my memory and question myself, I can look at that photo and *see* that my doubts aren't true. Having that external record is something I value about social media. When used mindfully, it helps me be more honest with myself. Because even though the caption of that photo said, "I will not forget this time in my life and the perspective it is giving me," the reality is that I already have. The specifics are blurred, in part because I don't *want* to remember them. But that photo helps tie me to that moment.

That's what social media, at its best, can do. It can help us feel less alone in times when that's monumentally important—it can save our lives, as it did for me that summer, when my friend Alex and a DM chat of semianonymous shitposters kept me tethered to the world, giving me as much love and support as I needed but not more than I could handle. But, all the more, it can help us see ourselves more honestly, even with all the filtering and editing we do. If we're willing to look at our social media output critically, we can see in that filtering, that editing—and in the moments when the facade cracks—things that help us better understand how to be more human.

Which is good, because I may never again be as unfiltered online as I was that summer. I don't edit my photos as much anymore, and I'm trying to force myself to post different kinds of pictures, not just cute ones—but as of now all of the photos I post are still carefully selected to emphasize my better angles. I am trying, though. In March 2019, for example, I tweeted, "A few weeks shy of 32, I'm single, living in a studio apartment w[ith] my dog, making very little money as I work on my next book, and caring for a loved one a few days a week. My life looks a lot less conventionally successful than it did a few years ago, but it feels more meaningful." I'm not entirely sure why I posted it; maybe I was trying to say it out loud so I knew it was true. I didn't expect more than a dozen likes, so I was surprised when, within hours, it passed seven hundred.

Maybe it was just the right tweet reaching the right people in the right moment. So often our digital successes happen like that, an alignment of content and chance, and it's best not to read too much into them. But this felt different. It felt like a small confirmation of my suspicion that people are relieved when someone online acknowledges that their life has intermingling challenges and joys. Because so often it feels like social media is split between the two—between cries for help or attention and the parade of personal successes.

I'm still not very good at disrupting the parade. I wish I could say I was free of the pressures, liberated from the desire for affirmation. But those battles are bigger than the internet.

Once, when I was traveling for a speaking engagement, I matched with a ridiculously attractive guy on Tinder. I don't even know why I was on Tinder, because I was only in the city for another day, but we matched, he was cute, and I was bored, so we started chatting. I told him right away that I was just in town for work and not looking to hook up, but he said that was fine and that he'd still like to meet up just to chat if I was interested. I told him it would depend on how tired I was after my event, because I'm usually pretty wiped after speaking, but that I'd let him know.

Sure enough, by the time I was done I was exhausted. I messaged him and said that I was sorry, but I couldn't meet. He pushed, asking for just a quick hello. I continued to say no, and sorry. His unwillingness to accept that it wasn't going to happen felt more jarring with each new message. By the end of our brief exchange he was insistent, angry, then demanding. Finally, he wrote, "I just want to know if any of this was real." I began typing again that I was sorry (as a Minnesotan it's one of the only things I know how to say when things go that wrong), but I couldn't send it because he had already blocked me.

The entire thing lasted just a few minutes. I couldn't understand his intensity; we had barely chatted. I stayed in my room for the rest of the night, hardly moving, chewing on the words. *I just want to know if any of this was real.*

I've had many conversations with people over the years, especially online, in which I sense a growing desperation for a meaningful and sincere connection. Which means that, if we're not careful, we can project a feeling of realness onto a blank space. I've done this numerous times. But no matter what that stranger on the other end of my Tinder match felt, realness can't emerge in a second. The digital age sometimes makes us feel like everything can and should happen instantly, but realness is a process. "It doesn't happen all at once," the old toy horse tells the velveteen rabbit. "You become. It takes a long time." We need to be patient if we want to feel real. And we need to be honest with ourselves about what's actually happening and what we really want.

A velveteen habit is meaningless if we can't be honest with ourselves first. But when honesty with ourselves and others becomes a part of our digital habits—and we learn to sit in the discomfort of uncertainty, as amateurs—we'll be that much closer to feeling real.

———■———

One thing that scares people most about Alzheimer's—one of the reasons some want to tuck those living with it into society's dark corners—is that it reveals a hard truth about what it means to be human. That truth is that who we are, our very identity and sense of self, is profoundly fragile, bound up in things that we often cannot control.

We like to think of our personalities as fixed, but we are forever in transition. While it's obvious for those with Alzheimer's, all of us are always changing. "Human beings," says Harvard psychologist Dan Gilbert, "are works in progress that mistakenly think they're finished."

What it is to be real is not fixed, either; it changes. Thus, in a time when realness sometimes feels like it's eroding, it may actually just be that the conventions of realness are changing. Real can mean something else now, which makes *The Velveteen Rabbit* a great touchpoint. Because it's not just a dark story about realness—one that reveals that becoming real involves confronting difficult things within yourself, experiencing loss, enduring change—but, like Alzheimer's, it also challenges the very foundations of what "real" means in the first place. In the story, the rabbit goes from an inanimate object to becoming a flesh-and-blood rabbit, all because he is loved.

I do worry sometimes about how we'll navigate a world where it is more and more difficult to determine what's real and what's not. I mean, we already live in such a world—think about how easy it is to fall for an edited image (I have!) or fake news on Facebook. It's only going to get worse. So it matters that we invest in working to promote values to combat the impulses to manipulate and lie. That means pushing our platforms to change but also cultivating habits of critical thinking within ourselves. And it also means treating our digital platforms as spaces where real life happens.

I once took a community college literature class that changed my life because it put Flannery O'Connor's short story "A Good Man Is Hard to Find" in front of me. The story's defining moment comes when the protagonist, a woman determined to control the world around her and bend the will of those she cares about to the vision she thinks is best, inadvertently puts herself in the path of a killer. Right before she's murdered, we see, for the first time, a moment of sincere compassion from her. "She would have been a good woman," the killer says after she's dead, "if it had been somebody there to shoot her every minute of her life." Confronted with her own mortality, she summons her best self. This situation reveals her to herself; if she had always lived *as if* someone were about to shoot her, she would have been the person that situation brought out in her.

A couple years later, while I was studying O'Connor's works as a religion major, my advisor Lori Brandt Hale introduced me to Lutheran theologian Dietrich Bonhoeffer, who wrote that we should live *as if* there's no God. We shouldn't expect a higher power to intervene in human events, he argued; instead, he thought Christians should work to determine the moral actions required to serve the world on God's behalf. (In his case, this included participating in a plot to assassinate Adolf Hitler. Badass, I know.)

I'm not sure I've fully convinced you—or even myself—that the digital world is entirely real. But whatever we think of the internet, real or unreal, we will be far better off if we treat our digital circumstances *as if* they are real. That means working to bring the same values and goals to our digital lives as we do every other part and treating the digital pieces of our lives as just as capable of teaching us things about ourselves, just as much spaces for finding meaning and belonging, as any other. After all, what we call things shapes our relationship to them.

As a teenager I trained myself to speak low and steady. The act was meant to protect me, shield my queerness, keep me safe from a world antagonistic toward people like me. Dropping my voice felt like a matter of survival, a way to hide, to ensure I didn't give myself away. Because I spoke that way during my formative years, in this low-pitched "vocal fry" tone, it's often how I still speak today. Over time, my body adapted to what I taught it to do; I only gave it a certain range in which to operate, and it obeyed. My voice does go to higher registers when I'm excited, but it always returns to the depths before long. A lower register is where my voice is most comfortable now. It is its home.

The voice I speak with today is probably different from the one that would have formed had I not spent my adolescence curating tonal ranges. But I wouldn't call the voice I use today "fake," either. It's not an act I put on. My voice today is what I made it. I built it through practice.

So much of who we are is the result of our circumstances and actions, especially the things we reinforce through repetition. Today we construct big chunks of that self on digital platforms designed to encourage repetitive behavior, building and rebuilding ourselves through actions both big and small. It's worth thinking about the consequences of those actions—and the actions themselves—more intentionally.

How we move through the world informs what we become. So it follows that the ways we use social media will become the ways we move through the other areas of our lives. That every tweet informs who we will become, that every status update is an act of building ourselves into being.

The voice we use online shapes how we speak and how we are heard. It is our voice. It's real. How does it sound? Do we pitch it down in the hope that changing it will protect us somehow—will make us safer, more desirable, more valuable, more real? And, whatever its timbre, how will we use it? What will we say?

For years my family called me "Tiffer Talks a Lot" because I wouldn't shut up, so enthusiastic and expressive was I as a young child. But when I realized I was gay and felt I needed to mask it, I went quiet. I dropped my voice, got soft and mumbly. In my voice today I can hear those years of effort, of adjusting myself to fit the expectations of the world around me. Years of stripping myself down and making myself less, doing what I thought would keep me safe and make me worthy of love. And there are moments when I look at old tweets and blog posts, old selfies and shitposts, and have the same feeling. I can see myself trying so hard to look smarter, more interesting, more attractive, kinder, more worthy.

But those posts have built me into the person I am now. The tattoos on my arms, my teenage blog posts, the tweets of my twenties—each of these willful acts of self-building have shaped me into who I am today. It's just that I haven't always been aware that I was building myself.

I have spent a lot of time trying to be something other than what I am. It's how I was taught to be. I am not ashamed that I do this, but I am trying to learn how to do it less, with greater intention and awareness. It is largely thanks to social media that I am now able to recognize the problem more completely, catch myself, and attempt to course correct.

When I first began writing this book, I would explain to people that I was trying to sift through what it means to be a "real" person today. Without my prompting, these conversations would inevitably trace back to the internet. In coffee shops, outside bars, and in backyards buzzing with mosquitos, people told me about investing countless hours in curating an Instagram aesthetic, only to find themselves unable to determine how much of it felt like an authentic expression of themselves and how much was for the benefit of others. About posting the things from their lives that made them seem interesting and hiding the rest. About seeing a friend share something online that they had told them in confidence. About scrolling through their comments and likes and not feeling like their friends understood them at all, not really. About feeling always connected but always alone. About comparing their lowest moments with other people's highlight reels.

None of it sounded new to me. I've felt many of these things online, too, but it was more than a recognition of shared digital habits. It all sounded like grappling with the kinds of questions I've grappled with my whole life and others in earlier generations have grappled with, too.

Yes, they've taken on a different flavor, perhaps even a new intensity, but ultimately the roots are the same: we're all struggling with how to show up in the world and understand ourselves and others. Social media shines a light on the curation, posing, and self-editing that's always occurred. Maybe it's taken on a more explicit life now, a life in which we're all amateurs—but that makes the problem easier to identify, and hopefully easier to address.

There's an Albert Einstein quote (I can already feel the eye rolls) that I keep coming back to: "The world as we have created it is a process of our thinking. It cannot be changed without changing our thinking." The way we use the internet is a product of our own desires, needs, and interests. But we can change it if we look at our desires, needs, and interests honestly. Acting *as if* the digital pieces of our lives aren't real, or are less real, doesn't encourage us to engage with them in ways that express our values.

However, we need to be careful not to turn our velveteen habit into just another vehicle for self-improvement. In the age of optimizing, of watches that track your steps and apps that monitor how much deep sleep you're getting, it's in the air (or, rather, right at our fingertips). These aren't new impulses, but they're much easier to indulge as we seek certainty—the kind that we think will keep us safe from risk and harm.

Ultimately, this desire to self-improve, and to find meaning more broadly, can be just another way of keeping ourselves busy—our incessant clicking. My whole life I've wanted to be working *toward* something, to be growing as a person. Serving as a chaplain in Ivy League institutions, it often felt countercultural to offer students the opportunity to do things that weren't about achievement, that were about being and becoming instead of accomplishing and showing off. But it was in those activities, apart from the pressures of performing and doing, that those students could explore many of the things that gave their lives meaning.

The ways we close distance and establish boundaries between ourselves and others; how we publicly and privately chart our lives and render ourselves visible; the ways we mark our lives permanently and fleetingly; the places we find meaning and belonging—these are what make us real. These are the practices that give our lives meaning, the habits that connect us to one another. Whatever we think of social media, doing these things online is a big part of our world now, or at least it is *for* now. It might be wise to put our faith in the ways it can transform us. To let it make us amateurs, digital novices fumbling in the dark.

One day, when I was a teenager, my stepdad picked me up from the community college campus where I took that literature class and said we were going to have a driving lesson. He directed me to a street near my house that I feared, because it was the steepest hill in town, and right at the very top there was a stoplight. It was a family rule that we had to learn how to drive on a manual transmission, which, when you're first learning, is hard enough to start on a flat surface. Starting on a steep incline, with a bunch of cars right behind you, is almost impossible. When we got to the top of the hill, I sobbed and told him I couldn't do it. I was sure I was going to hit the car that had pulled up right behind my bumper. That I would crash the car and open myself up to the anger of a stranger. But he turned to me and said I could do things I didn't know I could.

As Thomas Page McBee writes in *Amateur*, "To face and own what most disturbs you about yourself, [psychoanalyst Carl] Jung believed, is among the central moral tasks of being human." So I guess I'm ending where I began, without answers, trying to do something I'm not yet good at. Like it was in those high school cross-country races, the ones I was immensely bad at but kept doing anyway, sometimes the finish line and the starting line are the same. This search wasn't one that led to answers; rather, it led me to a commitment to a certain way of being in the world. A commitment to face reality honestly, as it is, online and off, and to learn from the trial and error of our new digital lives.

In *Rising*, Elizabeth Rush writes about finding this phrase in an essay on Alzheimer's: "Sometimes a key arrives before the lock." Rush says she understood it as a "reminder to pay attention to my surroundings. That hidden in plain sight I might discover the key I do not yet know I need, but that will help me cross an important threshold somewhere down the line."

For me, the threshold came when my stepdad—a man who has never had a Facebook profile or tweeted—was diagnosed with Alzheimer's. Spending days with him changed me. Our time together slowed down the pace of my life, and I unplugged more. I wish he could know just how much our time together has altered the way I see the world. And though I had no idea at the time, the key had arrived years earlier—when a series of disruptive events propelled me not only back to Minnesota but on a search for what it means to be real in the digital age.

Unlike most of the things that defined my twenties, the time I spend with my stepdad isn't about career advancement, status, productivity, or trying to change the world. It is about paying attention. I need to pay attention to him because he can't be left alone—but when I'm with him, I pay more attention not only to him but to myself and the world around me. In the slowness of our time together, all the noise of my Twitter timeline fades away, and I can focus on what is right in front of me.

Attention is how we attach ourselves to things. This search for realness began because I was feeling disconnected from my life, like I couldn't invest in the things around me, online or off. But in the time I've spent with my stepdad—time I wouldn't have if I hadn't moved back to Minnesota, which wouldn't have happened if everything I thought made me who I am hadn't fallen away—I've found myself attaching again. Sometimes a key arrives before the lock.

Earlier I wrote about constellations and why I love them; about the learning that happens at the points where we draw lines to connect things. But learning doesn't just happen in life's intersections—it also happens in its transitions. All the growing pains we experience in liminal periods like the last few years of my life, or like my stepdad's, when both of us went through major career, relationship, and life changes.

In the summer of 2019, I had to have a few surgeries. The day after my third and most intensive procedure, I sat in my mom's living room. We were both reading, she on an e-reader tablet and I with a stack of bound books at my side, casually picking them up and putting them down as conversation stopped and started between the ebbs of reading. The windows were open, and a late-August breeze ushered warmth inside as it pushed clouds along overhead. All day we sat together, talking on and off about the new transition we found ourselves in. While things with my stepdad had changed a great deal over the last few years, we were in the middle of the biggest shift yet. A few days before my surgery, we had helped him move into a memory-care facility down the road from my mom's place. It was no longer feasible for us to take care of him on our own, and fortunately the insurance company agreed to cover more intensive care. We talked about what we would lose in this change but also what would be gained, for him and for us. There was sadness in this transition but also new things to come. For my mom, especially, who had spent years caring for him, the transition was going to be a time of learning how to live alone again. A period of immense change, of difficulties and possibilities not unlike those I'd been navigating the last few years myself.

We are, all of us, in a time of significant transition. We sit at the end of an old age and the beginning of a new one (how long this new one will be is up to us), where the predigital age and the digital age overlap. Moments like this can be times of immense learning, where we can approach old questions concerning who we are in new ways. But they're also a place of pain. Change is hard. It's full of uncertainty. Things have to die in order to make space for the new.

Challenges and opportunities emerge from this change. Because not only is the world shifting from a predigital one to an increasingly digital one, but the internet itself is a kind of transitional space where boundaries blur. The digital critics are partially right: digital life is not entirely the same as offline life. But the internet's champions are partially right, too: it's a place where entirely new things are possible. It is simultaneously less and more real than offline life. Online, the real and the fake meet and intermingle.

There are places in the ocean where saltwater and freshwater meet, called haloclines, and they are unlike anywhere else on earth. Certain forms of life are only possible in a halocline because its conditions are utterly unique. In some ways, the internet is like that. In this strange, unique space, new ways of being can take shape and flourish. This transitional digital moment—and the transitional quality of the internet itself, where the online and offline meet—may make this the perfect time and space to cultivate a velveteen habit, an approach to life that leads us in the direction of openness instead of isolation.

Alzheimer's feels like a kind of in-between zone, too. I don't mean between life and death, as some might, but rather between the person who was and something else, something new. Something we don't yet fully understand, like how we didn't understand what we were doing to our planet when we first began burning coal, or how much we still don't understand about our digital lives. Or, rather, people with Alzheimer's stand between what we've traditionally thought it means to be human and the full spectrum of what it actually means, what it includes. Online we sit in the in-between, too. In the space between what we once understood as what it means to be human and real, what that means now, and what it will mean in the future. As people leave traditional institutions and move to digital ones that look and feel totally different, we will need to stretch our imagination. But if we do so, we can uncover new ways of being human. Because the habits we form now will determine what kind of humans we become.

Barring some currently unimaginable global event, the internet isn't going away. But if we look at what we use it for, we can better understand how to be human. The purposes we employ the internet for now—meaning, belonging, and the search for realness—aren't casual things. The fortunes we try to tell, the maps we create, the distances we traverse and shrink, the designs we ink into our digital skin, the games we play, and the certainties we seek—all of these things require honesty and self-awareness, time alone and time together. Honesty and awareness alone won't move us in the direction of the real, but without them we'll never get there. In the words of James Baldwin, "Not everything that is faced can be changed. But nothing can be changed until it is faced."

I can't give you the code for being real online. There aren't ten simple steps to a velveteen habit. Like the rabbit, you're going to have to find your own way. But I think it starts by treating the digital pieces of our lives as real—as spaces where we can love and be loved, and where we can hurt and be hurt. It starts with letting ourselves be vulnerable and attached to the world around us instead of treating our digital lives as spaces where we can optimize and design ourselves out of discomfort. If a toy rabbit can experience the realness that comes from connecting and disconnecting, there may be hope for the rest of us, too.

One summer day, as we sat on a patio, my stepdad offered to set me up with "a girl from the marching band." (The detail seemed random until I learned that a magazine I'd subscribed him to had an old photo of three women in marching-band uniforms on the cover that month.) I laughed, but my heart sank. Early on in our relationship, within the first years of us knowing each other, I'd come out to him as gay. In fact, he was one of the first people I came out to. Now he doesn't remember that I'm queer.

The transition in our relationship brought about by his Alzheimer's has had its gifts. But there has been immense loss, too. Yet that loss is also a part of what has made us both real. If I didn't care, it wouldn't hurt. But I do. I am attached.

Is my stepdad less real? No. But he is different. Changed.

In the swirl of change, of gain and deficit, that being online has created, it is still a space where we should care about what happens. A space we should treat as real, even when that means we get hurt. To make it so, we will need to pay close attention to how our digital lives are transforming us and instill in ourselves a velveteen habit—one that helps us connect but also allows us to be alone and attuned to the uncertainty and questions that arise in silence and solitude. Only then will we reap the rewards of being amateurs. Only then will we be soft and vulnerable like the baby rabbits my stepdad taught me about, or the fictional rabbit who first taught me what realness means and what it requires.

ACKNOWLEDGMENTS

There are so many people to thank and I'm going to do my best not to miss any of them here, though I surely will. If your name does not appear below but should, please know it has nothing to do with you. I am very forgetful, and very sorry.

My incredible agent Erik Hane, without whom this book wouldn't exist: thanks for seeing the pearl in this project when I was first figuring it out. I can't imagine doing this without your wisdom, humor, or dedication at every step. When it comes to agents, friends, humans, and human agents who are friends, you're as good as they come.

My editor Lil Copan, who was a complete joy to work with: thanks for your indispensable insight, incisive eye, and your belief in this project. Everyone at Broadleaf and Fortress (past, present, and contracted) who worked so hard on this, including but certainly not limited to Jill Braithwaite, Andrew DeYoung, Silas Morgan, Claire Vanden Branden, Madeleine Vasaly, Emily Benz, Mallory Hayes, Annette Hughes, Alison Vandenberg, and dozens of others: thank you for your commitment, advocacy, and effort. Thank you also to the wonderful writers who offered such generous endorsements. I'm awed by your talent and kindness.

The core readers who gave invaluable feedback on various drafts: Kelly Lundquist, Evan Stewart, Carrie Poppy, Nathan Goldman, Ryan Berg, Lia Siewert, and James Croft. Thank you for helping me get this book to the finish line; you asked all the right questions and pushed on all the right places. Thank you also to JP Brammer, Jacob Erickson, Timothy Otte, Nico Lang, Alison Dotson, Douglas Green and his fall 2019 creative nonfiction class, and anyone else who read pieces of this and gave feedback at some point.

My immense thanks to the many others who gave helpful input or pointed me in the direction of resources: Erica Stonestreet, Ronda Farah, Kirsten Delegard, Ryan Mattke, Jon Ozaksut, Jeff Tidball, Travis Winter, Cam Banks, Michael Lansing, Jacqui Frost, Matt Croasmun, Kaya Oakes, Jared Beverly, Laurie Santos, Mark Hanson, Liza Veale, Tyler Hower, Rachel Kambury, Alana Massey, Lia Bengston, Monica Miller, Jason Mahn, Brian Wagner, everyone at the RCC Campus Chaplaincy Project, all the campuses and communities that invited me to speak during the years I worked on this, and so many others. My deepest thanks also to everyone I interviewed for this book, who trusted me with your lives and stories, especially Zain, Merisa, Olivia, and Steve (and Mars and the Barking Points crew, too). Thanks also to those who provided space and support for a couple short, focused writing retreats: Ben and Kelly Lundquist, IFYC, and Danielle and Billy at the Mangy Moose.

Thanks to all of the people who supported me in so many other ways during the years I worked on this book, including many of those I mentioned already, and many others I will surely fail to mention here: Erik Roldan and Andrew Leon, Shelby Lano and Ollie Moltaji, Safy-Hallan Farah, Lori Brandt Hale, Ony Obiocha, the Lais, Jena Roth Falconi and Cara Falconi, Kate and Nate Wells, Kaitlin and John Sobieck, Raymond Thomas and Paul Fosaaen, Noah Barth, Alex Dimitrov, Patrick Comerford, Oliver Goodrich and Will Schultze, Fernando Giron, Malena Thoson, Elliott Powell, Michelle Ishikawa, Seth Kaempfer, Nathan Erisman, Julie Maxwell, Drew Spears, Zack Rosen, Craig Gronowski, Vlad Chituc, Chelsea and Sean Blink, James Croft, Bruce Johansen, Jacqueline Bussie, Nick Jordan, Sharon Kugler, Ryan Khosravi, Natalie Román and Josh Lindgren, Kenny Morford, Grace Patterson, Sadeeq Ali, Maytal Saltiel, Anthony Driscoll, Sharon Welch, Donovan Schaefer, Tony Pinn, A. Andrews, Archie Bongiovanni, Brian Konkol, Anthony Smith, Joan Wasser, Katie Heaney, Andreas Rekdal and Kristi Del Vecchio, Jessica and David Stearns Guerette, Aliyya Swaby, Joan Linley, Chris Bogen, Kari Henkelmann Keyl, Jeff Chu, Jason Weidemann, Michael Bourret, Sarah Jones and Ed Beck, Simran Jeet Singh, Nat DeLuca, Cody Nielsen, Tom Krattenmaker, Mary Dansinghani, Derek Kiewatt, Olga Verbeek, Ellen Koneck, Bradley Sterrenberg, Kristin Wintermute, Nick Hayden, Brenna Horn, Emilie Tomas, Emanuel Aguilar, Elaine Eschenbacher, Rita Allen, Brandon Musser and Alexandra Bodnarchuk, First Unitarian Society of Minneapolis and the Humanists of Minnesota, the Five Watt Kingfield crew, Twin Cities DSA, everyone at the Christensen and Sabo Centers and the Department of Religion and Philosophy (and so many others) at Augsburg University, friends at Beacon and Other Press, colleagues at IFYC and Yale and Harvard, the *IRL* launch team, and literally hundreds of other people. Special thanks to my dear Twitter DM chats, especially my longest-running one.

And Derek Weber, thanks for your support in the final year of writing this. I'm grateful we found each other when we needed one another.

Alex Dakoulas: it's funny to be thanking you in the acknowledgements of another book after what happened last time, and also all that's happened since, but I'm so grateful for you. Thanks for continuing to support me as our relationship changed, for being who you are, and for being behind this project without strings attached.

My beloved Alex Small, who I wish I could say this to: you're one of the primary reasons I got through 2016 in one piece, and this book wouldn't be here without you. You've taught me more about what it means to be real than just about anyone, and I'll carry you with me always. To Alex's sweet friends and family—Shoshi Small, Lexie Newman, Beth Stelling, Duje Bezina, James Lock, and the many other amazing people he loved and who loved him—thank you for friendships that allow me to be myself like I could with Alex.

My wonderful and strange family full of real (and really weird) ones: Mom, Casi, Colton, Cahlor, Halden, Henrik, Hazel, Dad and Sherry, and my extended family. I'm so fortunate to belong to a family that not only supports me in being exactly who I am, but encourages it. Thanks for showing me the way.

Charlie: I know you won't read this, but thank you for helping me finish this book. I'll never forget the day we were on our way to a museum and you asked how it was coming. It was the most lucid conversation we'd had in months. I told you it was almost done and you smiled and said "good, I know you're working hard." I was, but I wish you knew how much of it was because of you.

Finally, Matt Roberts: we met when the journey of this book was just beginning, but I didn't *really* know you until it was coming to an end. It's hard not to feel like that wasn't an accident, like the years that shaped this book were also shaping me for what would follow. You know, the key and the lock. Thanks for waiting on the other side of the door. You're the ultimate example of what being real can look like, and knowing you is the ultimate example of what I stood to gain from deciding to take the risk of being real, too.